NICOLAS

POUSSIN

A NEW APPROACH

WALTER FRIEDLAENDER

THE LIBRARY OF GREAT PAINTERS

HARRY N. ABRAMS, INC., *Publishers*, NEW YORK, N.Y.

To the Poussiniste,

JANE COSTELLO

Patricia Egan, *Editor*

Library of Congress Catalog Card Number: 64-10763
All rights reserved. No part of the contents of this book may be
reproduced without the written permission of the publishers,
HARRY N. ABRAMS, INCORPORATED, *New York.*
Gravure plates printed in Japan. Colorplates
and text printed in West Germany. Bound in West Germany.

CONTENTS

List of Colorplates   6

List of Black-and-White Illustrations   8

Preface   11

     I.   Poussin's Youth in France   13

     II.   Early Activity and Study in Rome   15

     III.   Poussin and Antiquity   17

     IV.   Poussin and the High Renaissance: Titian and Raphael   24

     V.   Poussin and His Contemporaries   27

     VI.   Poussin's Artistic Character and Method of Working   32

     VII.   Poussin as Theorist: The Theories of the Modes and Affetti   35

     VIII.   Poussin as Moralist: The Stoical Subjects   37

     IX.   Subject Matter: Paintings Before 1635   39

     X.   Subject Matter: Paintings 1635–1641   51

     XI.   Maniera Magnifica   57

     XII.   Landscapes   75

     XIII.   Poussin's Old Age   82

Description of Poussin   89

Biographical Outline   90

Colorplates and Commentaries   93

Index   201

Bibliographical Note   204

LIST OF COLORPLATES

SELF-PORTRAIT *The Louvre, Paris* *Frontispiece*

1. HOLY FAMILY (PEARSON MADONNA) *Landesmuseum, Karlsruhe* 95
2. DEATH OF GERMANICUS *The Minneapolis Institute of Arts, Minneapolis* 97
3. TRIUMPH OF FLORA *The Louvre, Paris* 99
4. MARTYRDOM OF ST. ERASMUS *Picture Gallery, Vatican, Rome* 101
5. LAMENTATION *Pinakothek, Munich* 103
6. NYMPH CARRIED BY A SATYR *Gallery, Cassel* 105
7. PLAGUE OF ASHDOD *The Louvre, Paris* 107
8. MASSACRE OF THE INNOCENTS *Musée Condé, Chantilly* 109
9. NARCISSUS AND ECHO *The Louvre, Paris* 111
10. MIDAS AND BACCHUS *Pinakothek, Munich* 113
11. MIDAS BATHING IN THE RIVER PACTOLUS *The Metropolitan Museum of Art, New York* 115
12. ET IN ARCADIA EGO *Chatsworth Settlement, Chatsworth* 117
13. MARS AND VENUS *Museum of Fine Arts, Boston* 119
14. LUNA AND ENDYMION *The Detroit Institute of Arts, Detroit* 121
15. AURORA AND CEPHALUS *National Gallery, London* 123
16. INSPIRATION OF THE POET *The Louvre, Paris* 125
17. REALM OF FLORA *Gallery, Dresden* 127
18. NURTURE OF BACCHUS *The Louvre, Paris* 129
19. TRIUMPH OF PAN *Morrison Collection, Sudeley Castle, Gloucestershire* 131
20. TRIUMPH OF NEPTUNE AND AMPHITRITE *Philadelphia Museum of Art, Philadelphia* 135
21. BACCHANALIAN REVEL BEFORE A TERM OF PAN *National Gallery, London* 137
22. ADORATION OF THE GOLDEN CALF *National Gallery, London* 139
23. PAN AND SYRINX *Gallery, Dresden* 141
24. RAPE OF THE SABINE WOMEN *The Metropolitan Museum of Art, New York* 143
25. GATHERING OF THE MANNA *The Louvre, Paris* 147
26. MADONNA ROCCATAGLIATA *The Detroit Institute of Arts, Detroit* 149
27. ET IN ARCADIA EGO *The Louvre, Paris* 151
28. NURTURE OF JUPITER *State Museums, Berlin-Dahlem* 153
29. EXTREME UNCTION *Collection Earl of Ellesmere, on loan to the National Galleries of Scotland, Edinburgh* 155
30. EUCHARIST *Collection Earl of Ellesmere, on loan to the National Galleries of Scotland, Edinburgh* 157

31. REBECCA AND ELIEZER AT THE WELL   *The Louvre, Paris*   *159*

32. MADONNA ON THE STEPS   *National Gallery of Art, Washington, D.C.*
     (Kress Collection)   *161*

33. JUDGMENT OF SOLOMON   *The Louvre, Paris*   *165*

34. HEALING THE BLIND OF JERICHO   *The Louvre, Paris*   *167*

35. TESTAMENT OF EUDAMIDAS   *State Museum of Art, Copenhagen*   *169*

36. MADONNA WITH A BASIN   *Fogg Art Museum, Harvard University, Cambridge*   *171*

37. SELF-PORTRAIT   *The Louvre, Paris (see Frontispiece)*   *173*

38. LANDSCAPE WITH ST. JOHN ON PATMOS   *The Art Institute, Chicago*   *175*

39. FUNERAL OF PHOCION   *The Louvre, Paris*   *177*

40. LANDSCAPE WITH A SNAKE   *National Gallery, London*   *179*

41. LANDSCAPE WITH ORPHEUS AND EURYDICE   *The Louvre, Paris*   *181*

42. LANDSCAPE WITH POLYPHEMUS   *The Hermitage, Leningrad*   *183*

43. HOLY FAMILY WITH ST. ELISABETH AND INFANT ST. JOHN
     The Louvre, Paris   *187*

44. ANNUNCIATION   *National Gallery, London*   *189*

45. BIRTH OF BACCHUS   *Fogg Art Museum, Harvard University, Cambridge*   *191*

46. SUMMER (RUTH AND BOAZ)   *The Louvre, Paris*   *195*

47. WINTER (THE DELUGE)   *The Louvre, Paris*   *197*

48. APOLLO AND DAPHNE   *The Louvre, Paris*   *199*

LIST OF BLACK-AND-WHITE ILLUSTRATIONS

1. DEATH OF CHIONE
   Engraving

2. CHIONE SLAIN BY DIANA
   Drawing   *Royal Library, Windsor Castle*

3. SCENE FROM THE COLUMN OF TRAJAN
   Drawing   *Collection Armide Oppé, London*

4. EQUESTRIAN STATUE OF MARCUS AURELIUS
   Drawing   *Musée Condé, Chantilly*

5. TRIUMPH OF TITUS
   Drawing   *National Museum, Stockholm*

6. MELEAGER SARCOPHAGUS
   Capitoline Museum, Rome

7. DEATH OF GERMANICUS
   Drawing   *Musée Condé, Chantilly*

8. TWO DRAPED FEMALE FIGURES
   Drawing   *Royal Library, Windsor Castle*

9. THE ALDOBRANDINI WEDDING
   Vatican Museum, Rome

10. Claude Mellan, after Poussin
    FRONTISPIECE,
    Horace's *Works*.   Engraving

11. Paris Bordone
    DEAD CHRIST SUPPORTED BY TWO ANGELS
    Palazzo Ducale, Venice

12. Titian
    BACCHANAL OF THE ANDRIANS
    The Prado, Madrid

13. Titian
    WORSHIP OF VENUS
    The Prado, Madrid

14. Raphael
    DEATH OF ANANIAS
    Cartoon   *Victoria and Albert Museum, London*

15. VISION OF ST. JAMES THE GREATER (MADONNA DU PILIER)
    The Louvre, Paris

16. Guido Reni
    MASSACRE OF THE INNOCENTS
    Gallery, Bologna

17. Domenichino
    SCOURGING OF ST. ANDREW
    S. Gregorio Magno, Rome

18. TRIUMPH OF DAVID
    Dulwich College Picture Gallery

19. Domenichino
    TIMOCLEA AND ALEXANDER
    The Louvre, Paris

20. Pietro da Cortona
    ST. BIBIANA REFUSING TO SACRIFICE TO IDOLS
    Sta. Bibiana, Rome

21. Pietro da Cortona
    RAPE OF THE SABINE WOMEN
    Capitoline Museum, Rome

22. STATUE OF ANTINOUS
    Engraving

23. Leonardo da Vinci   *Page from*
    TRATTATO DELLA PITTURA
    Drawing   *Vatican Library, Rome*

24. PARNASSUS
    The Prado, Madrid

25. CORONATION OF DAVID
    The Prado, Madrid

26. CONTINENCE OF SCIPIO
    Drawing   *Musée Condé, Chantilly*

27. SCHOOLMASTER OF THE FALERII
    The Louvre, Paris

28. DEATH OF VIRGINIA
    Drawing   *Royal Library, Windsor Castle*

29. ADORATION OF THE SHEPHERDS
    National Gallery, London

30. ADORATION OF THE MAGI
    Gallery, Dresden

31. FLIGHT INTO EGYPT IN A BOAT
    Dulwich College Picture Gallery

32. INSPIRATION OF ANACREON
    Landesmuseum, Hanover

33. DANCE TO THE MUSIC OF TIME
    The Wallace Collection, London

34. Guercino
    ET IN ARCADIA EGO
    Palazzo Corsini, Rome

35. COLORING OF CORAL
    Drawing   *Royal Library, Windsor Castle*

36. CHILDREN'S BACCHANAL
    Collection Marchese della Rocchetta, Rome

37. TRIUMPH OF BACCHUS
    Nelson Gallery-Atkins Museum, Kansas City

38. BACCHANAL BEFORE A TEMPLE
    Drawing   *Royal Library, Windsor Castle*

39. RINALDO AND ARMIDA
    Dulwich College Picture Gallery

40. ABANDONMENT OF ARMIDA
    Drawing   *The Louvre, Paris*

41. RESCUE OF THE INFANT PYRRHUS
    The Louvre, Paris

42. Leonardo da Vinci   *Page from*
    TRATTATO DELLA PITTURA
    Drawing   *Vatican Library, Rome*

43. PASSAGE OF THE RED SEA
    National Gallery of Victoria, Melbourne

44. MOSES FOUND BY THE PHARAOH'S DAUGHTER
    Drawing   *The Louvre, Paris*

45. HERCULES AND DEJANIRA
    Drawing   *Royal Library, Windsor Castle*

46. MOSES STRIKING THE ROCK
    Drawing   *Royal Library, Windsor Castle*

47. BAPTISM OF CHRIST
    National Gallery of Art, Washington, D.C.

48. Raphael
    BAPTISM OF CHRIST
    Vatican Loggias, Rome

49. BAPTISM
    National Galleries of Scotland, Edinburgh

50. CONFIRMATION
    National Galleries of Scotland, Edinburgh

51. PENANCE
    National Galleries of Scotland, Edinburgh

52. ORDINATION
    National Galleries of Scotland, Edinburgh

53. PENANCE
    Drawing   *Musée Fabre, Montpellier*

54. CRUCIFIXION
    Wadsworth Atheneum, Hartford

55. CARRYING OF THE CROSS
    Drawing   *Museum, Dijon*

56. ENTOMBMENT
    National Gallery of Ireland, Dublin

57. HOLY FAMILY WITH TEN FIGURES
    National Gallery of Ireland, Dublin

58. HOLY FAMILY WITH ELEVEN FIGURES
    Chatsworth Settlement, Chatsworth

59. MADONNA ON THE STEPS
    Drawing   *The Louvre, Paris*

60. HOLY FAMILY
    Drawing   *Musée Condé, Chantilly*

61. HOLY FAMILY
    Drawing   *National Museum, Stockholm*

62. HOLY FAMILY WITH INFANT ST. JOHN THE
    BAPTIST
    The John and Mable Ringling Museum of Art, Sarasota

63. REST ON THE FLIGHT INTO EGYPT
    The Hermitage, Leningrad

64. SCIPIO AND THE PIRATES
    Drawing   *École des Beaux-Arts, Orléans*

65. FINDING OF MOSES
    Collection Mrs. Schreiber, Bellasis House, Dorking

66. ACHILLES AND THE DAUGHTERS OF LYCOMEDES
    Museum of Fine Arts, Boston

67. CHRIST AND THE ADULTEROUS WOMAN
    The Louvre, Paris

68. DEATH OF SAPPHIRA
    The Louvre, Paris

69. Raphael
    BLINDING OF ELYMAS
    Cartoon   *Victoria and Albert Museum, London*

70. FIVE TREES
    Drawing   *The Louvre, Paris*

71. LANDSCAPE WITH FIGURES
    Drawing   *The Hermitage, Leningrad*

72. ST. MATTHEW AND THE ANGEL
    State Museums, Berlin-Dahlem

73. LANDSCAPE WITH DIOGENES
    The Louvre, Paris

74. GATHERING OF THE ASHES OF PHOCION
    Collection Earl of Derby, Prescot, Lancashire

75. After Poussin
    LANDSCAPE WITH THREE MONKS
    Engraving

76. LANDSCAPE WITH PYRAMUS AND THISBE
    Städel Institute, Frankfurt am Main

77. LANDSCAPE WITH TWO NYMPHS AND A SNAKE
    Musée Condé, Chantilly

78. After Poussin
    LANDSCAPE WITH A STORM
    Engraving

79. MERCURY AND PARIS
    Drawing   *The Louvre, Paris*

80. APOLLO SAUROCTONOS
    Drawing   *The Louvre, Paris*

81. PALESTRINA MOSAIC,
    detail   *Museo Prenestino Barberiniano, Palestrina*

82. CONVERSION OF ST. PAUL
    Drawing   *Musée Condé, Chantilly*

83. ACHILLES ON SKYROS
    The Virginia Museum of Fine Arts, Richmond

84. BLIND ORION SEARCHING FOR THE RISING SUN
    The Metropolitan Museum of Art, New York

85. RAPE OF EUROPA
    Drawing   *National Museum, Stockholm*

86. HOLY FAMILY (REINHART MADONNA)
    Collection Oskar Reinhart, Winterthur

87. Annibale Carracci
    TRIUMPH OF BACCHUS
    Farnese Gallery, Rome

88. Pietro da Cortona
    MARTYRDOM OF ST. ERASMUS
    Drawing   *Gabinetto dei Disegni, Uffizi, Florence*

89. DEATH OF ADONIS
    Museum, Caen

90.   Marcantonio, after Raphael
PLAGUE OF PHRYGIA
Engraving

91.   Marcantonio, after Raphael
MASSACRE OF THE INNOCENTS
Engraving

92. MASSACRE OF THE INNOCENTS
Drawing   *Musée Wicar, Lille*

93.   Titian
DIANA AND CALLISTO
National Galleries of Scotland, Edinburgh

94. MIDAS AT THE RIVER PACTOLUS
Musée Fesch, Ajaccio

95. MARS AND VENUS
Drawing   *Musée Condé, Chantilly*

96. MARS AND VENUS
Woodcut

97.   Annibale Carracci
DIANA AND ENDYMION
Farnese Gallery, Rome

98.   Agostino Carracci
CEPHALUS AND AURORA
Farnese Gallery, Rome

99. TRIUMPH OF PAN
Drawing   *Royal Library, Windsor Castle*

100. TRIUMPH OF PAN
Drawing   *Musée Bonnat, Bayonne*

101.   After Poussin
TRIUMPH OF SILENUS
National Gallery, London

102.   Raphael
GALATEA
Palazzo della Farnesina, Rome

103. TRIUMPH OF GALATEA
Drawing   *National Museum, Stockholm*

104.   School of Raphael
ADORATION OF THE GOLDEN CALF
Vatican Loggias, Rome

105. ISRAELITES WORSHIPING THE GOLDEN CALF
M. H. de Young Memorial Museum, San Francisco

106.   Gian Bologna
RAPE OF THE SABINE WOMAN
Loggia dei Lanzi, Florence

107. RAPE OF THE SABINE WOMEN
The Louvre, Paris

108. GAUL KILLING HIMSELF AND HIS WIFE
Terme Museum, Rome

109. HOLY FAMILY WITH NUDE FIGURES
Drawing   *Royal Library, Windsor Castle*

110.   Giulio Romano
INFANT JUPITER GUARDED BY THE CORYBANTES
ON CRETE
National Gallery, London

111. NURTURE OF JUPITER
Dulwich College Picture Gallery

112. THE EUCHARIST
The Louvre, Paris

113. MADONNA ON THE STEPS
Drawing   *Museum, Dijon*

114.   Michelangelo
LUNETTE OF NAASSON
Sistine Chapel, Vatican, Rome

115. JUDGMENT OF SOLOMON
Drawing   *École des Beaux-Arts, Paris*

116. HEALING THE BLIND OF JERICHO
Drawing   *Musée Bonnat, Bayonne*

117.   Jean Pesne, after Poussin
SELF-PORTRAIT
Engraving

118.   Titian
PORTRAIT OF JACOPO DE STRADA
Kunsthistorisches Museum, Vienna

119. NYMPHS SPIED UPON BY SATYRS
Drawing   *École des Beaux-Arts, Paris*

120.   Claude Lorrain
ACIS AND GALATEA
Gallery, Dresden

121.   Raphael
CANIGIANI MADONNA
Alte Pinakothek, Munich

122. HOLY FAMILY WITH ST. JOHN AND
ST. ELISABETH, AND ST. JOSEPH PRAYING
The Louvre, Paris

123. ANNUNCIATION
Musée Condé, Chantilly

124. INFANT BACCHUS ENTRUSTED TO THE NYMPHS
Drawing   *Fogg Art Museum, Harvard University,
Cambridge*

125.   Jean Verini, after Poussin
BIRTH OF BACCHUS WITH VENUS AND
CUPID IN THE SKY
Engraving

126. BIRTH OF BACCHUS
(detail, Jupiter)

127. BIRTH OF BACCHUS
(detail, Naiads)

128. SPRING
The Louvre, Paris

129. AUTUMN
The Louvre, Paris

130. APOLLO AND DAPHNE
Drawing   *The Louvre, Paris*

PREFACE

When I was asked in 1957 to write commentaries on forty-eight of Nicolas Poussin's paintings, I thought it would be a quick and easy enterprise. I assumed that I would have little more to do than to make extracts from the biography of Poussin which I had written about forty years before, and to bring them up to date. However, as I quickly learned, it was not an easy task, because research on Poussin had made great progress in the intervening years, and moreover, my views and opinions had changed considerably. Although a manuscript had been completed, the publication could not appear as originally planned before the great exhibition which opened at the Louvre in May, 1960.

This very important and fundamental show, in which most of Poussin's oeuvre was collected together for the first time, offered an opportunity for Poussin's work to be seen in totality, and this made a great impression on me, as on so many others. The passionately intense controversies which it provoked among the "Poussinists," and the new facts and ideas which appeared in the two large volumes of the *Actes du Colloque Nicolas Poussin*, reinvigorated the interest in Poussin. A Poussin renaissance had begun to flourish—at least among connoisseurs and amateurs.

Now I was again captivated by the general enthusiasm for Poussin. I requested my manuscript back—which was graciously conceded by the publisher—and began to write with greater intensity and pleasure. I did not try to compete with the extremely acute observations made by such eminent experts as Anthony Blunt—my co-editor on *The Drawings of Nicolas Poussin*—Denis Mahon, and Charles Sterling. Their several results, however, were used with great interest and gratitude.

Of course I wanted to see order in the rather confusing chronology of Poussin's paintings; without this no further study would be possible. But what concerned me more was their meaning. By "meaning" I do not imply only iconography or the solution of puzzles. The intention of the painter, and the impression he wished to evoke in the spectator for whom he created his work, were what I wanted to investigate. If possible, I wanted to show the change of his intention in different periods so as to stabilize a sort of chronology of content which would demonstrate the internal development of Poussin's style. In this way, I have tried to characterize certain periods by their predilection for humanistic subjects, for fables and poetry, for Bacchanals and Old Testament scenes, for devotional subjects, and finally for the vagueness and poetic revival of Poussin's old age.

Because of my advanced years, I could never have finished the work without the help of my various assistants and friends. I am very thankful to all of them. I would like to mention in particular Donald Posner, Guy Walton, and, for his help in the correction of the text, Donald Keyes. The indefatigable Lucie Bauer made the laborious final revision of the proofs and considerably ameliorated the style. Professor Charles Sterling sacrificed his precious time to read parts of the manuscript and made several very valuable suggestions.

W. F.

√Pouſſin

I. POUSSIN'S YOUTH IN FRANCE

For himself as well as for us, the life of Nicolas Poussin really began in 1624, when he went to Rome as a man of thirty. The remarkably little that we know about his pre-Roman years we mostly owe to his biographer and friend Giovanni Pietro Bellori, who devoted a long chapter to Poussin in his *Lives of the Painters* (published in Rome, 1672). Bellori's account of Poussin's youth in France seems to be drawn from the old master's fragmentary, perhaps reluctant recollections. Félibien, Poussin's other important contemporary biographer, based his account of those early years on Bellori's information.

Nicolas Poussin was born in 1594 in a hamlet near Les Andelys, a small town in Normandy, and his character and will power indeed showed the qualities of northern French peasant stock. His people were small farmers, although his father, Jean, came originally from Soissons and had been a soldier in the terrible religious wars that had devastated France. Nicolas Poussin's parents were not so poor that their son did not receive some education, including even a little Latin. He had a natural talent for drawing, and in his eighteenth year he ran away to Paris. His knowledge of painting had been acquired before that time mostly on his own, with perhaps some assistance from the older Noel Jouvenet in Rouen, and almost surely from Quentin Varin, a quite experienced traveling painter who was then painting altarpieces in a coarse Flemish manner for various churches in Les Andelys.

In Paris, Poussin had no great help or instruction from local painters, whose schools he attended only briefly, for the state of painting was then at a very low level—to quote Bellori: "The manner of painting, which in Italy had just begun to recover through the Carracci school, was in France as a whole still very bad!" Nevertheless, the young painter taught himself by studying the treasures of Italian art that had been collected in France during the reign of Francis I, early in the preceding century. With the help of the friends he made in Paris, Poussin was able to study intensely the engravings by Marcantonio Raimondi, after designs by Raphael and his school. Thus Poussin could later say that he had been nourished, as if by mother's milk, on the classical art of Raphael.

Poussin encountered the usual difficulties of young artists who must stand on their own feet. He seems to have earned his livelihood by painting, in the trend of the later Fontainebleau School, bacchanals and the like in various provincial châteaus, and by making portraits. None of these has been preserved. Because our information about Poussin during these years is not precise, attributions to him of work from this pre-Roman period have no real foundation. Poussin tried several times to go to Rome, his particular goal and the goal of all young painters. Once he traveled as far as Florence, but for some reason had to return almost immediately. Another time he had to use the money he had saved for his Italian trip to pay debts in Lyons, and could not continue the journey.

Not until he was almost thirty did some success come to him: he was commissioned by the Jesuits in Paris to paint six large panels in tempera, commemorating the canonization of several saints, including Ignatius of Loyola and Francis Xavier. These paintings attracted the attention of that strange personality, Cavaliere Marino, the famous Italian poet who was

Figure 1. DEATH OF CHIONE from *Les métamorphoses d'Ovide* (Paris, La Veuve Langelier, 1619).
Engraving. *Collection Mr. and Mrs. Philip Hofer, Boston*

also a connoisseur of painting, at that time living in Paris at the court of Marie de' Medici. Marino recognized the superiority of the paintings Poussin had made for the Jesuits, that they were different from the work of contemporary painters in France. He invited Poussin into his household and eventually made it possible for him to go to Rome. Marino's admiration probably enhanced Poussin's reputation, and the next year (1623) he was commissioned to paint a *Death of*

the Virgin for the Cathedral of Notre Dame. His painting remained there until the French Revolution; it then disappeared, and is now known from a tiny sketch by Gabriel de Saint-Aubin.

THE MARINO DRAWINGS

Poussin's friendship with Marino also enabled him to make the set of drawings now in the Royal Library of Windsor Castle, the only works we have that Poussin unquestionably made before he left for Italy. According to Bellori, Marino commissioned Poussin to illustrate *Adone*, the long poem that made Marino almost as well known as Ariosto and Tasso in sophisticated European circles; unfortunately this set of drawings, if it was ever made, has not been preserved. What are now called the "Marino Drawings" seem to be illustrations for an edition of Ovid's *Metamorphoses* which may have been planned under Marino's auspices. Such illustrated Ovids were still popular in the seventeenth century, as they had been in the sixteenth. Poussin's Marino Drawings already display his talent as a "great narrator and storyteller," as Lorenzo Bernini later called him. Bellori reports that Marino was extremely pleased by Poussin's power as a graphic artist, discovering in him "incisive and spontaneous inventiveness, especially in the rendering of emotion, so that he seems inspired by the Muses as poets are." He adds that one can see in the drawings that the young artist had "fertilized his mind with the

Figure 2. CHIONE SLAIN BY DIANA. 1622–23. Drawing, pen and bistre with dark gray wash, $7^1/_4 \times 12^3/_8''$.
Royal Library, Windsor Castle (by gracious permission of H. M. the Queen)

14

good example of Raphael and Giulio Romano," and that in Marino's company he had enriched his imagination with "poetic color." Even though the Marino Drawings fall short of the stirring fullness and force of Poussin's mature style, they are remarkably advanced and "modern" in comparison with earlier illustrations of Ovid.

In the interests of clearer form and emotion, and in contrast to the most recent illustrations, Poussin selected the most significant moments in Ovid's stories and presented them as on a stage. In an edition of the *Metamorphoses* published by Langelier in 1619, the engraving of the *Death of Chione* (fig. 1) still shows what is called "continuous narration": the illustration consists not only of Diana shooting Chione, the main action in Ovid's story, but also of two earlier incidents that have been inserted into the composition: Chione receiving Apollo, then Mercury, as her suitors. But Poussin, avoiding the frivolous episodes of Ovid's complicated story, has concentrated on the conclusive act of vengeance (fig. 2). His rendition dramatizes the climax wherein promiscuous Chione, who has been so unwise as to disparage the beauty of the chaste Diana and allude to her sterility, lies dying, shot through the tongue by the embittered goddess. Poussin, even before going to Rome, had already attained the eloquent and direct simplicity that, extended and enriched, was later to make him the great master of classicism (see J. Costello, *Journal of the Warburg and Courtauld Institutes*, XVIII).

II. EARLY ACTIVITY AND STUDY IN ROME

Poussin did not make the journey to Italy with his patron Marino, who left for Rome in April, 1623. He was obliged to remain in Paris and execute the painting for the Cathedral of Notre Dame. We do not know how long this task required but the young painter certainly did not tarry, and he probably left for Italy within six months. Instead of taking the usual route to Rome, via Marseilles and Civitavecchia, he went first to Venice and stayed there for some months. In March, 1624, he had just arrived in Rome, and in a census made at that time he is listed in the house of the French artist Simon Vouet.

Giulio Mancini, from whom we know of Poussin's trip to Venice, wrote a brief, fragmentary note on Poussin in his *Considerations on Painting*, about 1627. Mancini, the personal physician to Pope Urban VIII, undoubtedly heard praise of the young painter in the society around the Pope's art-loving family—especially from Marino, who was a close friend of the Pope's nephew, Cardinal Francesco Barberini. Because Mancini was on intimate terms with the circle that first acknowledged the newcomer, his remarks about the young artist have significance:

> After M. Poussin had learned Latin and acquired a good knowledge of histories and fables he dedicated himself to the study of painting. Having made sufficient progress in this art he came to Italy. He stayed in Venice for some time and then, imbued with Venetian ideas and manners, he came to Rome. Here he practiced making studies from the live model according to the principles of his teacher [Domenichino], but he enriched them with elements that he had learned in Venice. Studying in this way, his art attained a remarkable level, and he now enjoys a good reputation through many of the works he has made which are to be seen in private houses.
>
> He is a man of noble bearing, and—what is rather important—because of his literary erudition, he is familiar with almost any story (*historia*), fable (*favola*), or poem (*poesia*), so that he can express them—as he does in the most felicitous way—with his brush . . . .

According to Poussin's letters, and to the recollections he shared with Bellori, his first years in Rome were difficult. Soon after his arrival his influential protector and supporter, Cavaliere Marino, died in Naples, having already recommended him to Marcello Sacchetti (the patron of Pietro da Cortona), who in turn introduced the painter to Cardinal Francesco Barberini. Late in 1625 Poussin was commissioned by the latter to paint a *Conquest of Jerusalem* (this version has been lost), for which in 1626 he received 61 scudi. Unfortunately, the cardinal had to leave for Spain on a diplomatic mission, and with him went his secretary, Cassiano dal Pozzo, the famous antiquarian who later became Poussin's close friend and patron. Consequently, Poussin at first had no one to recommend him for larger commissions. He later recalled bitterly to Bellori that even after he had been in Rome several years, he had sold two large battle scenes for the ridiculously low price of 8 scudi apiece. In addition, he suffered recurrent attacks of a malady he had contracted in France. In a quite piteous, almost begging

Figure 3. SCENE FROM THE COLUMN OF TRAJAN. C. 1626. Drawing, pen and bistre wash, 10³/₈×15⁵/₈″. *Collection Armide Oppé, London*

letter to dal Pozzo, probably written in 1627, not long after the latter returned from Spain, Poussin complained of his sickness and his lack of commissions. He sent "as a present" a drawing or painting of *Hannibal Crossing the Alps* (see chap. IX), for which the generous dal Pozzo sent him 40 scudi. However, the return of Cardinal Barberini in the autumn of 1626 renewed and stabilized the patronage of the Barberini family and their circle, and thus marked a turning point in Poussin's economic life. Through them he received, directly or indirectly, several large commissions: of greatest artistic value was the *Death of Germanicus* (colorplate 2); officially, the most important was the *Martyrdom of St. Erasmus* (colorplate 4) for St. Peter's, finished in 1629. Poussin, as Mancini had predicted, had privately made his name more and more known and it is significant that, by the end of the 1620s, such art dealers as Roccatagliata and the diamond "merchant" Valguarnera ordered and bought the works of the newcomer, sometimes even with an extra copy because they were such good investments. This we know from Valguarnera's subsequent trial (J. Costello, *Journal of the Warburg and Courtauld Institutes*, XIII), which provides us with many interesting and elucidating facts.

During his illness Poussin was nursed by the family of the French confectioner Dughet, and in 1630 he married their eighteen-year-old daughter, Anne-

Marie. In his newly acquired house in Via Paolina, Poussin could now dedicate himself more fully to his artistic mission.

Figure 4. EQUESTRIAN STATUE OF MARCUS AURELIUS. C. 1626. Drawing, pen and bistre wash, 12×7¹/₄″. *Musée Condé, Chantilly*

Rome, in Poussin's day, was the Rome of Pope Urban VIII and had become the unique center of European art, offering everything an artist from the Netherlands or France could wish: the dazzling riches of the surviving relics of Antiquity; the glories of the High Renaissance—Raphael, Michelangelo, and Titian; the vegetating residue of the late *maniera*—Roncalli and d'Arpino; the revival of classic art in the neo-Renaissance of Annibale Carracci and his school, especially Domenichino; the psychologically deepened realism of Caravaggio and his followers; the Baroque style being formed by Lanfranco and developed by Pietro da Cortona and Lorenzo Bernini, with, as its countermovement, the simplification of this style by Andrea Sacchi. The young artist had only to choose.

III. POUSSIN AND ANTIQUITY

Poussin was never an antiquarian in the sense of Pirro Ligorio, but he wanted to be thoroughly informed about every aspect of life in Antiquity that could be of value to him in his work. For this purpose, nothing could have been of greater help to him than his close and lifelong connection with Cassiano dal Pozzo, an antiquarian in the grand style, who opened to him the riches of his house and of his precious library.

Poussin was entirely right when he declared himself a "disciple of the house and the museum of the Cavaliere dal Pozzo," because the extraordinarily rich material that he found there continually augmented his knowledge of Antiquity and facilitated his work. Thus, for instance, Poussin's beautiful drawing of an assembly of soldiers from the Column of Trajan was probably not made directly after the original relief, but after one of the casts Cassiano had ordered which Poussin could have studied at his leisure in dal Pozzo's library (see fig. 3). To name another example, dal Pozzo owned precise drawings of the mosaic with Egyptian scenes (fig. 81), recently discovered in Palestrina, which Poussin studied and used for his own purpose. Whether Poussin directly participated in the forming of dal Pozzo's museum, and if so to what extent, is not clear. It was a "paper museum" (*museo cartaceo*) consisting of an immense number of drawings commissioned by Cassiano from such young artists as Pietro Testa, and included copies after remains of all kinds, from great works of art to the paraphernalia of daily life. However, it is difficult to find any traces of Poussin's individual draftsmanship within the many volumes of drawings after ancient art in dal Pozzo's collection (the majority are now in the Royal Library, Windsor Castle).

Poussin as a young man was not the eager copyist that Rubens was. His meditative and reflective method

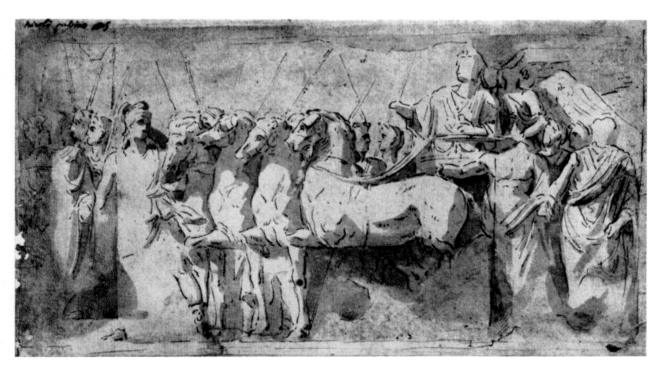

Figure 5. TRIUMPH OF TITUS from Arch of Titus. c. 1626. Drawing, pen and bistre wash, $5^7/_8 \times 10^7/_8''$. *National Museum, Stockholm*

Figure 6. MELEAGER SARCOPHAGUS. Mid-2nd century A.D. *Capitoline Museum, Rome*

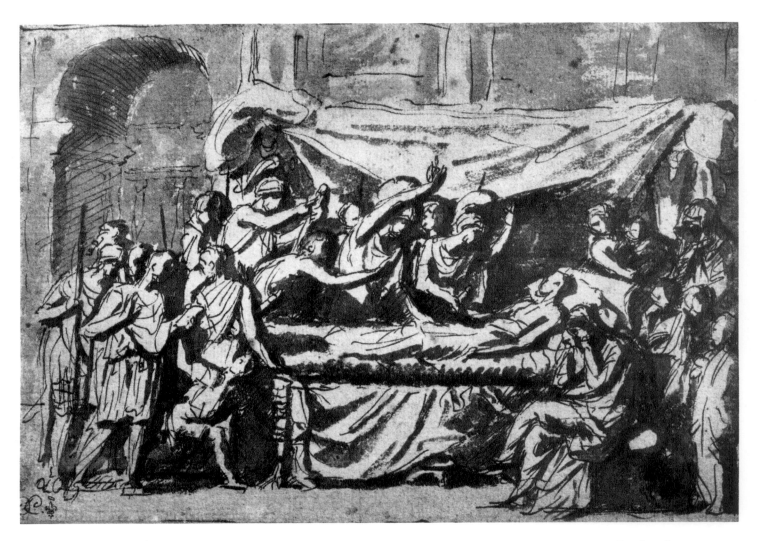

Figure 7. DEATH OF GERMANICUS. Early 1630s. Drawing, pen and bistre wash, $6^7/_8 \times 9^1/_2''$. *Musée Condé, Chantilly*

was more given to observing, studying, and analyzing an object than to tracing it impulsively and directly on paper. He said himself that a painter acquires greater skill by intense observation than by exhaustive copying, and Félibien reports that when Poussin encountered an ancient piece which merited his attention, he often did not make a sketch of it, but studied it in detail and impressed its image so strongly upon his mind that eventually he could use it, if he so desired. Therefore, Poussin's authentic drawings after ancient works are fewer than once was estimated. However, since his name and fame in the eighteenth and nineteenth centuries were so closely connected with classical Antiquity, many anonymous drawings

18

after ancient monuments were attributed to him by collectors, amateurs, and dealers; today it is often not easy to decide whether the more impressive of these drawings are authentic, or whether they merely show the similar technique of minor, but gifted, artists, sometimes even working in direct imitation of Poussin.

On the other hand, Félibien also reports that Poussin, on his frequent walks through Rome and its environs, jotted sketches of ancient monuments in a book he carried with him. It seems that he did not make many detailed studies of ancient statues in the round—even the well-known drawings in pen and bistre of the equestrian statue of Marcus Aurelius on the Capitol (the drawing of the side view is preferable to that of the front view) have been tentatively considered to be Poussin's own copies after an engraving by Perrier (fig. 4). Some of Poussin's almost casual pen drawings, those in light brownish bistre, reproduce scenes from such famous Roman monuments as Trajan's Column and the Arch of Titus (figs. 3, 5). Other compositions are taken from reliefs on marble sarcophagi: the Meleager sarcophagus was the source for Poussin's drawing the *Death of Germanicus* (figs. 6, 7). His interpretation is especially strong and personal, and he intentionally omits parts of the Roman relief to permit its essential spirit, as Poussin wanted to see it, to appear almost violently. In his drawing after the Endymion sarcophagus the youthful, proud pose of the goddess Diana-Luna reflects that of the original, except that she is now in a strong chiaroscuro produced by powerful light from the side. Poussin may have made the drawing as a preliminary study for his marvelous painting *Luna and Endymion* (colorplate 14), using not the original marble but a cast—perhaps also in the house of dal Pozzo.

Whether Poussin drew from figures and scenes in the original ancient sculptures, or copied and adapted them from sixteenth-century engravings, or, perhaps, embedded the images so firmly in his mind that he was able to transcribe them freely without direct reference to a specific model, is irrelevant to the final problem of the insertion of these models into his compositions. It is characteristic of Poussin that he never imitated relief compositions *in toto*. He picked out a single figure—an Apollo (in *Midas and Bacchus*, colorplate 10), or a Diana (in *Luna and Endymion*, colorplate 14), or a

Figure 8. TWO DRAPED FEMALE FIGURES. C. 1626.
Drawing, pen and ink, 6⅜×4⅝″. *Royal Library, Windsor Castle (by gracious permission of H. M. the Queen)*

Victory (in the *Coronation of David*, fig. 25)—and adapted its proportions, gestures, or characteristic attributes to those of the main figure in a quite different composition. These figures are isolated by their intentional and undeniable classicality; they do not lose their sculptural character; unlike the ancient figures in Rubens' work, they do not melt into a full, warm stream of color. For example, the famed ancient statue, *Gaul Killing Himself and His Wife* (fig. 108), occupies a prominent place in the foreground of the *Rape of the Sabine Women* (colorplate 24); the *Borghese Warrior* was selected for an important role in the *Rescue of the Infant Pyrrhus* (fig. 41). But it remains significant that such groups and figures, more or less directly borrowed, were used by Poussin only in the 1620s and 1630s. They do not appear in his works after his visit to Paris in 1642, because he was by then so satu-

Figure 9. THE ALDOBRANDINI WEDDING. Early 1st century A.D. Fresco. *Vatican Museum, Rome*

rated with the vocabulary of ancient art that he could improvise classical art on his own, without reference to particular models.

As might be expected, Poussin's main contact with the art of Antiquity was through Roman examples. He studied the historical reliefs from the Ara Pacis, the Arch of Titus, the Column of Trajan, and other famous monuments, all of which were common property. The examples he knew reflected a wide range of ancient art. However, the greatest number of them belong to the Hellenistic-Baroque; these include the well-known statues of the Ludovisi *Gaul Killing Himself and His Wife*, the *Dead Amazon* in Naples, the Pasquino group, the *Borghese Warrior*, the *Farnese Hercules*, and the *Apollo Belvedere* (a Roman, rather than Greek, work). Roman sculpture was built upon Greek art and derived many of its main elements by direct copy or by a process of amalgamating Greek material with Roman forms—a translation that itself evolved into a new language. But to call Poussin "Greek" or "Attic," as certain French critics have recently done in the attempt to demonstrate his affinity with French statuary, is to disregard the greater body of evidence—although after Poussin's sojourn in Paris he showed a preference for the abstract, ideal aspects of ancient art. In this later period he sometimes turned to such works as gems of the fifth and fourth centuries B.C., and to highly refined neo-classical monuments of Roman Imperial times: an instance is the Albani Puteal, which is the source for

his wonderful drawing of two draped women (fig. 8). But Poussin was no more "Greek" than "Roman," and it may be said that most aspects of ancient art were incorporated into his particular classicism.

Random borrowing was by no means the most important way that Poussin utilized ancient prototypes in his paintings. More systematically than any previous painter, Poussin turned to ancient reliefs to learn their spatial construction and organization. One of his early works, the *Death of Germanicus* (colorplate 2), and still more obviously his later drawing of the same subject (fig. 7), provide excellent examples of how he used the structural principles of ancient relief. With the Meleager sarcophagus as his model (fig. 6), he transposed into painting the fundamental system used in the relief to produce depth, not by perspective lines and foreshortenings, but by layers of planes added one behind the other, all parallel to the picture surface. This solution to the problem of transforming a two-dimensional area into a three-dimensional space is completely anti-illusionistic. No remote distances are implied. All action takes place in the plane close to the spectator, and the movement has great clarity and lucidity. The planimetric system, developed from Poussin's study of ancient reliefs, gains its greatest momentum and significance during the period of his Maniera Magnifica.

Poussin was not exclusively attracted to sculptural works from Antiquity. Ancient paintings and mosaics unearthed in Rome and the surrounding countryside also interested him highly, and Roman art of this kind had an important impact on the development of his later style. Perhaps on commission from dal Pozzo, he copied the celebrated fresco, *The Aldobrandini Wedding* (fig. 9), which had been found in 1606. This painting, in strictly parallel layers, helped no less than did the Meleager sarcophagus to form his pictorial relief style. He apparently knew other, less famous, frescoes that were later excavated, such as those in the house under SS. Giovanni e Paolo, which Mancini may have noticed about 1628. Either these works or others like them have left their traces in Poussin's compositions (see the drawings of *Bacchus and Ariadne*, now in the Royal Library, Windsor Castle; W. Friedlaender and A. Blunt, *Drawings*, III, No. 182). Likewise, his treatment of color in his later work shows his knowledge of ancient painting. He was certainly familiar with the

Figure 10. Claude Mellan, after Poussin: FRONTISPIECE, Horace's *Works* (Paris, 1642). Engraving. *Bibliothèque Nationale, Paris*

splendid Palestrina mosaic with Nilotic scenes, owned by the Barberini family (fig. 81): he transported the procession of priests of Isis from this mosaic to the background of his late *Rest on the Flight into Egypt* (fig. 63), and it is not improbable that the grotesque physiognomies and grimacing faces haunting some of his other late works were also inspired by the mosaic figures.

Much as he devoted himself to large-scale ancient art around Rome, Poussin did not neglect the minor arts—cameos, coins, medals, and so forth. From these he gleaned information about Roman life and customs, such as clothing (see, for example, fig. 8), hair styles, weapons, shields, and utensils for sacrifice. Many such details he copied in small pen drawings that are often not taken from the originals, but from antiquarian engravings by the Roman school of Marcantonio, or their successors (as G. Kauffmann has shown in *Zeitschrift für Kunstgeschichte*, XXIV, 2, 1961); or he used printed books of the same kind, such as *Le Discours sur la Religion des Anciens Romains*, by Jean du Choul (Lyons, 1556; see A. Blunt, *Revue des Arts*, X).

Poussin took great pains to design architectural settings that would be accurate and appropriate for historical paintings. For the *Rape of the Sabine Women* he re-created a Roman forum on the basis of Vitruvius (as J. Costello has shown in *Bulletin of the Metropolitan Museum*, V); the houses and temples in the background of the Phocion landscapes (colorplate 39; fig. 74) were not constructed arbitrarily, but only after consulting specific architectural books by, for example, Serlio. To maintain *costume*, or appropriate usage, Poussin painted both *The Last Supper* (*Eucharist;* colorplate 30) and *Penance* (fig. 51), from *The Seven Sacraments*, as Roman dinner scenes, the figures reclining at a three-sided table as though at a Roman triclinium. The idea of visualizing New Testament scenes in their historical milieu was not originated by Poussin. Lodovico Cigoli had already included a triclinium in his *Last Supper*, probably at the request of his patron, Girolamo Mercurialis, who had discussed the triclinium in his *Gymnastica* of 1569. In both Italy and France there had been much discussion of how the Christian mysteries might be presented in ancient pagan form, and especially of how the triclinium might be used in representations of the Eucharist. But in Poussin's hands the idea outgrew archaeological or clerical scope

Figure 11. Paris Bordone: DEAD CHRIST SUPPORTED BY TWO ANGELS. Fresco. *Palazzo Ducale, Venice*

to assume a monumentality and originality that justify Poussin's boast, in a letter to his friend Chantelou, that he had created something surprisingly new by introducing a triclinium into his representation of *The Last Supper*.

Mancini, even in his brief note, stresses Poussin's literary knowledge, and Roland Fréart de Chambray praises Poussin as one of the rare painters who has studied the "humane letters" and read the "beautiful books of the Antique," so necessary for anyone who aspires to the "Perfection of Art." Poussin was certainly very familiar with classical literature, partly from having moved as a young man in French society, notably in the circle of the poet Marino and the Hôtel Rambouillet. He knew some Latin—probably enough at least to consult classical texts in specific cases. In general, I think he used available translations in French and Italian. One can assume that he knew both the content of ancient mythologies, and the French stories and versifications of these anthologies that were appearing in France at that time. But because he was a conscientious man and a humanistic dilettante, he undoubtedly checked the original sources. Almost certainly he knew the *Metamorphoses* of Ovid by heart, for he sometimes literally transposed lines and scenes from it into his paintings. His source for the *Realm of Flora* (colorplate 17) was Ovid's less widely read *Fasti*.

He praised Virgil highly, and executed a beautiful frontispiece for an edition of Virgil's works published in 1641. Similarly, he made an engraving for a 1642 edition of the works of Horace (fig. 10). He translated into paint episodes from Plutarch (the Phocion landscapes, colorplate 39; fig. 74), from Livy (*Schoolmaster of the Falerii*, fig. 27), from Tacitus (*Death of Germanicus*, colorplate 2), and from Philostratus (*Apollo and Daphne*, colorplate 48), to mention only these authors. For his pictures of Old Testament scenes, he did not confine himself to the text of Exodus, but also consulted Josephus' *Jewish Antiquities*. He learned about some authors, with whose writing he was not acquainted at first hand, through a book he obviously always kept close by—Vincenzo Cartari's *Imagini de i dei degli antichi (Images of the Gods*, probably the Paduan edition of 1616). For instance, he used Cartari's Italian translation of Statius' lines on the praise of Venus by Mars for his painting *Mars and Venus* (colorplate 13). The more heuristic and complicated *Mythologiae* by Natales Comes provided Poussin with ideas for his landscape, *Blind Orion* (fig. 84). The great Barberini library and the private library of Cassiano dal Pozzo furnished vast material for the study of ancient culture. Poussin constantly availed himself of these resources, making excerpts or having passages copied that specially interested him. From these literary works as well as from ancient sculpture and painting, he continued to absorb throughout his life the principles that formed the deepest wellspring of his own work.

THE IDEAL OF PERFECTION

Nothing was closer to the heart and intellect of Nicolas Poussin than the spirit of classical Antiquity. Poussin's artistic character was in great part conditioned by his relation to this spirit. For him, ancient forms not only provided supplementary motifs to be used under certain circumstances in his own works, they were also representative parts of a general idea, an artistic conception having values that were beyond dispute. His ideal was not exclusively artistic; it also included cultural, social, and pedagogical matters. He wished to elevate artistic production to the highest level, to make it equal the works of ancient artists so celebrated by the authority of ancient writers. In a letter to Chantelou (June, 1655), Poussin gives Quintilian's list of the names of leading ancient painters and sculptors, and mentions the special virtue

that made each one superior and famous. "For everyone who considers the matter carefully," Poussin adds proudly, "it will be evident that among the famous painters of the last 350 years [that is, since the beginning of the Renaissance] he [Poussin] within the limits of his specialty and individuality had made himself a part of this illustrious tradition." This evaluation of Poussin's art as the equal to that of the most famous painters was already proclaimed in the master's lifetime; in 1662 it was expressed in the most enthusiastic way by Roland Fréart de Chambray, the brother of Poussin's patron and friend, Paul Fréart de Chantelou, in his *Idée de la perfection de la peinture.* In Fréart de Chambray's opinion, such "arbiters of antiquity" as Pliny and Quintilian, who immortalized the great ancient painters by their comments and by descriptions of these works, "have preserved the ideal of the 'Perfection of Art,' which would otherwise have been lost." And Nicolas Poussin, who has studied their writings, "is of the moderns the most 'perfect'—equal to the ancients." The *Sacrifice of*

Figure 12. Titian: BACCHANAL OF THE ANDRIANS. 1518–19. Oil on canvas, 68⁷/₈×76″. *The Prado, Madrid*

23

Figure 13. Titian: WORSHIP OF VENUS.
1516–18. Oil on canvas, 67³/₄×68⁷/₈″. *The Prado, Madrid*

Iphigenia by Timanthes, praised as the most ingenious and perfect picture of ancient times, can now be compared, according to Fréart de Chambray, only with Poussin's masterpiece, the *Extreme Unction* (color-plate 29) in the series of *The Seven Sacraments* for Chantelou. Poussin is the first great "classicist."

The difference between "classic" and "classicistic" in art corresponds to the contrast in late-eighteenth-century terminology between "naïve" and "sentimental" poetry. Raphael's approach to Antiquity was naïve and direct, as, in a different way, was that of Rubens. Poussin's was colored by sentiment and reflection. "It is man whom Poussin studied via the antique," says Delacroix in *Essai sur le Poussin*, "and it is he who revives in some way the male genius of the ancients." Not only did he take the figures from ancient monuments, but the whole Antique method—the planimetric construction and its special feeling for space. Poussin reached his goal, that of equaling Antiquity, only in his later years. His preceding work is complex and varied, although it is already filled with his feeling for, and knowledge of, Antiquity. Only in his Maniera Magnifica did Poussin achieve

full splendor and dignity as a classicist; and only thereafter was he considered a *maître sublime* by his friends and admirers in Paris.

IV. POUSSIN AND THE HIGH RENAISSANCE: TITIAN AND RAPHAEL

Poussin's preoccupation with ancient art and culture did not by any means suppress his innate love for colorful poetry, the *colori poetici* that Marino had praised so highly. The bucolic, erotic fantasies and the fairy-tale-like qualities in Hellenistic and Roman poetry and art quite early attracted the artist's fancy. In Mancini's admiring words, Poussin possessed, as a young man, an extraordinary knowledge of this area of Antiquity, especially the Ovidian stories; bacchanals, nymphs, satyrs, *putti*, and river gods appealed to his humanistic imagination. And where could he find mythological or romantic scenes of this sort expressed in such variety and, above all, such colorful richness as in the Venetian painting that had stemmed from Giorgione's and Titian's art? Mancini's report that Poussin was already influenced by Venetian ideas and manners when he arrived in Rome is confirmed by the Venetian tonality and character of his early paintings, which gave him a certain prestige in Roman "private houses."

Yet at the time of Poussin's visit, Venice was artistically stagnant. It was like a museum filled with marvels of color from the preceding century; it therefore attracted many seventeenth-century painters, especially those from northern Europe who were on their way to Rome, the city of draftsmanship (*disegno*) and monumentality. Poussin's painting in France seems to have been mainly in tempera and fresco; in Venice, as nowhere else, he could improve his oil technique, and study light and color (*lumine e colore*). Both Pietro da Cortona, in his early frescoes in Sta. Bibiana in Rome, and Poussin were influenced by the transparent, subdued light that radiates in the cool, refined color system of Paolo Veronese's canvases. In general, Poussin never imitated Venetian compositions directly; except for the posture of Paris Bordone's dead Christ (fig. 11) which Poussin may have borrowed for *Narcissus and Echo* (colorplate 9), there are no motifs recognizably

Figure 14. Raphael: DEATH OF ANANIAS. 1515–16. Cartoon, watercolor and charcoal on paper laid down on canvas.
H. M. the Queen, on loan to Victoria and Albert Museum, London

appropriated from the Venetian masters to be found in his entire oeuvre.

The one great exception to this, not to be compared with immediate borrowings, is the result of the enduring, profound impression made on Poussin by Titian's two great Philostratic Bacchanals: *The Andrians* (fig. 12) and the *Worship of Venus* (fig. 13; also called *Children's Bacchanal*). To these must be added Titian's *Bacchus and Ariadne* (National Gallery, London) and Giovanni Bellini's *Feast of the Gods*, finished by Titian (National Gallery of Art, Washington, D.C.; a copy ascribed by tradition to Poussin is in the National Galleries of Scotland, Edinburgh). But Poussin could only have seen these paintings in Rome, not in Venice, for they had belonged to the Este in Ferrara until some twenty-five years before, and from there had passed directly to Rome.

Joachim von Sandrart, who came to Rome in 1629, relates that in the company of Poussin, Pietro da Cortona, Claude Lorrain, and Duquesnoy, he saw one of

Titian's Bacchanals in the Palazzo Aldobrandini. Poussin may not often have had the chance to see these paintings, because their acquisition had been of dubious legality and they were not shown publicly. Nevertheless, the influence of Titian's Bacchanals is already obvious in Poussin's two tempera paintings of Children's Bacchanals which came from the Chigi family and are now in the possession of their heir, the Marchese Incisa della Rocchetta (fig. 36). They are probably dated about 1626, when Poussin worked with Duquesnoy, who was also interested in this kind of subject. However, Titian's strongest influence on Poussin is to be found during the late 1620s. We do not know whether Poussin ever made complete copies of Titian's Bacchanals, but he surely made partial copies, because he used figure types specifically from these paintings in his own works: some of the *putti*, for instance, and the type of the recumbent, sleeping Ariadne in *Midas and Bacchus* (colorplate 10), *Mars and Venus* (colorplate 13), *Nurture of Bacchus*

25

Figure 15. VISION OF ST. JAMES THE GREATER
(MADONNA DU PILIER). 1629–30.
Oil on canvas, 118$^1/_2$×95$^1/_4$″. *The Louvre, Paris*

(colorplate 18), and others (Titian had adapted this famous corner figure from a Roman sarcophagus relief). These marvelous Bacchanals initiated Poussin into the entire atmosphere of this part of Titian's imagination: light, color, and landscape motifs; Bacchic emblems; god-inspired drunkenness; and playful, rhythmical gestures and movements.

Poussin's Bacchanals are to be sharply distinguished from Titian's, however; between the two masters intervened the neo-classic revival embodied in Annibale Carracci's splendid, but rather cool, mythologies painted on the ceiling of the Farnese Gallery (fig. 87). In Titian's Bacchanals there is a seemingly uncontrolled mingling of figures, atmosphere, and colors, and a deep, natural lustiness; this degree of pagan mystery is not present in Annibale's neo-classic works. For example, in Poussin's magnificent *Triumph of Pan* for Richelieu (colorplate 19), he rejects the transitory and frieze-like procession in Annibale's *Triumph* in favor

of significant, dramatic actions; but his intertwined groups, frozen into rationalized ornament, do not approximate Titian's glowing fire.

By acknowledging the force of colorful light, Poussin goes beyond Annibale's essentially linear manner. Poussin's classicistic "glamour" is of his own making and absolutely different from that of Annibale or his followers. The cool blues that dominate such mythological and fantastic paintings as *Luna and Endymion* (colorplate 14) or *Aurora and Cephalus* (colorplate 15) are surrounded by warm earth colors, based on a deep reddish ground underneath. This extremely painterly technique is developed from Titian's coloristically "dissolved" manner. It is very clear in the landscape backgrounds of Poussin's compositions from the late 1620s throughout most of the 1630s. The powerful masses of trees, a diffused light shining through the leaves, are drawn from those in Titian's middle period. The arrangement of open sections that lead to atmospheric distance, in contrast with elements in the foreground, is also Titianesque. It has recently been demonstrated, moreover, that Poussin used Titian's drawing technique for his own landscape drawings (J. Shearman, in *Actes du Colloque Poussin*, I). Unlike many contemporary artists who were influenced by Titian, Poussin derived inspiration almost exclusively from Titian's Bacchic works. Nothing from the whole of Titian's impressive religious painting seems to be reflected in Poussin's art—neither Titian's dramatic scenes in Sta. Maria della Salute from the 1540s (which fascinated Rubens), nor the grandiose Passion scenes (for example, Titian's late *Crowning with Thorns*, which inspired Lodovico Carracci).

It is true that Titian's influence upon Poussin had altogether ceased by the period of the Maniera Magnifica. But he never entirely forgot the example of Titian, and in Poussin's old age it re-emerges in a new, perhaps richer way. Poussin, whose highest desire was to recapture the glory of ancient painting, found or regained inspiration from Titian's most pagan mythologies—such as *Diana and Actaeon*, or similar marvels—for his own grandiose pagan works: the *Birth of Bacchus* (colorplate 45) and *Apollo and Daphne* (colorplate 48).

Just as Titian's art was a vital source of inspiration for Poussin, so from the first Raphael furnished another source. Michelangelo, rather than Raphael, had dominated vast artistic territories during the preceding century; his irrepressible genius, especially his anatomical *disegno* and his figure types, deeply impregnated many sixteenth- and seventeenth-century minds. (Poussin used a number of Michelangelo's figures and motifs, especially from the Sistine Chapel, as part of the accepted artistic vocabulary.) In reaction to Michelangelo's intensity came the return to Raphael's art, softer and harmonizing, yet monumental. The revival of Raphael was marked in the early seventeenth century by the publication, in an edition engraved by two artists from the circle of Annibale Carracci, of the Biblical stories in the Loggias of the Vatican known as the "Bible of Raphael"; it was furthered, toward the end of the century, by the discourses on Raphael by Poussin's biographer and friend, Bellori. Therefore Poussin's Raphaelism was founded on the vogue for the *divino Raffaello* which, together with the passion for Antiquity in the seventeenth century, formed the core of conservative and classicistic art. The closer Poussin approached, in his mature work, to a conscious classicism aiming at compositional clarity and expressive, stagelike representation, the more he took Raphael's later art for his model. Between the mid-1640s and the mid-1650s, Poussin re-created the structure of certain Holy Families by Raphael and his school, including Giulio Romano. And, in compositions such as the *Death of Sapphira* (fig. 68) or *Christ and the Adulterous Woman* (fig. 67), Poussin approached more closely than anyone else the abstract classical space in Raphael's tapestry cartoons. An artistic classicism, however, was a natural expression for an artist like Raphael; Poussin arrived at classicism only through strong-willed intention. He could achieve the simplicity, clarity, and spatial abstraction so prominent in Raphael's style (see the *Death of Ananias*, fig. 14) only by subduing the impulsive vehemence and passion which his drawings show to be deeply ingrained in his artistic nature. This suppression of spontaneous feeling may be seen in his finished paintings, and for this reason Poussin's work has been called overcalculated and rigid. The conscious crystallization that takes place in Poussin's *modus operandi* explains the difference in spirit between the two masters, Poussin and Raphael.

These forms of art, so great that they seem eternal—Antiquity; the classical style of Raphael and Raphaelism; the Venetian tonality of Titian, Veronese, and others—these are the main sources of Poussin's noble art. Their influence on him differed in vitality by time and degree. Also Leonardo's influence should not be overlooked, especially in Poussin's paintings of the *affetti* in the 1630s. All other "influences" (for instance, that of Mantegna on Poussin's *Crucifixion;* fig. 54) are sporadic and ephemeral; they either disappear, or become submerged in the broad stream of his clear and conscious art.

V. POUSSIN AND HIS CONTEMPORARIES

Poussin remained, on the whole, an absolutely independent artist. He did not belong to any school,

Figure 16. Guido Reni: MASSACRE OF THE INNOCENTS. C. 1611. Oil on canvas, 105$\frac{1}{2}$×66$\frac{7}{8}$". *Gallery, Bologna*

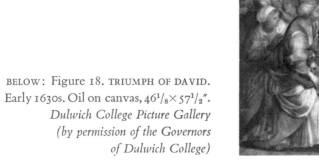

Figure 19. Domenichino:
TIMOCLEA AND ALEXANDER.
c. 1612–14. Oil on canvas,
44$^1/_2$×58$^5/_8$″. *The Louvre, Paris*

but, at least in his formative years, neither did he keep aloof from contemporary artistic trends and innovations. Occasionally he competed with contemporary masters, Guido Reni or Pietro da Cortona, and he borrowed ideas and schemes from artists of the preceding generation, such as Domenichino. Poussin's concern for the progressive ideas of his own time, as well as the art of the past, gave his works a vitality that attracted the new generation of French painters, and he thus became the undisputed leader of a new school of painting.

By the time Poussin came to Rome, the humanizing, dramatic chiaroscuro introduced by Michelangelo da Caravaggio had gone out of fashion. It had been supported mostly by "foreigners" from the Netherlands, Germany, or France, not to mention occasional visitors from Naples and elsewhere. An outstanding Caravaggist was Poussin's competitor in St. Peter's and also his countryman, Monsù Valentin of Boulogne. Poussin's connection with this serious artist was apparently not close; he had even less sympathy with the versatile and skillful Simon Vouet, and certainly none with the latter's experiments in Caravaggism. It is now a documented fact that Poussin, on his arrival in Rome in March, 1624, was acquainted with Vouet and the whole French artistic colony, but he does not seem to have paid much attention to their

works and activities. When in later years he took any note of his French confrères, he used terms of open contempt. On the other hand, Caravaggio's provocative art, like that of Michelangelo, was not easily suppressed, and its influence appears occasionally in the works of Poussin; the near crudeness of St. Joseph's naked foot, so daringly and unconventionally exposed in *Madonna on the Steps* (colorplate 32), may well have stemmed from Poussin's direct observation of Caravaggio's "naturalism."

The chiaroscuro that Poussin used in his so-called Baroque period at the end of the 1620s had less in common with Caravaggism than with the dark-tone style that had originated with Jacopo Bassano and spread throughout northern Italy. The protagonist, in the second decade of the seventeenth century, of this kind of chiaroscuro was Giovanni Lanfranco (born 1582), a turbulent and courageous student of Annibale Carracci; he was a native of Parma, the city of "illusionism," where he worked between 1610 and 1612. He did not handle chiaroscuro in a "static" way, as Caravaggio and even Bassano had done, but he made it seem to move in masses, according to principles that can be called "Baroque" and ultimately depend on the styles of Correggio, Schedoni, and Lodovico Carracci. One can discover in Poussin's large altarpieces, such as *Madonna du Pilier* (fig. 15), particular Baroque tendencies reminiscent of Lanfranco. However, Poussin's darkish style, which appears in a number of works in this period, is not a "surrender" to the Baroque. His clear, rational French spirit protected him from further steps in this direction.

But the attitude of the young painter toward the Carracci was quite different. Annibale Carracci, at least in the eyes of Poussin's generation, had rescued virtue and nature in art from the plague of Mannerism and *maniera;* he was the savior who had restored to art the dignity it had had for Raphael. The praise first bestowed on Annibale by Agucchi in his *Trattato,* written sometime between 1607 and 1615, became generally accepted, and Bellori, Poussin's friend and later his biographer, strengthened this appreciation in the introduction to his *Vite.* Poussin was undeniably indebted to Annibale in conceiving his artistic ideal, and advanced in a similar direction toward the *grande manière.* Nevertheless, Poussin throughout his life remained astonishingly independent of Annibale, both in details of form and, generally, in invention. Poussin painted the same subjects that Annibale had chosen for the Farnese Gallery—*Aurora and Cephalus, Luna and Endymion, Polyphemus*—but with a fundamentally different point of view; they are no longer graceful and amorous showpieces, but dramatic psychological problems.

Of the other followers of the Carracci (the Roman-Bolognese school, in the old terminology), there are only two artistic personalities who had importance for Poussin: Guido Reni (born 1575) and Domenichino (born 1581). The difference between the two was already well known by then, and often passionately discussed. Poussin admired, no doubt, the fascinating "beauty line" of Reni's figures and the much-refined, enamel-like colors, which he sometimes tried to emulate (for example, the head and helmet of the mounted *capitano* in the *Martyrdom of St. Erasmus;* colorplate 4). But he did not absorb what I call the "operatic" manner of Reni, which Reni partly shared with Lodovico Carracci. Reni, as Bernini relates, was personally not very amiable toward his French competitor, and his art was a challenge to Poussin. Poussin's large *Massacre of the Innocents* (colorplate 8) is in some respects an answer and correction to Reni's famous composition of the subject, so decorative and melodious (fig. 16). Poussin, like Reni, restricted this

Figure 20. Pietro da Cortona:
ST. BIBIANA REFUSING TO SACRIFICE TO IDOLS.
1624–25. Fresco. *Sta. Bibiana, Rome*

usually many-figured composition to a few persons. But he went further: intentionally avoiding any trace of Reni's elegant, lyrical beauty, he concentrated the dramatic action into one group of powerful, rustic Romans (reminiscent of *Gaul Killing Himself and His Wife;* fig. 108) and, using the motif of the soldier stepping on the neck of an infant, he stressed the cruelty of the murderous action somewhat in the brutal manner described in the poem by his friend, Marino (see Commentary 8).

Well known and often repeated is the contemporary anecdote of the old woman who, standing before Domenichino's *Scourging of St. Andrew* (fig. 17), explains to her child all the events to be seen in the fresco; but before Reni's counterpart, *St. Andrew Led to Martyrdom,* she can find nothing to say. Poussin must have known and liked the anecdote, because it demonstrates the clear readability of Domenichino's narrative style, which corresponded to Poussin's fundamental intentions.

Domenichino's influence on Poussin in his early Roman years was, however, neither immediate nor

30

decisive. Mancini observed clearly that Poussin, although he learned academic discipline in Domenichino's drawing academy, deviated by embroidering these principles with Venetian ideas. When Domenichino left Rome for Naples about 1630, Poussin, according to Passeri, continued to draw from the model in the studio of Andrea Sacchi. Sacchi in the early 1630s was the leader of the anti-Baroque movement whose principles underlay his controversy with Pietro da Cortona, in the Academy of St. Luke; he fought for simple, lucid composition against Baroque profusion and illusionism. The two ceilings in the Palazzo Barberini, one by Sacchi, the other by Cortona, are documents of these opposing principles: extremely different from one another, they nevertheless provide admirable models, practically and theoretically, for the styles evolved later, classicistic and Baroque. Quite possibly (see D. Mahon, *Gazette des Beaux-Arts*, LX) the restrained, abstract style inaugurated by Sacchi provoked and fortified Poussin's latent classicizing tendencies. Sacchi, too, probably admired Domenichino above other artists of the older generation because in Domenichino's purified art, linear tactility (*disegno*) was emphasized at the expense of color.

It is remarkable that Domenichino had no direct or even visible influence on Poussin while the latter, a newcomer to the Roman art world, was studying in Domenichino's drawing academy. Only when Poussin, in company with Sacchi and Duquesnoy, definitely revolted against the popular and powerful Baroque tendencies represented in painting by Lanfranco and Pietro da Cortona, did he become converted to Domenichino's art—and only to a relatively early phase of his art. The unexpectedly monumental works that Domenichino created in the 1620s, after Poussin came to Rome (especially the important frescoes in the apse of S. Andrea della Valle), did not impress Poussin. He preferred instead the simple linearism and clear narration that characterize Domenichino's style in S. Gregorio Magno (1608), in Grottaferrata (1608–10), and in the St. Cecilia frescoes in S. Luigi dei Francesi (1614; although these are more complicated).

In Poussin's interesting, but stylistically rather disturbing, *Triumph of David* (fig. 18), painted in the early 1630s, is the first complete confession of his strong interest in the planimetric construction and sober factual style that are manifest in Domenichino's *Scourging of St. Andrew* (fig. 17). In this and similar works by Domenichino Poussin found support for his own anti-Baroque sentiments of the beginning of the 1630s. Thus he composed *Schoolmaster of the Falerii* (first version, c. 1635) in a purely narrative manner based on Domenichino's charming oval painting, *Timoclea and Alexander* (fig. 19). Still more important

Figure 21. Pietro da Cortona:
RAPE OF THE SABINE WOMEN.
c. 1629. Oil on canvas,
9'1¼"×13'10½". *Capitoline Museum, Rome*

31

for the structural quality of Poussin's mature art was Domenichino's planimetric arrangement of the pictorial surface: in compositions like *St. Cecilia Distributing Alms* (S. Luigi dei Francesi), which show many figures in the foreground and nearly cubic buildings behind, these elements are arranged parallel to the surface. In addition to his studies of ancient art and of Raphael, Poussin, in many of his compositions of the 1640s and 1650s, was indebted to Domenichino's space construction.

The more that Poussin, in his later monumental phase, found his ideal of form and space in Raphael's art, the more he was inclined to follow Domenichino, who has occasionally been called the Raphael of the *seicento*. Poussin's painting of the *Vision of St. Paul* (1643; Museum, Sarasota) for his friend, Chantelou, resembles Domenichino's *St. Paul* even more than it does Raphael's *Vision of Ezekiel*, although the patron wanted it to be a pendant to the latter work.

The greatest difference between the younger and older masters is in the realm of color. The dichotomy in importance between color and line is less great in Poussin's art than in Domenichino's; Poussin chose to hold a book entitled *De Lumine et Colore* in one of his self-portraits (fig. 117). Even in Poussin's later paintings, where *disegno* is more emphasized than in his youthful productions, the volume of the figures remains conditioned by a strong system of color. Poussin's feeling for color is already clear in his drawings, with their astonishing, deep-toned washes of bistre. Domenichino, in his rather schoolmasterly drawings, never aimed at such splendor.

Abraham Bosse, in his treatise on the different manners of painting, drawing, and engraving, declared that, among the good painters in his time, only two —a Frenchman, Nicolas Poussin, and an Italian, Pietro da Cortona, both of whom were living in Rome— could truly be called excellent. By the time of writing, 1649, Poussin and Pietro da Cortona were the leading exponents in Rome of two diametrically opposed tendencies. However in the 1620s, when Poussin first arrived in Italy, their differences were less clear.

Pietro da Cortona was not then the illusionistic wizard he was later to become; his easel paintings and his frescoes of Sta. Bibiana seem to have a linear and ornamental style that is more "Early Baroque" than "High Baroque." Poussin was two years the elder,

but still somewhat *en retard* in his métier. He was certainly impressed by the frescoes Pietro was then painting in Sta. Bibiana (fig. 20). When one studies the clear color scheme of Poussin's *Martyrdom of St. Erasmus* (colorplate 4), the only comparison one can find in Roman works of the time is with these frescoes. In fact, Poussin is indebted in his *Erasmus* to Pietro da Cortona for more than color; the commission for the altarpiece itself had first been Pietro's and he had already made a sketch for it (fig. 88).

Differences between the two painters emerge in the mid-1630s. Poussin, in his second version of the *Rape of the Sabine Women* (colorplate 24), challenged Pietro da Cortona much as he had challenged Reni in *Massacre of the Innocents* (colorplate 8). In his second *Sabine Women* the figures are taller and the colors more vivid, and thus he came closer to Cortona's masterpiece of the same subject (fig. 21). But the great difference between their works is what Poussin added to his version, that was lacking in Pietro da Cortona's in spite of its color and brilliant ballet gestures—namely, drama and passion.

Nothing could be more significant than the artistic moral that is implicit in the work of these two great artists. Poussin had surely not been tempted to follow the great protagonists of the Baroque illusionistic trend, Pietro da Cortona, Bernini, and Borromini. The division between Italian Baroque and French Classicism, epitomized in the work of Pietro da Cortona and Nicolas Poussin respectively, was definitely and forever decided in the 1640s.

VI. POUSSIN'S ARTISTIC CHARACTER AND METHOD OF WORKING

If we interpret Poussin's words correctly, both natural impulse and assiduity are essential to the formation of an artist. Natural impulse is given by the Fates. One has it or one has it not, and nothing can be done to acquire it. The other factor, which particularly concerns Poussin in his maturity, is assiduity—the indefatigable, obstinate will to transform an impulse, a first idea, into a work of high perfection. This can be obtained only by knowledge and methodical thinking.

Figure 22. STATUE OF ANTINOUS.
Engraving. *Bibliothèque Nationale, Paris*

The "inventions" of his early years in Rome were mostly lyric and poetic. Later, in his maturity, his mind turned to more serious themes, dramatic or moralizing. But no matter what Poussin painted, his imagination was only the basis for a perfection, a finality, that far exceeded the preliminary steps or trials. He overlooked no information pertinent to the whole painting, no detail that might contribute to this final goal. Consequently, his studies went beyond what was customary for most painters in his day. He read learned treatises on perspective and optics—Félibien mentions that he admired Albrecht Dürer's books on proportion and Leon Battista Alberti's treatise on painting. In the library of the Barberini he studied manuscripts on perspective by Matteo Zoccolini, the Theatine monk who had taught perspective to Domenichino, and he had them (or parts of them) copied by his secretary Jean Dughet in the later 1630s. His own studies of the proportions of ancient statues, for which he collaborated with the Flemish sculptor François Duquesnoy, consisted of making elaborate measurements to determine the anatomical proportions of well-known Roman statues, for example, the so-called *Antinous* (the engraving of this famous statue, marked with proportional notations, was published by Bellori as an addendum to his *Life of Poussin;* see fig. 22). Poussin himself made wax models after the *putti* in Titian's *Worship of Venus* (fig. 13), and is said to have much helped Duquesnoy to understand and appreciate the beauty of classical statuary. At different times of his life, Poussin tried the medium of sculpture. He is said to have made a wax copy of the famous *Sleeping Ariadne* in the Vatican, and he later modeled a series of herms for the *Surintendant* Foucquet. The technical procedure that he adopted to give form to his ideas was characteristic. As Bellori describes it, Poussin first composed a story or fable in the form of a rough sketch, and fashioned little wax models about four inches high of all the figures in their proper attitudes in order to study the natural effect upon them of light and shadow. He then made larger, clothed models to study the arrangement of the drapery on the nude body, using several small pieces of moist linen in a variety of colors. Poussin's method is very different from that of Caravaggio and his followers, who composed directly on the canvas; but it had been used in Venice, especially by Tintoretto, and

Lorenzo Bernini seems to have cleverly understood and appreciated both components of Poussin's art. During his visit to Paris in 1665, guided by Poussin's enthusiastic patron and friend Chantelou, he had occasion to look at quite a number of paintings by Poussin, and his remarks on them are very interesting. On seeing a Bacchanal by Poussin in Chantelou's house, he praised Poussin's natural talent for inventing a lively, poetic scene, and exclaimed: "What an incomparable narrator and storyteller is this man!" But, on another occasion, when he saw Poussin's landscape with the story of Phocion, he alluded to the other ingredient of Poussin's art, pointing to his head and saying, "Poussin works from here" (*Il signor Poussin lavora di là*). Bernini's reactions provide a key to the understanding of Poussin's artistic character, so abundantly endowed with fanciful emotion and co-ordinating intelligence.

From the Marino Drawings, his earliest project, to the storied landscapes of his old age, Poussin never lacked ideas and *invenzioni*.

33

also by Federico Barrocci (see Bellori's *Life of Barrocci*).

In Rome Poussin continued the anatomical studies which he had already begun as a young man in Paris. It is related that he studied the writings and figures in the famous work on anatomy by Vesalius, and also took part in the lectures and dissections of the learned surgeon, Ambroise Paré. Poussin never lost the wish to understand the theoretical and practical bases of artistic construction. When he was nearing sixty his vivid interest in theories and controversies about proportion and artistic geometry is still evident in his remarks in a letter (c. 1651) to the engraver Abraham Bosse, a belligerent theorist.

Apart from this research in construction, Poussin also found it necessary to inform himself of more general matters pertaining to the art of painting. He read erudite books on history, music, dialectic, and philosophy. Poussin's aim was to make his compositions so accurate that they would have convincing truth—truth, in the sense of credibility, which would be enhanced by the visual beauty of movement and color. Having painstakingly verified his work in every part, Poussin could proudly declare (as it has been related), "I have neglected nothing." One is reminded of the dictum of Descartes, who shared Poussin's passion for truth: "Do not take to be true that which is false, but strive to attain the knowledge of all things."

Poussin distinguished between two ways of seeing (in a letter of 1642 to Sublet de Noyers): one, the *aspect*, is simple perceiving, and is a natural function; the other, the *prospect*, or seeing with consideration and attention, is an activity of reason. This separation of the lower, mechanical function of the eye from its higher, rational potentiality clarifies the description he gave of himself: "My nature forces me to search for and to love well-ordered things, fleeing confusion, which is as contrary and inimical to me as deep darkness is to light." Poussin held strongly to the conviction that the original idea must be crystallized, if a painting were to have utmost clarity and perspicuity. By this crystallization, the conception was elevated beyond the merely naturalistic to a higher intellectual plane. A comparison of his drawings with his finished paintings, or of his earlier and later versions of the same subject, demonstrates Poussin's constant effort toward clearer form and content.

Figure 23. Leonardo da Vinci: Illustration in *Trattato della Pittura* (Codex Vaticano Urbinate 1270). Drawing, pen and ink. *Vatican Library, Rome*

The difference between the preliminary sketches and drawings and the final paintings is sometimes striking. The former are often quick impressions of scenes perceived subjectively—impulsive, emotional, the composition often in apparent confusion; the latter are idealized, the execution of the theme being carefully planned and controlled. Many of Poussin's drawings are impetuous in this way—sketchy and sweeping, the light and shade often handled with a tremendous violence that is comparable to some of Rembrandt's drawings; they reveal what Poussin intentionally disguised in his paintings.

The fundamental changes between the first and second (and even third and fourth) versions are perhaps even more exciting than those between drawings and paintings of the same theme. No other artist's work shows such a conscious change of treatment in the second version of a painting. Titian, for instance, painted two versions of Danaë and of the Crowning with Thorns, but their variations come less from a changed intention than from the artist's developing style. Poussin's second versions are always more precise and concise, more concentrated and epigrammatic. The transformation may move from the informal to the hieratic (*Et In Arcadia Ego*, colorplates 12, 27; or *Inspiration of the Poet*, colorplate 16; fig. 32), or from a painterly, coloristic treatment to a severe, late-Hellenistic relief style (*Nurture of Jupiter*, colorplate 28; fig. 111). Invariably, however, the last version is final,

34

Figure 24. PARNASSUS.
1626–27. Oil on canvas, 57¹/₈×77⁵/₈".
The Prado, Madrid

completely thought out; it would be impossible to change. A prominent instance of first and second versions is his two series of *The Seven Sacraments.* Poussin was unwilling to copy for Chantelou the series he had first made for Cassiano dal Pozzo. Instead he made for his French patron seven completely new paintings, expanding the modest, more loosely organized series he had painted earlier into a grandiose second version. Reason and intelligence dominate this series, replacing the more visual aspect of the first set (see colorplates 29, 30). The steps that have led from the imperfect to the perfect seem part of an organic development, thus making us forget the intervening intellectual endeavor.

VII. POUSSIN AS THEORIST: THE THEORIES OF THE MODES AND AFFETTI

Poussin's deliberate classicism in his later years made him by definition a theorist. On the other hand, he did not explain his theories in writing as clearly as he

demonstrated them in his compositions. With his theory of the modes he attempted to systematize the relation between content and sentiment. In Poussin's opinion, more than in other painters', different subjects require different manners of representation. Angered by Chantelou's remark that he preferred a painting made by Poussin for Pointel to one made for him, Poussin defended himself by answering simply (perhaps a little rudely): "Pray do not count me among those who in singing take always the same note: I can vary when I wish." The so-called theory of the modes that Poussin expounded in another letter to Chantelou (Nov. 24, 1647) is actually a translation of excerpts from a sixteenth-century book on music theory, *Istituzioni Harmoniche,* by Giuseppe Zarlino (a splendid discovery by A. Blunt, in *Bulletin de la société de l'histoire de l'art français,* 1933). Poussin, always pleased to have a classical precedent for his own methods, transposed the idea of the classical Greek modes of music, used to express different moods, into a kind of rule for painting. Accordingly, the Phrygian mode was to be used for violent scenes, such as battles; the Lydian mode was applied to tragic and mournful subjects; the Ionic mode was joyous, appropriate to

Figure 25. CORONATION OF DAVID. Late 1620s–early 1630s. Oil on canvas, 39×51¹/₈″. *The Prado, Madrid*

festivals and bacchanals; the Hypolydian mode suited sacred subjects; and so on.

Poussin did not systematically formulate his theory of the modes, lifted from ancient musical theory, until 1647. But ten years earlier, without using the exact Antique terms "Doric" and "Ionic," he had written in a letter to Jacques Stella, perhaps feeling the need to justify himself, that he had made a painting (either the lost *Rinaldo and Armida* or the brilliant *Pan and Syrinx*, colorplate 23) in a "soft" *(mol)* manner, different from *Schoolmaster of the Falerii* (fig. 27) for Phélipeaux de la Vrillère which he painted in the same year in a more severe manner, "as is reasonable, considering that the subject is heroic." This tendency to make different subjects conform with different modes (to which he did not always adhere strictly, especially in his earlier paintings) is surely founded on Poussin's deep conviction that he must give to each subject its proper "decorum" or *costume*.

Poussin's theory of the *affetti* reflects a similar aim toward clarity of expression as that which underlies his theory of the *modi*. The *affetti*, or emotions, meant to Poussin and to the seventeenth century in general the outward manifestations, in movement or gesture, of inward reactions, either psychic or physical.

Through systematizing the *affetti*, Poussin delineated certain clear, unmixed emotions, associating with each emotion a distinguishing attitude. To create his vocabulary of gestures, Poussin followed in general the dictates of Roman rhetorical writers (Cicero, and especially Quintilian, who describe appropriate oratorical gestures in detail). Poussin also illustrated, and therefore must have known well, Leonardo's *Trattato della Pittura* (first published in French and Italian, 1651), which contains Leonardo's naturalistic observation that an inward emotion must be depicted by its outward physical effect (figs. 23, 42).

A renewed interest in systems governing the emotions or passions prevailed in philosophic and artistic circles in France, culminating in the *Traité des Passions*, published in 1649 by René Descartes. Poussin's fame in the French Academy was largely the result of his special gift in portraying emotions. Such works as the *Gathering of the Manna* (colorplate 25) and *Moses Striking the Rock* (Collection Earl of Ellesmere) were greatly admired by Le Brun and his fellows and meticulously analyzed for their epigrammatic strength and didactic potentiality, each figure being "read" separately for its particular psychological expression. This method of analysis was intended and approved by Poussin him-

36

Figure 26. CONTINENCE OF SCIPIO. c. 1642. Drawing, pen and bistre wash, 6⁷/₈×12″. *Musée Condé, Chantilly*

self, for he instructs Chantelou, in a letter of 1639 about the *Gathering of the Manna*, to observe the movements of each figure and thereby to discover its particular emotion (see chap. IX).

VIII. POUSSIN AS MORALIST: THE STOICAL SUBJECTS

The general affinity which has often been observed between Nicolas Poussin and two of his French contemporaries, Descartes and Corneille, is based partly upon the Stoic conceptions underlying the work of all three. The revival of Stoicism at the end of the sixteenth century (particularly in Holland, under the influence of the new humanism) provided a fundamental part of the entire spiritual complex in France in the seventeenth century. This neo-Stoicism is dependent upon the philosophical thought of Seneca, as it was expressed in his letters; very famous was the French translation by Seigneur de Pressac of the *Epîtres Morales de Sénèque* (Lyons, 1598), dedicated to Henri IV of France. In the preface, the leaders of France are asked to study especially those philosophical discourses which create in the soul a firm and absolute resolution to resist accidents of fortune and death. The well-known French moralist Pierre Charron, friend and successor of Montaigne, was deeply indebted to Seneca: Poussin surely knew well Charron's *Traité de la Sagesse* (Bordeaux, 1601), which undoubtedly influenced his spiritual development.

The Stoicism of the seventeenth century was somewhat different from that taught in the ancient Stoa. The neo-Stoics recognized that passions are inherent in the nature of man; they should not be despised or suppressed, but governed and controlled by reason. Corneille, in his great tragedies, incarnates the human passions in various characters who are in each case the embodiment and condensation of a particular passion. In contrast to Shakespeare, he leaves aside details of personality and emphasizes only the particular trait. The dramatic action in his plays depends on the action of the will; thus the role of external circumstances in the development of the plot is diminished. The restraint in Poussin's pictures is in some respects parallel to that in the plays of Corneille, and to the structure of Descartes' logic.

The moralizing and didactic element in Poussin's mature paintings distinguishes him clearly from his

37

Figure 27. SCHOOLMASTER OF THE FALERII. 1637.
Oil on canvas, 99¼×105½″. *The Louvre, Paris*

Figure 28. DEATH OF VIRGINIA. C. 1648. Drawing,
pen and bistre wash, 6⅞×9⅛″. *Royal Library, Windsor Castle
(by gracious permission of H. M. the Queen)*

Italian contemporaries; it is derived in great part from the French neo-Stoical milieu, as well as from Poussin's own upper-bourgeois morality. Through the

process of "crystallization" Poussin brought his art not only to a highly classicistic beauty, but to a strongly didactic impressiveness. When he said "La fin de l'art est la délectation," he was not referring only to the delight of the senses; he meant that the purpose of art is a more sublime delectation of the soul. To some extent, even Poussin's paintings having subjects which seem to be simply sensuous (such as the Bacchanals) lead to a delectation that in some way has been purified by his clear and rational forms. However, the moralizing Stoical subjects which he chose when painting in his grandiose and mature style clearly "instruct as well as delight," and they tangibly ally Poussin not only with Stoical tendencies but with Corneille and Descartes as well.

In his first Roman period, Poussin was not deeply interested in the stories of Stoic virtue and heroism told by ancient writers. He was still captivated by the typical humanistic hero of the High Renaissance, who is endowed by the gods with physical or intellectual powers and rewarded by them with the laurel wreath. Poussin's *Parnassus* (fig. 24) is nothing but an assembly of such heroes in accordance with the Renaissance tradition. In several other paintings of the 1620s and early 1630s, he singled out a solitary hero—the poet, the intellectual spirit (*Inspiration of the Poet*, colorplate 16), or David, crowned as a personification of virtue and strength (*Coronation of David*, fig. 25; see chap. IX). Poussin preferred a quiet, lyric treatment for representing the elevation of the artist whose virtue is inherent in mental superiority (for example, his two versions of *Inspiration of the Poet;* colorplate 16; fig. 32). Using the same method to depict David, Poussin comes close to the Herculean hero painted by Annibale Carracci (Palazzo Sampieri, Bologna, and National Museum, Naples), and by Rubens (the *Crowning of the Hero*, Dresden Gallery).

In much later works, painted after his return from Paris, Poussin had begun to abhor these vanities and to praise a quite different hero, the *honnête homme*. The virtue of this hero resides entirely within himself, and is the product of his own strong will. Poussin found examples of such men of virtue in the collections of moralizing stories by Roman writers. Livy, Plutarch, Valerius Maximus, and others tell of *exempla virtutis* (examples of virtue) that demonstrate the perseverance of a particular hero in the face of evil fortune, great

Figure 29. ADORATION OF THE SHEPHERDS.
c. 1637. Oil on canvas, 38×29″. *National Gallery, London
(by courtesy of the Trustees)*

temptation, or despair. Poussin's subjects illustrate many of these themes: Phocion, whose honor is reaffirmed after his unjust execution (colorplate 39; fig. 74); Scipio, who magnanimously renounces his right to a Numidian princess and returns her, with her dowry, to her betrothed (fig. 26); Camillus, who refuses to accept as hostages the children of the Falerian nobility, when their traitorous schoolmaster presents them to him (fig. 27); Eudamidas, who trusts the friendship of his townsmen so firmly that he wills his penniless family to their care (colorplate 35). Poussin had less interest in the Stoical bravura pieces that emphasize physical courage (Marcus Curtius, Mucius Scaevola, Horatius Cocles); apart from his drawing *Death of Virginia* (fig. 28), he always portrayed the virtues of the mind. Subjects such as *Et In Arcadia Ego* (colorplate 27) and *Dance to the Music of Time* (fig. 33) express in a more general way the same triumph of the mind over the vicissitudes of fate and calm acceptance of inevitable death.

The concept of the *honnête homme* was particularly suited to the educated, strong-minded class of the *bourgeoisie;* less influential and magnificent than the aristocracy, this class was nevertheless a dominant part of French cultural and political life. Poussin was much admired in these circles, and during the 1640s (especially after his trip to Paris) he was commissioned by such patrons as Fréart de Chantelou, Pointel, and Cérisier for many Stoical subjects. These patrons included some of Poussin's closest friends, who encouraged him to continue this line. However Poussin's *Death of Germanicus* (colorplate 2), painted for the Barberini about 1627, already gives us direct evidence that as a young man he had great feeling for such moralizing scenes—in this case the dying soldier-hero surrounded by loyal soldiers who pledge to avenge his murder.

IX. SUBJECT MATTER: PAINTINGS BEFORE 1635

The method an artist uses to project, develop, and execute his works has been often observed, and it sometimes provides the only criterion of real interest in the evaluation of his work. Equally important, though less frequently analyzed, is the consideration of what the artist wished to express in his finished work, and of how he wanted to impress the spectator by illustrating a chosen theme with new power, more profoundly than it had been previously treated. To Poussin it seemed especially important to present the various episodes replete with psychological tension; his efforts to show the refined relationships among the characters intensified as his work developed.

Poussin's development was slow and irregular. Had he, like Raphael, Caravaggio, or Mozart, died at the age of thirty-seven (or even forty-five), many of his works would certainly have been appreciated and admired, but posterity might not have esteemed him much higher than Fetti, for example, or than his countryman, Louis Le Nain. He would not have been proclaimed the standard-bearer of classicism, the undisputed leader of the French art in "le grand siècle." "Greatness" was attributed to him for the singularly outstanding works that he painted when he was fifty, or older; only these consolidated his fame and glory.

39

Figure 30. ADORATION OF THE MAGI.
1633. Oil on canvas,
63×71¼". *Gallery, Dresden*

Thus there is a particular difference between the respective oeuvres of Poussin and of Titian—and, to a lesser degree, of Rubens. Nothing in Poussin's early and middle periods has the historical significance of Titian's *St. Peter Martyr*, or Rubens' *Descent from the Cross* in Antwerp Cathedral. In comparison with these artists, Poussin was definitely handicapped: he had not Titian's advantage of the superb tradition of Bellini and Giorgione, nor Rubens' aristocratic, humanistic education. His was a longer struggle than theirs for his livelihood and education. Therefore, despite his strong personality and his undeniable energy (the "furia del diavolo" of which Marino speaks), Poussin as a young man had to wait for favorable occasions; meanwhile, the commissions he accepted limited his time for choosing topics adequate to his talent and imagination.

The limitations imposed by the existing art market of course affected Poussin most strongly at the beginning of his career. In France, he had painted what was in demand: devotional paintings, altarpieces for small churches (later, for more important ones), portraits, and decorative murals for country castles—

mythological subjects and bacchanals. One can assume that he specialized more and more in the last category, for the mythological drawings he made with such facility and skill for Marino (see chap. I) show that the young artist was already remarkably experienced in the genre of "fancy," which presupposes an extensive knowledge of ancient literature, especially poetry. Presumably this gentle art and knowledge continued, after he left his country, to be his main stock in trade with the Roman public.

BATTLE SCENES AND MASSACRES

Poussin's drawings for Marino were not only from Ovid's *Metamorphoses*, but also included a number of battle scenes, mostly from Virgil's *Aeneid* (see J. Costello, *Journal of the Warburg and Courtauld Institutes*, 1955). The earliest works Bellori mentions Poussin having painted in Rome are two oblong pieces showing fighting soldiers, based on the Old Testament (*Victory of Joshua Over the Amalekites*, The Hermitage, Leningrad; *Victory of Joshua Over the Amorites*, Pushkin Museum, Moscow). A third painting of an Old Testament battle has been found recently in the Vatican. These compositions are in the manner of reliefs on Roman battle sarcophagi, but they are also Raphaelesque (for example, the *Battle of Ostia*, Stanza dell'Incendio, Vatican). Engravings of works by Raphael, as well as numerous sarcophagi, were available in France, and these battle pieces could, from a stylistic point of view, have been executed in Paris. It was possibly this type of work that brought Poussin his first commission in Rome, *Conquest of Jerusalem*, for which he received payment from the Barberini in February, 1626; this, too, was a battle scene, though enlarged by the addition of more precise historical detail. (This version is lost; the version now in the Kunsthistorisches Museum, Vienna, was painted much later.) The vogue for turbulent, ferocious fighting scenes had been propagated in the late sixteenth century by Antonio Tempesta, and the series of battle scenes that Giuseppe Cesare d'Arpino began in the mid-1590s was greatly admired by Pietro da Cortona; one, in the Borghese Gallery, is particularly close to Poussin's battle scenes. This genre was later favored by Giovanni Lanfranco, who gave it a curious roman-

Figure 32. INSPIRATION OF ANACREON. Late 1620s. Oil on canvas, 37×27¹/₄". *Landesmuseum, Hanover*

Figure 31. FLIGHT INTO EGYPT IN A BOAT. 1637–38. Oil on canvas, 44×37". *Dulwich College Picture Gallery (by permission of the Governors of Dulwich College)*

tic-historic turn (among other examples, *Fight of the Gladiators*, The Prado, Madrid). Poussin's interest in Roman military events may also be behind his *Hannibal Crossing the Alps* (recently discovered by Charles Sterling, though only in a copy). Hannibal, in full Roman armor and a big helmet, is mounted on a gigantic elephant and rises above scattered small figures of Roman soldiers. Poussin mentions this work in his first letter, c. 1627, to Cassiano dal Pozzo (see chap. III). Possibly painted during these Roman years (c. 1625–26) was the violent *Massacre of the Innocents* (Petit Palais, Paris; damage and overpainting make it difficult to date); it is a cruel scene, in the sense of the descriptions in the poem "Massacre of the Innocents" by Poussin's friend and patron, Marino (see chap. V). In Poussin's probably later, much superior *Massacre* (colorplate 8) there are only a few figures, and their sculptural nobility tempers the cruelty of their actions. After this early period, Poussin avoided topics of

41

bloodthirsty violence, which may be not without interest for the artist's psychology. Except for his second *Conquest of Jerusalem* (Kunsthistorisches Museum, Vienna), painted on special commission for the Barberini, he did not return to subjects of this kind.

Figure 33. DANCE TO THE MUSIC OF TIME. 1638–40.
Oil on canvas, 32¹/₄×41³/₈″. *The Wallace Collection, London (by permission of the Trustees)*

Figure 34. Guercino: ET IN ARCADIA EGO. C. 1620.
Oil on canvas, 32×35⁷/₈″. *Palazzo Corsini, Rome*

Subjects from the New Testament are relatively rare in Poussin's oeuvre during the 1620s or 1630s. At that time, he was less interested in devotional, specifically Christian topics than he later became, although his drawings show that he must already have been occupied with compositional problems presented by the figuration of certain New Testament subjects.

Around 1630 or even earlier he made quite a few sketches and versions of the Annunciation to the Virgin: the only painting now preserved is the interesting, and certainly genuine, *Annunciation* (fig. 123) which seems to foreshadow in its turbulence the *Annunciation* of 1657 (colorplate 44). There are also numerous versions of the Adoration of the Shepherds preserved, for the most part, in engravings or sketches (see W. Friedlaender and A. Blunt, *Drawings;* Andresen, in his useful and excellent catalogue of engravings after Poussin, enumerates no fewer than seven versions of this venerable topic). The only extant painting from about 1636 is the beautiful, very classical *Adoration of the Shepherds* (fig. 29) recently acquired by the National Gallery, London (engraved by Picart); the customary group is enlarged to include a Raphaelesque shepherdess bearing a large basket of fruit. The scene is set before the fantastic ruins of a temple, through whose columns may be seen the Annunciation to the Shepherds.

The *Adoration of the Magi* (fig. 30) is one of the few paintings that Poussin signed and dated; at one time it was thought to be his reception piece for the Academy of St. Luke. Excellently and diligently designed and painted, it is an accomplished work of academic perfection: with its severe, classical Renaissance forms, it presents a rather official and strained appearance. If (as D. Mahon maintains in *Gazette des Beaux-Arts*, LX) it really marks the turning point from *colore* to *disegno* in Poussin's art, then it would be the almost pedantic beginning of an evolution that was to be far from pedantic. The two drawings for this painting are similarly classical, academic, and dull.

From this period, the various groups of the Holy Family and the Rest on the Flight into Egypt, of which the best known are the *Pearson Madonna* (colorplate 1) from the end of the 1620s, and the somewhat later *Holy Family (Reinhart Madonna;* fig. 86), are fresh and

Figure 35. COLORING OF CORAL. Late 1620s.
Drawing, pen with brown wash and red chalk,
13⁷/₈×20¹/₄″. *Royal Library, Windsor Castle*
(by gracious permission of H. M. the Queen)

lovely in their color and composition. But one cannot seriously compare them with the grandiose, profoundly original type of Holy Family Poussin created in the 1640s and 1650s. The *Flight into Egypt in a Boat* (fig. 31), with its soaring angels who carry the large cross in the sky, is iconographically interesting. But the bearded ferryman with the characteristic band around his forehead is Christophoros; he is not Charon on the River Styx, as has been suggested, nor is he a symbol of Charon.

Apart from the early *Annunciation*, Poussin made few scenes of the Life of the Virgin that were of any importance during his first two decades in Rome; this is quite in contrast to the innumerable Assuntas and other supernatural mysteries painted, for example, by Lanfranco. Nor are representations of saints at all numerous, although there are such agreeable exceptions as *St. Cecilia* (c. 1628–29; The Prado, Madrid), who looks from her keyboard to a broad music book held by *putti* (the painting in much the style of the *Pearson Madonna;* see Commentary 1); or *The Marriage of St. Catherine* (c. 1632–34; Heathcote Amory Collection, England), in which the saint's powerful figure much resembles that of a Roman matron, and the composition is of the utmost classicality. Even scenes of the Life and Passion of Christ are rare before 1640; the *Deposition from the Cross* (The Hermitage,

Leningrad) and the *Lamentation* (colorplate 5) are almost the only ones. Both of these relatively early paintings are impressive, the one painted in full chiaroscuro, the other illuminated by its clear, strong colors. They are dramatic but emotionally not very profound, and they contain no surprising innovations.

Two large altarpieces, the *Martyrdom of St. Erasmus* (colorplate 4) and the *Vision of St. James the Greater* (*Madonna du Pilier;* fig. 15), typical Roman *seicento* paintings, both present subjects certainly not of Poussin's own choice (see chap. II). From the viewpoint of material and artistic advancement, these works could have been important for Poussin, a newcomer in Rome, particularly the *Martyrdom of St. Erasmus* painted for St. Peter's. But in spite of his artistic and technical excellence, his debut in the profitable field of large-scale paintings for churches was no great success. Rather than compete with his Roman colleagues in huge decorative altarpieces, Poussin could employ his special narrative and philosophic imagination to far better effect in canvases of medium size.

POUSSIN AND HUMANISM

Whereas Poussin's early religious paintings occur sporadically and are often of lesser importance, there is another small group of very personal early works that characterize Poussin's spiritual and artistic attitude

RIGHT: Figure 36. CHILDREN'S BACCHANAL.
c. 1626. Tempera on canvas,
22×29⁷/₈″. Collection
Marchese Incisa della Rocchetta, Rome

BELOW: Figure 37. TRIUMPH OF BACCHUS. 1635–36.
Oil on canvas, 48⁷/₈×58⁵/₈″.
Nelson Gallery–Atkins Museum, Kansas City

44

at that time. Poussin's humanistic attitude is certainly based on his own extended and profound studies of Antiquity, but it is also specifically influenced by the revival of Antiquity in the Florentine-Roman Renaissance. The apotheosis of the artist, that doctrine of genius and divine (Apollonian) inspiration so overemphasized by the Neoplatonists and in general so dear to many of the intellectuals of the *cinquecento* (brought to absurdity in Federico Zuccari's inaugural speech in 1592 to the Academy of St. Luke), was revived, somewhat anachronistically, by Nicolas Poussin.

As his starting point for representing the apotheosis of the artist in *Parnassus* (fig. 24), Poussin uses Raphael's famous *Parnassus* (Stanza della Segnatura, Vatican). But he transforms Raphael's more general representation into the apotheosis of one individual, placing the poet's dedication to Apollo at the center, where he is crowned by the Muses in the ceremony that makes him accepted as an equal in the community of famous poets. In this case, Poussin has even represented a definite personality—his friend and patron, the poet Marino (according to the spirited observation of E. Panofsky in *Nationalmusei Skriftserie, 1960*). The painting may thus be considered a humanistic

tribute to the man who introduced Poussin to learned Roman society.

There are other paintings made around 1630 that belong to this small group of humanistic works. They have as a common denominator the enraptured poet directly inspired by the god Apollo (the coronation by a *putto* is less important). The relatively small painting in Hanover (fig. 32; see Commentary 16) was arbitrarily entitled *Inspiration of Anacreon* in the late eighteenth century. This charming composition has a bucolic, informal character; its main feature is the inspiration of the poet by Apollo, who administers a draft of sacred water from the spring of the Muses. The lyric nature of the inspiration is specified by the presence of Euterpe, the Muse of lyric poetry.

The second painting, widely known as the *Inspiration of the Poet*, is more famous (colorplate 16). Poussin here represents the poet in a much more elevated action, his pen poised as he prepares to write under the direction of Apollo. On the bindings of the books are titles of epic poems, indicating that the Muse on the left is Calliope.

Poussin's humanistic feeling is also transposed, in a most interesting way, into a subject from the Old Testament, the *Coronation of David* (fig. 25). Among the innumerable representations that have been made of David, Poussin's has a unique, almost pagan character. Victory, a half-naked Antique figure, carries in her right hand the crown of David; with her left, she holds a laurel wreath over the head of the victorious hero of the Jews, who is seated before a fluted column. In his right hand is a large sword, in his left the shield of Goliath; Goliath's head is on the heaped-up armor on David's left, but at his right, *putti* play with his harp. David is thus glorified as both the warrior and the great poet of the Psalms.

These humanistic pictures were all painted within the short interval between the end of the 1620s and the beginning of the 1630s. Poussin never again painted either Muses or victors, and when he later represented Apollo, it was not as the inspiring *numen* but as the almost human god, tormented, or even slightly ridiculed, by love.

HISTORICAL PAINTINGS

Two relatively early paintings which do not belong to any of these categories have, nevertheless, a special importance in Poussin's development because they inaugurate him as a history painter. One is the *Death of Germanicus* (see Commentary 2). It would be interesting to know if Poussin himself, about 1626–27, chose this topic from Tacitus, or if it was commissioned by the Barberini—perhaps, as in the case of the *Conquest of Jerusalem*, under the influence of the erudite Cassiano dal Pozzo. In any event the impressive painting follows ancient examples in an exceptionally solemn and monumental manner for its early date, and anticipates the deathbed scenes of virtuous men, that favorite topic of Poussin's in the 1640s. The other example is *Plague of Ashdod*, painted in 1630–31 (see Commentary 7). It is not impossible that this painting was connected with a contemporary outbreak of the plague; but the right half of the composition was inspired by Marcantonio's engraving, *Plague of Phrygia* (fig. 90). This was the first of Poussin's historical paintings with an important architectural setting, and his first essay in expressing a wide range of human emotions.

MYTHOLOGIES AND STORIES FROM OVID

The topics that Poussin treated in his first working years in Rome did not develop consecutively, and were directed mostly by chance. Military, religious, and humanistic subjects appear in no particular order. Huge altarpieces alternate with smaller "recreation pieces" (*divertimenti*). Only one category is quantitatively and qualitatively outstanding in his production between 1626 and 1636; in these ten years the gentle and beautiful art of Nicolas Poussin as an illustrator and narrator becomes triumphant in the realm of ancient fairy tales and mythological short stories. Imaginative and poetic themes (*idee fantastiche*), mythologies, and romances form at least half of Poussin's production during this period. They become rarer after 1635 and disappear almost totally in the 1640s (except for his revisions of earlier themes); they reappear around 1650 in two or three isolated instances in his landscape paintings, and they are rejuvenated in a few sublime paintings and drawings of his old age style.

In contrast to the enigmatic creations of his old age, the mythologies, bacchanals, and romances that Poussin invented so abundantly in his early Roman years are purely narrative and illustrative. They were meant to be easily understood and enjoyed; to use a Poussinesque expression, they are for "reading." No meanings are deliberately hidden—at least not from a public familiar with the tradition of the classics.

Poussin's clear mind and hatred of confusion made him avoid allegories and farfetched symbolism. He used, of course, those attributes that were easily understandable as part of the artistic vocabulary of the time. For example, the doves of Venus, or the hares chased by *putti*, were almost universally recognized in the seventeenth century as Philostratic symbols of fertility or sexuality. But Poussin nevertheless abstained, on the whole, from obscurities in his early, and certainly in his middle, period. When he was later obliged on a few occasions to represent complicated, though somewhat trivial, topics—as, for instance, *Time Revealing Truth*, painted during his trip to Paris, for Richelieu—the result was rather disappointing. Poussin was evidently little interested in the full allegorical significance of the figures in his famous *Dance to the Music of Time* (fig. 33) for the prelate Giulio Rospigliosi, and he did not clearly indicate their attributes. Allegory was favored in the leisure class of the courts, but the Stoical outlook of the middle class, in which Poussin was so firmly rooted, strictly opposed it.

Poussin had the storyteller's ability to make the

sense and the content of his paintings both readable and meaningful; this talent becomes more evident from one year to the next — and certainly from one period to the next. His repertory, apart from some of his last works that show such a remarkable psychological change, consisted in large part of relatively uncomplicated subjects in all the categories in which Mancini tells us Poussin excelled: *historia*, *favola*, and *poesia*. Just as Poussin was fundamentally not a lover of allegories, he also did not search out obscure stories to paint. The mythological tales that he chose, largely from Ovid's *Metamorphoses*—Apollo and Daphne, Aurora and Cephalus, Luna and Endymion, and the Abduction of Europa—were in his time as well known as fairy tales, and they were used frequently for paintings, engravings, and book illustrations. As a great and original artist, however, Poussin made any subject into something that had a radically new style, composition, and general tenor. He created one of his most remarkably original pictures, the final version of *Nurture of Jupiter* (colorplate 28), by remodeling the interesting composition of Giulio Romano's *Infant Jupiter* (fig. 110). And following Guercino's *Et In Arcadia Ego* (fig. 34), he used the iconography of the *memento mori;* in his earlier painting of this subject

(colorplate 12) he followed it rather closely, but in his later version (colorplate 27) he changed many of its implications (as E. Panofsky has demonstrated in *Meaning in the Visual Arts*, 1955).

However, there are also many delightful paintings in which Poussin's fanciful and inventive spirit went its own way, selecting from well-known stories episodes that had never been treated before. In later years, when friends suggested that Poussin should paint the often-illustrated Abduction of Europa, he was immediately enthusiastic, finding the subject "full of richly flavored episodes" (*rempli d'épisodes fort goûtés*). Indeed, in drawing the *Rape of Europa* (fig. 85; chap. XIII), a masterpiece of his late style, Poussin used the story only as a motif, like a musical theme, and added passages of his own choice. The episodes in his early *Luna and Endymion* (colorplate 14) and *Aurora and Cephalus* (colorplate 15) are depicted with far deeper psychological significance than the more obvious love scenes to which his predecessors, the Carracci, limited themselves in the frescoes of the Farnese Gallery. In the same manner, he did not take from the legend of King Midas the often-painted Judgment of Midas in which Pan succeeds over Apollo; he chose instead the earlier part of the story, when the

Figure 39. RINALDO AND ARMIDA. 1635.
Oil on canvas, $31^1/_2 \times 42^1/_8''$.
Dulwich College Picture Gallery
(by permission of the
Governors of Dulwich College)

Figure 40. ABANDONMENT OF ARMIDA. Late 1640s. Drawing, pen and bistre wash, 7¹/₂×10″. *The Louvre, Paris*

once-greedy king tries to rid himself of the golden touch he had begged of Bacchus, because it threatens to destroy him (colorplate 11). Poussin overlooked the usual scene from the Perseus legend, the Liberation of Andromeda, in favor of its much rarer, and wonderfully poetic, conclusion: the *Coloring of Coral* (fig. 35). Before 1631–32, Poussin's mythological paintings derive their warmth of color and poetic tenor, if not so much their form, from Venetian, especially Titianesque, models.

Among Ovid's many stories, the metamorphoses into flowers seem to have especially attracted Poussin at the end of the 1620s. He treated them in an extremely original and independent way: the episodes of metamorphosis, humans changed into flowers, are subordinate to the gay procession in the *Triumph of Flora* (colorplate 3), and the *Realm of Flora*, inspired by Ovid's *Fasti*, is an exquisite garden scene (color-

plate 17). These myths and tales provided Poussin with tragic motifs. In *Narcissus and Echo* (colorplate 9), Poussin was the first to add to the scene of Narcissus' death the desperate figure of Echo as she fades away, destroyed by the invincible egocentrism of the youth.

BACCHIC SCENES

From the many-sided legends of Antiquity, Poussin chose a number of erotic subjects from the Bacchic realm. Some were openly sensuous, as *Jupiter Swimming to the Naked Callisto* (Royal Library, Windsor Castle), for instance, or *Venus Surprised by Satyrs*, a scene from ancient sarcophagi which Poussin still favored in his later years; but they did not descend to the regions of the *basse cuisine* that appear in some works of the Carracci, especially Agostino, and their school.

Bucolic genre scenes of a Bacchic character are to be

48

seen in two of Poussin's relatively small paintings: one depicts a satyr family enjoying a *déjeuner sur l'herbe* (The Prado, Madrid); the other (colorplate 6), a nude nymph carried on the back of a satyr, on their way to such a feast. Poussin's well-known and charming works in the Louvre—the *Nurture of Bacchus* (colorplate 18), in which the recumbent and sleeping nude is taken from Titian's *Bacchanal* (fig. 12), and the so-called *Bacchanal with the Lute Player* (The Louvre, Paris)—both have this rustic character, and show rather peaceful family scenes transposed into the Bacchic world. Their color retains all the warmth of the earlier mythological paintings, and in their paradisiac inactivity they are not unlike Dosso Dossi's Bacchic figures. More *mouvementés* are the *Children's Bacchanals*, two pleasant, small paintings in tempera, that formerly belonged to the Chigi family (fig. 36). These go back, of course, like the many sculptures of children by Poussin's friend, Duquesnoy, to Titian's incomparable *Worship of Venus* (fig. 13), which both friends had eagerly studied.

Poussin placed the scene of Bacchus' encounter with the deserted Ariadne, which Titian painted so splendidly (National Gallery, London), in the center of a great bacchanalian composition (The Prado, Madrid), painted still in the late 1620s, probably one of his earliest in this genre. He made two sketches (Royal Library, Windsor Castle) of Bacchus offering a bowl of wine to the seated Ariadne, who, in a curious way, is accompanied by another female figure (perhaps Peitho, the goddess of persuasion—very similar to an ancient Roman fresco; see chap. III). In Annibale Carracci's famous fresco in the Farnese Gallery, Ariadne shares Bacchus' triumph as he returns victorious from India, but in Poussin's impressive painting in Kansas City (possibly a copy; fig. 37), Bacchus is alone on his chariot; an excited host of maenads and bacchantes jubilantly precede him in a tumultuous procession, including two wild centaurs, male and female, who draw the chariot.

The *Triumph of Bacchus* belongs to the great series of bacchanals that Poussin made in 1635–36, commissioned by Cardinal Richelieu (see Commentary 19). These bacchanals (partly preserved in copies) are among the most famous works that Poussin made after 1635. Bellori praises them because they are "the best examples of his compositions based upon the study of antique marbles, and because they are full of poetic inventions from Poussin's most felicitous genius." The uncommonly rich number of ancient motifs in these compositions are not adapted from one model, but put together from studies of many models. One can see the value he placed on the spirited ornamentation of his work from the great variety of motifs in his sketches, gathered not only from ancient sculptures, but also from literary sources, such as the poetry of Catullus, or Vincenzo Cartari's useful chapter on Bacchus in *Images of the Gods*.

However, beyond this lavish ornamentation, something else distinguishes these later bacchanals, especially the *Triumph of Pan* (colorplate 19), from earlier manifestations of Bacchic joy and revelry: all of them are mysteries—*misteri*—in a religious sense, as in the mysteries of the Sacraments: baptism, confirmation, and extreme unction. The Bacchic rites are religious performances in honor of a god: Pan (or is it Priapus?), whose herm is wreathed by a priestess in a solemn attitude. In the striking *Bacchanal Before a Temple* (fig. 38), known to us in wonderful, deep-toned drawings, a Saturnalian festival seems to unfold in gestures and frenetic dancing, extremely pagan. Parallel to this work, and of particularly high quality, is the drawing in deep and warm chiaroscuro of a bacchanal with not one, but two herms (The Louvre, Paris). The splendid painting, *Bacchanalian Revel Before a Term of Pan* (colorplate 21), is also ritualistic, corresponding exactly to *Adoration of the Golden Calf* (colorplate 22) in its form, and, in this sense, in its meaning.

Supplementary to the earthly triumphs of Bacchus, Silenus, and Pan is the large *Triumph of Neptune and Amphitrite*, also made for Richelieu (see Commentary 20). These Bacchic or maritime dances and triumphs (*thiasoi*) are spectacles in the *grande manière*. Like Titian's, they are revelries, but they are ceremonial, ritualistic revelries. After the 1630s, Poussin painted bacchanals only exceptionally.

SCENES FROM TASSO

Within the epic literature of his time, only Torquato Tasso's *Jerusalem Delivered* inspired Poussin for a series of paintings and drawings that equals in quality and invention the bacchanals and fanciful Ovidian tales he painted in the 1630s. His rendering of the romantic, emotional love story of Rinaldo and Armida (fig. 39), previously illustrated by many others, shows Poussin to be the most profound interpreter of Tasso's poetry (as R. Lee terms him in *The Art Bulletin*, XXII). Poussin, the splendid and sensitive narrator, represented the love drama from its very beginning to its tragic end, omitting only the often-painted love scene in the garden. He illustrated the beginning of the romance in two remarkably fine versions. Armida's abrupt psychological change, from murderous hatred of the Christian hero to overwhelming passion for his beauty (*di nemica diviene amante*), is analyzed in accordance with different emotional nuances: in the first (fig. 39), her state seems still to be one of delighted surprise; in the second (Pushkin Museum, Moscow; painted a few years later), she appears totally, irrevocably, fascinated.

Poussin then depicted Armida and her companions carrying the unconscious Rinaldo to the magic chariot, which will transport him to the Fortunate Island. In a later scene, Carlo and Ubaldo, Rinaldo's patriotic and bellicose companions, fight the guardian dragon to liberate Rinaldo from the amorous enticements of the sorceress, so that he will return to his military duty in the First Crusades (Harrach Collection, Vienna). Finally, there is a large, wonderful drawing, probably of a later date, in which the steep fairy-tale mountain recalls Monte Circeo near Terracina; here Poussin illustrated most dramatically the abduction of the reluctant Rinaldo and the abandonment of Armida, who lies on the rocks of the beach in a deep faint, attended by a lamenting, bewildered *putto* (fig. 40). Another rapid sketch of the abduction scene, also in the Louvre, shows the anguished youth being dragged away, a marvel of force and spontaneity.

In addition to the Rinaldo series, Poussin also illustrated Tasso's description of the dramatic and heroic

Figure 41. RESCUE OF THE INFANT PYRRHUS. c. 1637–38. Oil on canvas, 45³/₄×63¹/₈″. *The Louvre, Paris*

Figure 42. Leonardo da Vinci: Illustration in *Trattato della Pittura* (Codex Vaticano Urbinate 1270).
Drawing, pen and ink. *Vatican Library, Rome*

scene in which Hermione cuts her hair with a sword to dry the wounds of Tancred, who lies outstretched before her, supported by the Christian warrior Vafrin (The Hermitage, Leningrad). Hermione's striking white horse seems to participate in the action, as St. Paul's very different horse joins in the scene of Caravaggio's *Conversion of St. Paul*.

X. SUBJECT MATTER: PAINTINGS 1635–1641

In the second half of the 1630s, or perhaps somewhat earlier, we may observe a remarkable change occurring in Poussin's artistic character. It is as if he had left his youth behind—a rather protracted youth—and entered with determination a phase of maturity. This is true not only of his use of color and his painterly conception, but also of his choice of subjects. He is still far from the self-conscious classicism he will develop in the 1640s and 1650s, but he is no longer so experimental. Tackling different subjects of a religious, humanistic, or lyrical-humanistic nature, he brings them to a certain pitch, then he more or less deserts them. He now abandons (though not completely) the colorism of Titian, which he had perfected to such a

degree, and with it the lyricism of his youthful style and the poetry of Ovid. Already some of his scenes from Tasso have a character more Virgilian than Ovidian, an expression less playful and more epic-dramatic; his later bacchanals are less pleasantly bucolic and lyrical, and more solemn, serious, and monumental—almost religious. The masculine character of this new period is very evident, and Poussin now chooses subjects that display this significant mutation.

At the same time, the theoretical questions that Poussin had always found stimulating became more important in this relatively untroubled period, and his opinions more firmly consolidated. He found time to make a whole series of drawings (see chap. VII) for Leonardo da Vinci's *Trattato della Pittura*. He renewed his earlier studies of the proportions of the human body. And by 1640 we hear that Chantelou (later his great friend and patron), together with the painter Charles Errard (with whom Poussin collaborated on the French edition of Leonardo's *Trattato*), were following Poussin's example, and measuring ancient statues. It was probably at this time that Poussin and his circle were discussing not only color and design, but also the theory of the *affetti* (see chap. VII), the doctrine of the agreement between external gestures and inner emotions. This doctrine, which found its most practical and varied exposition in compositions involving masses of people, may account partly for Poussin's new predilection for illustrating, in many-figured compositions, historical and semihistorical episodes from Roman legends and the Old Testament.

The *Rescue of the Infant Pyrrhus* (fig. 41) is directly related to Poussin's illustrations for Leonardo's *Trattato*. The two young men in the left foreground who throw the stone and the lance across the river to the people of Megara are excellent examples of forceful, passionate movement that is directed by, and correspondent to, their emotions (seen also in the preparatory drawing). Poussin transformed two tiny figures from Leonardo's manuscript of the *Trattato* (figs. 23, 42) into these large sculptural figures (J. Bialostocki, *Actes*, I); he also used famous ancient statues such as the *Borghese Warrior*. The figures recur in Poussin's illustrations for the French *Traité*. The message the men are conveying is that they have the king's infant son Pyrrhus, who, being pursued by enemies of the royal family, is in mortal danger. They are asking for help, and their vigorous and athletic performance makes more vivid the sense of emergency of the whole scene; contributing to this effect are the excited women in the center who guard the child and, quite far in the right background, the soldiers who fight off the approaching enemy. Poussin found this extraordinarily crucial and exciting moment in a story by Plutarch that, so far as I know, was never before illustrated.

With the *Rape of the Sabine Women* (colorplate 24) Poussin returned to a subject that had been frequently illustrated. In common with *Pyrrhus* it has the dramatic intensity of a moment of climax, but it provided Poussin with a greater opportunity to express his predilection for the *affetti*, since it permitted him to manipulate an anonymous multitude of struggling figures, each one reacting differently to the assault. The first version (fig. 107) has still some affinity with the relatively primitive *Plague of Ashdod* (see Commentary 7), but already the actions and passions of the separate groups of figures have become characterized. The influence of Leonardo is more apparent, however, in the second version (colorplate 24): the groups are clearer, more separate in space, and the famous group of the Roman soldier lifting a Sabine woman closely resembles one of Leonardo's tiny illustrations of Hercules

and Antaeus (fig. 23). Consequently the second version has an important place among the paintings made about 1637, wherein Poussin attempted systematically to regulate violent emotions (see Commentary 24).

Poussin's large *Schoolmaster of the Falerii* (fig. 27) is the most rigid and unappealing of his historical paintings of this period. There is also an early version, c. 1634, which is more attractive, partly because it is smaller. The size of the Louvre painting (approximately eight by nine feet) is certainly too cumbersome for its purely anecdotal content. Moreover, its color is drab and leaden; this is probably intentional, for the subject is to be understood as an example of the severe Doric mode, in contrast to the light, shining color in the mythological *Pan and Syrinx* (see Commentary 23) which Félibien tells us was painted the same year, 1637. The story of the Roman general Camillus, who decreed the punishment of the treacherous schoolmaster of the Falerii by his pupils, had been painted before (for instance, by Francesco Salviati). But Poussin followed Valerius Maximus in using this topic as a moral example of justice. Apart from the *Death of Germanicus* (colorplate 2), this is Poussin's first painting of a Stoical subject; this may explain why he used for the composition a style of strong relief like that of

Figure 43. PASSAGE OF THE RED SEA. Late 1630s. Oil on canvas, $60^5/_8 \times 82^5/_8''$. *National Gallery of Victoria, Melbourne*

Germanicus. He also followed rather closely, as in the first version, the composition of Domenichino's *Timoclea and Alexander* (fig. 19; see chap. V).

OLD TESTAMENT

For Poussin, subjects from the Old Testament possessed a primarily artistic and emotional interest. He seems to have been fascinated by the stories of Moses and the Exodus, and did not consider them from an exclusively religious point of view (as, for instance, prefigurations of events in the life of Christ).

He admired them for their heroic character, finding them comparable to ancient stories such as those of Romulus and Scipio; the fabulous content of these Biblical tales also stimulated his innate talent as a "storyteller." An example of the same phenomenon in literature is the poem "Moyse Sauvé, Idylle Héroique" by Saint-Amant, 1653. Moreover, the Biblical descriptions of the suffering and salvation of entire communities interested Poussin from a sociological point of view. In the late 1630s his interpretations of mass psychology was based on his theoretical studies of the *affetti*—the effects of the passions on human movement. Nowhere could he have found material more suited to a display of his expressive ability and perspicacious observation than these exciting stories of the Exodus of the people of Israel (see chap. VII).

He had already made three large paintings of stories of Moses. None of these, however, has any psychological impact: neither the *contrapposto* seen in the large-figured *Exposure of Moses* (Gallery, Dresden), nor the almost *quattrocentesque*, thinly painted *Israelites Worshiping the Golden Calf* (fig. 105), and certainly not the rather ugly, Baroque (but very likely genuine) *Moses Sweetening the Waters* (Museum of Art, Baltimore). But the four spectacular miracles of Moses that Poussin painted one after the other in the short period of 1635–38/39 are almost paradigms of the illustration of differentiated emotions within a crowd, excited by events bringing unexpected salvation.

These Exodus pictures are *Moses Striking the Rock* (Collection Earl of Ellesmere), the *Passage of the Red Sea* (fig. 43), the *Adoration of the Golden Calf* (colorplate 22), and last and most famous, the *Gathering of the Manna* (colorplate 25). *Moses Striking the Rock* is Poussin's earliest of his two or three extant compositions on this topic. His extraordinary interest in the subject was noticed by Bellori, who praised the "rich mine of Poussin's imagination and his observation of the instinctive actions of men pertinent to their inner emotions." Indeed, we have many vigorous and impressive sketches, large and small, for *Moses Striking the Rock* (fig. 46), but most of them are for the later painting in The Hermitage, Leningrad.

The relatively loose composition of *Moses Striking the Rock* (Collection Earl of Ellesmere; c. 1637, or perhaps somewhat earlier) is stylistically related to Raphael's art, but owes still more to Domenichino's. The "caritas" group of mother and child in the right corner is reminiscent of Domenichino, and the Titianesque child misbehaving on the left had already been used by Poussin himself. The figures are composed somewhat in the manner of a relief and placed before an open, tripartite background. However, the painting already shows Poussin's new conception of the emotional characterization of the different groups, all of which have, nevertheless, a clearly recognizable common denominator. The action, similar to that in *Rape of the Sabine Women* (colorplate 24), is the simultaneous response of everyone to Moses' one gesture which brings the life-giving water. The reactions of the groups to this miracle are clearly described: some figures turn to Moses, their hands clasped in a prayer of thanks; others eagerly bend to drink from the refreshing stream. Poussin's grandiose repetition of the topic twelve or fifteen years later (The Hermitage, Leningrad) emphasizes the agitated, almost convulsive expressions of astonishment and awe.

The two many-figured paintings that Poussin made about 1637 for Amadeo dal Pozzo, Cassiano's cousin in Turin—the *Passage of the Red Sea* (fig. 43) and the *Adoration of the Golden Calf* (colorplate 22)—are perhaps the most forceful of the series. In their design and flourishing color they are stronger and more advanced than *Moses Striking the Rock;* less sculptural than the *Rape of the Sabine Women*, they are also less programmatic and didactic than *Gathering of the Manna.* Although these two paintings for Amadeo are the same size, and made for the same man at the same time, they are not pendants, for they do not closely supplement one another. They illustrate two very different scenes from Exodus: one shows the Israelites' miraculous escape from Egyptian servitude—more precisely, the

53

Figure 44. MOSES FOUND BY THE PHARAOH'S DAUGHTER. Mid-1640s. Drawing, pen and bistre wash, $6^7/_8 \times 10''$. *The Louvre, Paris*

moment of their salvation from the waters of the Red Sea (Exodus 14–15); the other depicts a much later episode (Exodus 32), the Israelites' dance around the golden calf, and, in the upper left, Moses breaking the Tablets of the Law as he discovers his people adoring the idol.

In both paintings there are expressions of emotion, but they are shown differently. Most prominent in the *Adoration of the Golden Calf* are six figures on the left who perform a solemn, almost hieratic, dance before the statue of the golden calf (reminiscent both of ancient reliefs and of compositions by Giulio Romano in the Palazzo del Tè). In the multitude compressed into the right side, the different gestures show the gratitude and joy that is provoked by the imperious gesture of Aaron, Moses' brother: Aaron points to the idol, fashioned at his command to represent the new savior of the people of Israel. The other powerful picture is wrongly called *Passage of the Red Sea*, for it shows the exaltation of the people after the danger is past. Their excitement lingers in their spirits and finds expression in many violent gestures. Poussin had certainly read Josephus' description in *Jewish Antiquities*, Book IV: the Hebrews "could scarce contain themselves for joy at their miraculous deliverance and the destruction of their foes, believing themselves assuredly

at liberty, now that the tyrants who would have enslaved them had perished and that God had so manifestly befriended them. After having themselves thus escaped from peril and furthermore beheld their enemies punished in such wise as within men's memory no others had ever been before, they passed that whole night in melody and mirth..." This is the attitude expressed in chapter 16 of Exodus, where Moses, and later his sister Miriam, deliver their paeans to Jehovah. Poussin, in a marvelous way, tries to render this atmosphere of mixed joy, surprise, and gratitude by showing a panorama receding into depth, which includes innumerable larger and smaller figures in different activities or moods. One curious detail, also inspired by Josephus, shows the Israelites in their pride of victory, fishing from the water the drowned enemy's armor and collecting the shields which have been swept into shore. Like the *Rescue of the Infant Pyrrhus* (fig. 41), this incident gave Poussin an occasion to place in the foreground a row of figures whose action has strong movement in the Leonardesque sense.

In some respects these two paintings, the *Passage of the Red Sea* and the *Adoration of the Golden Calf*, have a community of planned opposition. In the *Golden Calf* the passions of joy and gratitude are directed in a wrong way, toward sin that will be followed by severe

54

punishment. In the *Passage of the Red Sea* the joy and gratitude are rendered for true salvation.

Poussin painted the *Gathering of the Manna* (colorplate 25) in 1638, and sent it to Chantelou in 1639; it proved to be the last of this series of programmatic and analytical works. In his famous letters to Stella and to Chantelou, Poussin himself developed his program and his intentions (see Commentary 25), which are discussed and expounded thirty years later in Le Brun's conference on this painting. Poussin must have particularly valued *Gathering of the Manna*, because he was so eager that the public should understand his method. With great emphasis he instructs his audiences not only in how to see, but in how to read a painting group by group, as one reads a book, page by page.

> I believe that you will easily recognize which are those who languish, those who admire, those who have pity, who do charitable acts, of great necessity, of desire, or of a delight in consolation, and others, for the first seven figures on the left, will tell you all that is written here and all the rest is of the same thread. Read the story with the painting, in order to know if each thing is appropriate to the subject. (Letter to Chantelou, April 28, 1639.)

These sentences are parallel to the quotation from his letter to Stella, and they apply to *Gathering of the Manna* and to all the paintings we have here discussed.

With the stories of Moses from this period of the late 1630s belongs a subject that is definitely unheroic, but nevertheless connected with the life of that historic man. The *Finding of Moses* (fig. 65), which was once owned by André Le Nôtre, has beautiful, shining, tempera-like color, in harmony with the subject. Rather than the cramped torsion of the *Exposure of Moses* (Gallery, Dresden), this work has a ceremonious pattern. The princess is a truly regal figure, full of feminine, almost matronly, dignity and grace. Poussin was doubtlessly inspired by an ancient model, but a very different one from the figure on an ancient relief that he used for *Luna and Endymion* (colorplate 14). The young, beautiful matron appears for the first time in this painting; she recurs in drawings as the mother of Theseus, who orders her son to look for his father's sword, and she also acts as prototype for the woman in front of the pillar in *Rebecca and Eliezer at the Well* (colorplate 31). The whole composition, with its placid landscape and the new motif of a long bridge parallel to the surface of the picture, anticipates Poussin's later planimetric style.

Of Poussin's five or six mythological paintings from the later 1630s, made before he left for Paris, only one has the lyrical quality that gave such charm to his works only a few years before. This painting is *Pan and Syrinx* (colorplate 23), which tells a story similar to the myth of Apollo and Daphne. The god Pan per-

Figure 45. HERCULES AND DEJANIRA. c. 1638. Drawing, pen and bistre wash, $8^5/_8 \times 12^3/_8''$. *Royal Library, Windsor Castle (by gracious permission of H. M. the Queen)*

Figure 46. MOSES STRIKING THE ROCK. C. 1649. Drawing, pen and bistre wash, $5^5/_8 \times 14^3/_8''$.
Royal Library, Windsor Castle (by gracious permission of H. M. the Queen)

secutes and pursues the beautiful nymph Syrinx, who changes into reeds as he grasps her; swaying in the wind, the reeds give off a sweet sound, and from them Pan ingeniously fashions his famous panpipe or "syrinx." Poussin wrote to Stella that he enjoyed painting this subject: "If I have ever done anything good I believe that it is the manner in which this subject is treated. I painted it with love and tenderness. The subject demanded it so." Indeed the painting is one of Poussin's finest and most elaborate creations, especially in its color; he seems to have domesticated Titian's colors with new refinement. Poussin apparently derived much pleasure from painting this lyrical, tender theme at the time that he was primarily occupied with more severe historical, heroic paintings.

Among the other mythological paintings, *Phaeton Before Apollo* (State Museums, Berlin-Dahlem) and *Venus Arming Aeneas* (two versions; Art Gallery of Toronto, and Museum of Fine Arts, Rouen) have a more epic character. The most delightful of this group, *Hercules and Dejanira*, made for Stella about 1637, is preserved today only in vivid, amusing drawings (fig. 45).

THE SEVEN SACRAMENTS

In the period of the later 1630s which I have called "masculine," when Poussin's style found its main outlet in forceful scenes from the Old Testament, his mind was occupied for the first time with religious and meditative subjects that concentrate upon the mysteries of the New Testament. It has not yet, as far as I can see, been fully explained whether the idea of painting the Seven Sacraments in a series of seven paintings originated with Poussin himself, or was suggested by Cassiano dal Pozzo, whose intellectual circle included not only antiquarians and scholars of natural history, but philosophical clergymen. As a pictorial subject, the Seven Sacraments had more appeal in the North than the South; and it is not impossible that the source of this subject was in Piedmont, Cassiano's home province and the northernmost in Italy. In any case, the project captivated Poussin for many years to come.

Poussin was the first artist to monumentalize the Seven Sacraments in seven separate paintings. To depict all the Sacraments in one painting was not without precedent, but the shop piece by Roger van der Weyden (Museum, Antwerp) and the works of Northern graphic artists all seem to be irrelevant to Poussin's innovation. Poussin removed the whole subject from the strictly liturgical sphere and depicted each Sacrament in a historical form that is both precise and idealized. He based his representation of four Sacraments on the New Testament: the *Baptism of Christ* (fig. 47; Baptism), the *Giving of the Keys to St. Peter* (Ordination), *Mary Magdalen Washing the Feet of Christ* (Penance), *The Last Supper* (Eucharist). The other three, *Confirmation, Marriage,* and *Extreme Unction,* have a more general character but they, too, conform to Poussin's ideas of ancient Christian custom.

Poussin must have delivered all of the paintings, except for the *Baptism of Christ,* to Cassiano dal Pozzo sometime between 1637, when the series of the large bacchanals for Richelieu was probably behind him, and 1640. Cassiano was immensely proud of this great accomplishment by his early protégé, and showed them to all his friends; he later became rather unpleasant when Chantelou wanted to have copies for himself. These paintings have smallish figures, mostly arranged in a row and covering only about one third of the available space; the series lost public favor in the 1640s, after Poussin's new, grandiose versions of the same topic for his French friend, Chantelou. The early series, however, despite its relatively modest proportions, forms a decisive step toward the grandeur of Poussin's later work; many motifs—for instance, the use of the triclinium—are here developed for the first time. With this series of *The Seven Sacraments* (even though they were superseded by the later version: see colorplates 29, 30; figs. 49–52), and the astonishing number of powerful works he created in the last six or seven years before his departure for Paris, Poussin's artistic performance reached an extremely high level that was acknowledged in Rome and still more in his own country, France.

Apart from the advance in style and form that every great artist shows in manhood, Poussin distinguished himself by creating themes that had never been thought of before, impregnating them with new and original programmatic concepts. But Poussin's creation during these years in Rome, especially the preceding decade, had been extraordinary—not only in painting, but in thought and classification. No one in modern times had thought to represent a bacchanal as a sacrificial act; no one had conceived of a coronation, be it of a poet or a Jewish hero, as a humanistic ritual; no one had tried to resolve the Israelites' reception of Moses' miraculous deeds into a multitude of *affetti.* It is no wonder that a man of these high artistic and intellectual faculties so appealed to the French *esprit* of the seventeenth century, or that Richelieu and the French government, ambitious of centralization in every respect, wanted to use Poussin's eminently French genius for the glory of France.

Figure 47. BAPTISM OF CHRIST.
Early 1640s. Oil on canvas, 37^1/$_2$×47^1/$_2$″. *National Gallery of Art, Washington, D.C. (Kress Collection)*

Figure 48. Raphael: BAPTISM OF CHRIST. 1509–11.
Fresco. *Vatican Loggias, Rome*

XI. MANIERA MAGNIFICA

The interruption of Poussin's more original work and his absence from Rome for about two years (from October, 1640, to November, 1642) were forced upon the reluctant artist by Louis XIII and the French government, who wanted the artist to paint in Paris "pour la gloire de France." In some respects, his so-

RIGHT: Figure 49. BAPTISM. 1644–48.
Oil on canvas, 46$^1/_8$×70$^1/_8$″.
Collection Earl of Ellesmere, on loan to
National Galleries of Scotland, Edinburgh

BELOW: Figure 50. CONFIRMATION.
1644–48. Oil on canvas, 46$^1/_8$×70$^1/_8$″.
Collection Earl of Ellesmere, on loan to
National Galleries of Scotland, Edinburgh

journ in Paris was by no means disagreeable. Poussin was honored and flattered—and he was not at all insensitive to this. He lived in the style of a wealthy nobleman, and finally left Paris of his own free will. He had enlarged and deepened the friendships connecting him with certain educated men: high civil servants, bankers, and other members of the powerful upper middle class. In France he not only acquired new, eager customers, but he also became intimate with a small group of men who shared his opinions and passionately wanted to see them depicted by their adored friend. Paul Fréart de Chantelou, the secretary and cousin of Sublet de Noyers, *Surintendant* of the Royal Buildings, and Paul's brother, Roland Fréart de Cham-

58

bray, were the most prominent of Poussin's friends and patrons in Paris. He also became acquainted with a select circle of scientists, physicians, and philosophers (among them Gabriel Naudé, Pierre Bourdelot, and perhaps the *Abbé* Gassendi), most of them friends and correspondents of Poussin's great Roman patron, Cassiano dal Pozzo. Although this acquaintance was probably limited to social intercourse (as R. Pintard has suggested in *Actes du Colloque Poussin*, I), it is also quite possible that the doctrines and opinions of these advanced and learned men, some of whom belonged to the so-called *Libertins*, interested and enriched the mind of the painter.

Despite these social advantages, Poussin's sojourn

Figure 51. PENANCE. 1644–48.
Oil on canvas, 46¹/₈×70¹/₈".
Collection Earl of Ellesmere, on loan to
National Galleries of Scotland, Edinburgh

Figure 52. ORDINATION. 1644–48.
Oil on canvas, 46¹/₈×70¹/₈".
Collection Earl of Ellesmere, on loan to
National Galleries of Scotland, Edinburgh

in Paris was nevertheless a failure and temporarily a major deterrent to his art. Louis XIII and Richelieu intended to establish Poussin as the leader of a regulated and controlled style of art which would express the political and social conformity that was the highest goal of the French government (to be attained only later, under Louis XIV). However, the introduction of an uncompromising classicist into the vast domain of easygoing and tasteful decorative painting, as it was practiced by Vouet and his large school, the "Moderate Baroque," aroused envy and resentment. Louis XIII himself, on first meeting Poussin at Fontainebleau, brought the rift into the open by saying to the painter rather tactlessly: "*Voilà Vouet bien attrapé!*" (There is Vouet, well trapped). The consequences were quite natural: years later, Poussin still remembered and resented the intrigues and accusations of Vouet's coterie.

The deeper reason for Poussin's discontent was that he, no longer able to choose his own subjects, had become an employee of the royal administration; he was given commissions that would often have been better accomplished by established French painters, and did not inspire his own independent genius. After the limited success of his large altarpieces in Rome at the end of the 1620s, Poussin had returned by his own choice to compositions of smaller dimensions; but in Paris, he was again forced to fabricate large altarpieces—*The Eucharist* (fig. 112) and the *Miracle of St. Francis Xavier* (both commissioned by Sublet de Noyers, who also chose the subjects). These he painted with intelligence and with elegance, but he nevertheless maintained a certain classicistic distance. The paintings were severely criticized by his enemies; for example, they blamed Poussin for giving Christ the attitude of a *Jupiter tonans*. Poussin replied, he had not intended to give the Lord the face of a "sissy" (*père douillet*). Poussin also had to paint for Richelieu a trite and uninspiring allegory of *Time Revealing Truth* (The Louvre, Paris) in a round format, to decorate the ceiling of a room in the Cardinal's palace, and, for the mantelpiece in the same room, a rather unoriginal painting of Moses speaking with Jehovah—the *Burning Bush*. In addition to these commissions, Poussin was overburdened with numerous activities, including designs for a set of tapestry cartoons intended as pendants to Raphael's famous set. In consequence, he bitterly complained in a letter of April, 1642, that he was "employed without relief for mere bagatelles"—for frontispiece designs, cabinet decorations, fireplaces, bookbindings, and other "foolishness."

But the main disaster was a staggering commission for the Grande Galerie of the Louvre; planned in pungent anti-Baroque style, this project was to cover the ceiling with representations of reliefs from Trajan's Column (R. H. Hallett, "Studies for the Long Gallery," in Friedlaender and Blunt, *Drawings*, IV). It was a super-classicistic challenge to the decorative ceilings and wall paintings of the period, and it is not astonishing that it was much opposed. Poussin worked with intensity on the project in the first year, but, discouraged by the many difficulties and by the intrigues of his adversaries, he lost interest; giving a half-sincere promise to return eventually to Paris, he went back to Rome late in the autumn of 1642.

His subsequent letters to Chantelou show that he sometimes played with the idea of returning to Paris, but he never considered it seriously. Conditions in Paris changed: Richelieu and Louis XIII both died shortly after Poussin returned to Rome, and his art was less in demand under the new regime. But the situation in Rome was also changing. After the death in 1644 of Pope Urban VIII, a Francophile Barberini, and the subsequent disgrace of Cardinal Francesco, the Pope's powerful and cultivated nephew, Poussin could no longer count on the support and patronage that the Barberini and their circle had so persistently accorded to him. Instead he now worked almost exclusively for his French patrons and friends, who were, apparently, little affected by the turbulent political events of the Regency. Poussin began to be isolated from the brilliant artistic life in Rome: as a result of his experience in Paris, he now knew that he could not paint under the direction of anyone, but only alone. Undisturbed by outside pressures, he was free to develop his artistic personality and ideals.

Poussin himself had changed astonishingly in these two years; the change was a fundamental one, and deeper than that between his juvenile works and the more emotional paintings of the later 1630s. His creative genius, partly unused, partly abused during his stay in Paris, emerged as if newborn, with the force and virtue of the Hercules whose deeds were also planned to decorate the Grande Galerie. Poussin had passed the stage of the late 1630s when he endeavored

Figure 53. PENANCE. 1646–48. Drawing, squared, pen washed with bistre, $8^{1}/_{4} \times 12^{1}/_{4}$". *Musée Fabre, Montpellier*

to demonstrate the modes and make the *affetti* readable by illustrating them in numerous single examples, one next to the other. The elements that previously had been individualized and juxtaposed were now subordinated to a greater, more unified conception. Poussin became conscious of his role as the leader of moral and religious classicism. As a man of fifty, he had reached a high artistic maturity—the "maniera magnifica" as Bellori called it, or the "grande manière," as it was later called in France.

By "maniera magnifica" Bellori designated that manner of painting in which the possibility of ornamentation and perfection is contained in the subject itself. The concept, structure, and style of a painting must also be "great" (*grande*), for nothing should enter that detracts by its low or insignificant character from the decorum of the painting.

It is characteristic of Poussin's conception of the *grand idéal* (and corresponds to Bellori's definition) that as his style grew toward magnificence and perfection, during the 1640s and first half of the 1650s, he

almost completely abandoned all "light" subjects. Ovid's amorous mythological scenes, and Tasso's pathetic and colorful romances—those ancient and romantic Venetianized inventions in which Poussin, the teller of fables and stories, had earlier delighted— were suppressed, just as Titian's color was banished from his palette. Humanistic coronations of poets and heroes no longer interested Poussin's serious and Stoical mind. His "bacchanalian" phase of the mid-1630s came more or less to a close with the completion of the series for Richelieu. Narrative paintings showing historical subject matter, such as the *Rape of the Sabine Women* or *Pyrrhus*, are no longer prominent in this later period. He continued to paint stories of Moses from the Old Testament, but they are mostly variants of earlier compositions—although they have often great force and vigor, such as the impressive *Moses Striking the Rock*, painted for Stella in 1649 (The Hermitage, Leningrad).

As the number of Old Testament subjects diminishes during the 1640s, scenes based on the New Testament

Figure 54. CRUCIFIXION. 1645–46. Oil on canvas, 46^1/$_2$×84^1/$_2$″. *Wadsworth Atheneum, Hartford*

begin to predominate. Poussin's earlier religious production could be called, for the most part, indifferent, or even pagan. The great enterprise, the painting of *The Seven Sacraments* for Cassiano dal Pozzo in the late 1630s, may mark the beginning of Poussin's new attitude toward the representation of religious contemplation. But only after Poussin had returned to Rome did he become, at least for a while, almost exclusively a painter of religious and Christian themes. His allegedly close association in Paris (perhaps even earlier, in Rome) with the skeptical *Libertins* scarcely seems to have impressed him in religious matters. However, his sentiments were probably not in absolute accord with the opinions and demonstrations of the Roman *ecclesia Cattolica;* they were tinged by the Northern doctrines which separated the French clergy from Italian Baroque religiosity. Poussin's was a demonstrably rationalistic—a "classicistic"—religiosity. He was not unreasonably blamed when he was in Paris for having made the figure of Christ as a

Jupiter tonans. By far the greatest manifestation of his general attitude toward religious matters is his new series of *The Seven Sacraments.*

This second series (see colorplates 29, 30; figs. 49–52) was originally commissioned as a copy of the seven paintings Poussin had made in the later 1630s for his Roman patron, Cassiano dal Pozzo. When Poussin returned from his Paris sojourn, however, he had outgrown both the style and the dimensions he had used for the first series, and he decided to make fundamentally different, new paintings, to correspond with his new, grandiose conceptions. The change was already apparent in Paris when Poussin supplied the one picture, the *Baptism of Christ* (fig. 47), that the first had lacked. He was already dissatisfied with the small figures in his paintings of the 1630s, including those in the other six Sacraments for Cassiano. In the *Baptism* he enlarged the figures in proportion to the height of the painting, thereby giving them greater monumentality and representational power. The influence of Titian's art, which was waning at the end of the 1630s, is completely obliterated by the example of Raphael (see fig. 48). This composition marks the hesitant beginning of Poussin's grand, mature style.

The larger figures, deeper space, and synthesis of action with landscape distinguish Poussin's works after he returned from Paris. Moreover, Poussin's new conception of the subject, and of its value as a highly significant, educational means, moved him to devote the next four years to his new redaction of the Seven Sacraments. He writes to Chantelou (April 8, 1644) that he is giving his particular consideration to the work on *The Seven Sacraments* ("J'ai en singulière recommandation les Sacrements"): "I have made them my main object and I will give to them my whole study and all the force of my talent, such as it is." The seven paintings clarify with new penetration these examples of decisive moments in human life. The

Figure 55. CARRYING OF THE CROSS. C. 1645.
Drawing, bistre wash with traces of black chalk, $6^5/_8 \times 8^7/_8$".
Museum, Dijon

Figure 56. ENTOMBMENT. C. 1650. Oil on canvas, $38^5/_8 \times 52$". *National Gallery of Ireland, Dublin*

topic, the seven Sacraments illustrated by seven paintings, which itself is quite rare, corresponds more to French meditative, sober religiosity than to Italian Counter- or Post-Reformation emotionalism and bravura. In the second series for Chantelou, Poussin expressed the contemporary sentiment in France with restraint and abstraction. Nowhere is he closer to French High Classicism, that is to say, to Corneille, than in *The Seven Sacraments*; nowhere is he further from the Italian High Baroque.

On June 22, 1648, Poussin wrote Chantelou a curious letter that is extremely revealing with respect to *The Seven Sacraments*. Replying to the latter's news concerning the death of a friend (the writer Vincent Voiture), Poussin expresses his condolences in a somewhat philosophical but impatient manner, avoiding the usual pious phrases, and does not even mention God, or God's will:

> I would like, if it were possible, to convert these *Seven Sacraments* into seven other stories representing, in a most lively way, the strangest tricks that Fortune ever played on men, and especially on those who have ridiculed her efforts. These examples would not be fortuitous or unimaginative; on seeing them people would be reminded to consider the virtue and the wisdom that one must acquire in order to stand firm and

immobile against the efforts of this blind madwoman. But only by extreme wisdom or extreme stupidity can one be exempt from her tempests—the one being above, and the other below, and the people of medium stamp are bound to feel her severity.

Poussin's terminology in this letter is decidedly Stoical, and comes close to Pierre Charron's expressions in the preface to Book II of his *Traité de la Sagesse*, where a distinction is made between those who find peace and serenity, immune from misfortune through either high wisdom or obstinate ignorance, and those in the middle, the ordinary people, who suffer most from the "tempests and meteors" (see Montaigne, *Essais*, Book I, chap. LIV). Poussin, in his casual proposal to rework the sacred subjects of the Seven Sacraments into profane "tricks of Fortune," was certainly not deprecating his own much-admired work of some years before, still less its religious content. Rather it shows that Poussin's attitude toward religious mysteries was in common with that of his French confrères and in contrast with the pious emotionalism of his Italian contemporaries, Bernini and Pietro da Cortona. Characterized by sober common sense, this attitude was in no way heretical, but it was nonetheless rational and anti-superstitious. Just as Poussin added motifs of Egyptian

Figure 57. HOLY FAMILY WITH
TEN FIGURES. C. 1650.
Oil on canvas, 30⅜ × 39⅜″.
National Gallery of Ireland, Dublin

Figure 58. HOLY FAMILY
WITH ELEVEN FIGURES. C. 1650.
Oil on canvas, $39^3/_4 \times 53''$.
Chatsworth Settlement, Chatsworth

scenery to the *Rest on the Flight into Egypt* (fig. 63) and the *Finding of Moses* (fig. 65), so he also wished to illustrate the Seven Sacraments in a manner conforming to their historical and ideological content. Since the Sacraments are a fundamental doctrine of the Church, it was fitting to render them in utmost simplicity, with a naïveté proper to the spirit of early Christianity. Thus the personages are represented, as Bellori remarks, "in the manner of the first church" and their architectural surroundings correspond to the early Christian style: this is particularly true of *Confirmation* (fig. 50) and *Ordination* (fig. 52). As he had in other cases, so Poussin tried to give utmost verisimilitude to this especially important series.

In *The Seven Sacraments* Poussin wished to communicate virtually the same message that he wanted to express in the projected "Seven Tricks of Fortune," the preparedness of the wise and the virtuous. All the actions in the *Sacraments*, from Baptism to Extreme Unction, acknowledge the wisdom or higher *sagesse* which provides the believer with armor against the tempests (or the "tricks") of Fortune. He placed this highly moral and rationalistic concept—a kind of Puritan mystique—into an ambient almost geometrically co-ordinated, that is ultimately to be derived

from the constructed space in Raphael's tapestries. In this way proper decorum and dignity is accorded to the naked or half-dressed figures in the *Baptism* (fig. 49) by the grandiose, stylized landscape; or in *The Last Supper* (*Eucharist;* colorplate 30) and *Penance* (figs. 51, 53) by the rigorous spatial construction of a triclinium in the Roman manner. Poussin's new style and conception has often been considered too cold and rational, but it never fades into the flat linearism that was practiced by the later neo-Poussinists and abstract classicists. Poussin (who allegedly wanted at this time to write a treatise on light and color) vivifies the rigidity of his scheme by warm color and strong light. The sublime idea and masterly execution of these seven paintings for Chantelou make them in content and style Poussin's most remarkable and characteristic works.

The series of *The Seven Sacraments* is not the only manifestation of Poussin's recently awakened interest in religious subjects. Of more immediate impact is the large *Crucifixion* (fig. 54) which Poussin made for Président Jacques de Thou in 1645–46, during an interlude between the painting of two of the Sacraments for Chantelou. This grandiose (now much-darkened) painting is intentionally traditional in form

Figure 59. MADONNA ON THE STEPS.
c. 1650. Drawing, pen and bistre wash, $7^{1}/_{4} \times 9^{5}/_{8}''$.
The Louvre, Paris

Figure 60. HOLY FAMILY. C. 1650. Drawing,
pen and bistre wash, $4^{3}/_{8} \times 5^{1}/_{2}''$. *Musée Condé, Chantilly*

and conception, and in space and figural composition it is quite different from the planimetric order seen in *The Seven Sacraments*. From the viewpoint of seventeenth-century style it has an archaic character, which is stressed in the foreground by the medieval motif of Adam rising from the grave. There are some reminiscences of Mantegna, whose engraving Poussin is said

to have admired and collected. But no *Crucifixion* of similar grandeur had been created since the *Crucifixions* by Tintoretto and Veronese. Poussin seems to have been so saddened and depressed by this "*sujet triste*" that he attributed the grave illness that overcame him at this time to his prolonged occupation with it; he refused to paint another painful subject, the Carrying of the Cross, although he had already made a remarkably beautiful drawing for it (fig. 55)—he said it would kill him. Poussin's admirable *Entombment* (fig. 56) represents the same type of subject matter, scenes from the Passion of Christ, but is a product of his old age style, dating from the middle of the 1650s. Surprisingly, this impressive and serious composition is closely based upon High Renaissance models—Raphael, Fra Bartolommeo, and especially Sebastiano del Piombo (*Pietà*, Viterbo Museum)—but it, too, has an outspoken archaic solemnity. The various *affetti* of the past are here united in one grand expression of mourning shared by all in deep feeling. In comparison with Poussin's representation of the same theme made about 1630 (colorplate 5), full of gay colors and Antique references, the great change in his sentiments and his art is astonishing.

Poussin's progress toward the Maniera Magnifica is strongly and beautifully evident in the successive Holy Families that he painted in the late 1640s and the early 1650s. Before this time, Poussin could hardly be called a "Madonna painter," although he had painted elegant and modish specimens in his early picturesque manner (colorplate 1; fig. 86). About ten years later (1641) he made the interesting *Madonna Roccatagliata* (colorplate 26) and the attractive drawing, *Holy Family with Nude Figures* (fig. 109); both have a classicistic preciosity, and the stylized figure of the Virgin resembles an ancient Nike. The Holy Families composed in the Maniera Magnifica are more majestic and monumental. Without being modeled directly on Greek or Roman statuary, they come close to the spirit of Antiquity by adopting the cubic forms and the planimetric spatial conventions from ancient painting and relief sculpture. However, the basic conception of Poussin's figures and groups is derived from Raphael, the great Renaissance painter of Holy Families. Raphael and his school rendered natural beauty in idealized classic forms, and clarified natural gestures in a lawful and geometric order. Poussin goes further:

he sets the geometric figural groups into an elaborate system of cubic architecture, or into an equally clear landscape. The emphasis on the planar construction and the two-dimensionality of this pictorial system gives great dignity and new stature to the separated, yet dramatically connected, figures of the holy scene —placed as if they were on a proscenium.

The first of the later series of Holy Families was painted in the late 1640s, the splendid *Madonna on the Steps* (colorplate 32), a particularly fine example of an ancient scheme utilized for Poussin's new plastic and intellectual ideal. The composition of the work is thoughtfully planned to make every plane parallel as exactly as possible the surface of the picture, in the manner of an ancient relief. The broad triangular composition extends across the entire width of the canvas. The group is placed one step above the immediate foreground, on a narrow platform which, in the Venetian tradition, is adorned with three colorful, shining objects (perhaps these were taken from ancient models, and refer to the gifts of the Magi): a basket of red apples (à la Caravaggio), a precious golden-brown vase, and a shimmering casket or jewel box. Seen in this slight elevation, the group is at the same time close to the spectator and given an enhanced monumentality. Although the relation of the figures to the architectural elements is reminiscent of ancient prototypes (see Commentary 32), their grouping, and the figural types themselves, are obviously drawn from High Renaissance models. The strong colors—sharp yellow for Elisabeth's robe, sky blue for the Madonna, and deep brown for Joseph—stand out strikingly against the light ocher of the architectural background. The many background forms provide both a foil and a contrast to the foreground, adding vertical accents to the basically horizontal composition. These cubic elements appear in many of Poussin's paintings at this time; here they are particularly emphatic, transformed into a massive version of Renaissance or severe Baroque architecture. Serving to soften the rigid milieu are the round reflecting surfaces of the large vases set off by flowering bushes, and the softly curved movements of the figures; a strong, sudden light emanates from behind the staircase, and the sky is filled with billowy clouds that suggest an infinite space transcending the structural boundaries. It has been suggested (see Commentary 32) that this composition has symbolic connotations; this may be true, but the main effect, be-

Figure 61. HOLY FAMILY. 1649.
Drawing, pen and bistre wash, $6^1/_8 \times 7^1/_2''$.
National Museum, Stockholm

cause of the conception that amalgamates pagan and Christian elements, is that of a religious work of art in a late humanistic guise.

Equally grandiose are three other Holy Families of this period: *Holy Family with Ten Figures* (fig. 57), *Madonna with a Basin* (colorplate 36), and *Holy Family with Eleven Figures* (fig. 58). All combine Antique planimetric conventions with his monumental figure style of the Maniera Magnifica. They have in common a wide format, with figures arranged on a proscenium, and cubic architectural accents such as in the *Madonna on the Steps* (colorplate 32; figs. 59, 113). The predominant note is of gravity, tempered by an idyllic relaxation that comes from the greater number of playing children. In a vivid sketch of a Holy Family (fig. 60), this relaxed quality increases to make a scene that could almost be a Bacchic one, if St. Joseph's rigid

Figure 62. HOLY FAMILY WITH INFANT ST. JOHN THE BAPTIST. 1655. Oil on canvas, 76×50³/₈″.
The John and Mable Ringling Museum of Art, Sarasota

figure in the background were to be replaced by a herm of Pan. It is not by chance that broad landscapes appeared in Poussin's oeuvre at the end of the 1640s, coincident with this form of Holy Family in a bucolic setting, for landscape contributes greatly to the relaxed ease permeating these Holy Families, in spite of the subject's intrinsic stylization and abstraction. A beautiful drawing of the Holy Family (fig. 61; on the verso of the *Rape of Europa*, 1649) is stylistically similar to both the *Holy Family with Ten Figures* (fig. 57) and to the *Madonna on the Steps* (fig. 59). The ceremonial and hieratical qualities of this composition are stressed by the presence of the throne and the absence of landscape. The planimetric scheme of the *Madonna on the Steps* is combined with a severe, tightly controlled arrangement of figures which anticipates the more vertical compositions of Poussin's later Holy Families.

Rather different from the type of Holy Family with many figures are two Holy Families composed in a vertical format; these are extremely serious and ceremonial, even rather rigid; the figures are close to life size and dominate the entire picture plane. The resemblance to late Madonnas (The Prado, Madrid, and National Museum, Naples) by Raphael (and perhaps Giulio Romano) is evident. Poussin finished these two "Grandes Vierges" in the year 1655, but at least one (fig. 62) had been started much earlier for a "personne grande." The other, a *Rest on the Flight into Egypt* (fig. 63), was made for Madame de Montmort, who became Chantelou's wife.

Stoical meditation is in some way similar to religious introspection, and thus it is not astonishing that Poussin, the meditative moralist of *The Seven Sacraments*, was particularly interested at this time in stories having Stoical subjects. It has been noted above that Poussin had begun to illustrate examples of Stoical virtue as early as 1627 in the *Death of Germanicus*. Most of his works having Stoical subjects were painted in the 1640s. There are indications of Poussin's interest in *exempla virtutis* at this period to be found in two small pen and bistre sketches, both after Livy: one, in Windsor, shows the fight of the Horatii and Curatii; the other, in the Louvre, the story of Mettius Curtius riding out of the marsh (nos. 120, 121; W. Friedlaender and A. Blunt, *Drawings*, II).

In a rather rough sketch Poussin illustrated (*op. cit.*, no. 124) Plutarch's account of the suicide of Cato the

Figure 63. REST ON THE FLIGHT INTO EGYPT. 1655–57. Oil on canvas, 41³/₈×57¹/₈″. *The Hermitage, Leningrad*

Younger, who, after reading Plato's *Phaedo*, ran himself through with his sword. Also Stoical in flavor is the story of Queen Zenobia who, fleeing from her enemies, asked her husband to kill her lest she fall into their hands. Poussin's series of spirited sketches (probably from the late 1630s) describes her rescue from the waters of the river into which she had been thrown (*op. cit.*, nos. 131–33; A. 34 to A. 36). Typically Stoical is also the story of the general Coriolanus who, moved by the pleas of his mother and his wife, did not fight against Rome, his ungrateful homeland. Illustrating this famous incident are a drawing (*op. cit.*, A. 31; questionable) and a painting (now in Les Andelys, c. 1645). Poussin also represented two episodes from the life of the great Scipio Africanus, the hero of Stoicism. One rather finished drawing for Cassiano dal Pozzo, made at the very end of Poussin's sojourn in Paris (fig. 64), illustrates the intrepidity of Scipio, who allowed a horde of pirates to enter his villa at Linturnum, knowing they would do no harm, but intended to pay homage to him. The Continence of Scipio was a more popular subject; it was often represented before Poussin's time (e. g., by Beccafumi) and afterward, especially in the eighteenth century. It is probable that when Poussin had in mind the pirates' visit to Scipio for Cassiano dal Pozzo, he also

decided on the idea for his painting of the *Continence of Scipio* (Pushkin Museum, Moscow), which also belongs to the period after Poussin's return from his Paris sojourn. But the large, grandiose drawing (fig. 26), composed in strictest relief style, is clearly later, in his Maniera Magnifica, and should be thought of as an independent, finished work. The hero is seated in the center with the grateful bridegroom kneeling before him, and the tall, beautiful princess (Scipio's booty, whom he liberates in his magnanimity)

Figure 64. SCIPIO AND THE PIRATES. 1642. Drawing, pen and bistre wash, 11¹/₂×17³/₄″. *École des Beaux-Arts, Orléans*

Figure 65. FINDING OF MOSES. 1651. Oil on canvas, 45⁵/₈×69³/₄″. *Collection Mrs. Schreiber, Bellasis House, Dorking*

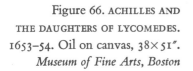

Figure 66. ACHILLES AND
THE DAUGHTERS OF LYCOMEDES.
1653–54. Oil on canvas, 38×51″.
Museum of Fine Arts, Boston

standing next to him. As a reward for his virtue, a Victory crowns Scipio with a wreath—a motif unusual in Poussin's later period.

The dramatic and forceful large drawing of the *Death of Virginia* (fig. 28) is one of the most exciting representations of the murder of Virginia by her father to save her honor, which was threatened by the decemvir, Appius Claudius. In political cast this representation of uproar against the tyrants is comparable to Botticelli's *Virginia*. The most penetrating and successful of Poussin's Stoical compositions is the *Testament of Eudamidas* (colorplate 35), which is as great in artistic merit—even greater in moral value—as the finest creations of the Maniera Magnifica. For its profound simplicity and for the disposition of the painting, the *Eudamidas* is the most religious, so to speak, of Poussin's non-religious paintings. (For the unusual use of Stoical motifs in landscapes, see chap. XII.)

Poussin had worked intensely and devotedly on *The Seven Sacraments* (1642–47), and he had not been in the mood to paint less profound subjects, except for the two amusing scenes for Camillo Massimi, taken from the early life of Moses: *The Child Moses Trampling on Pharaoh's Crown* and *Moses Changing the Rod of Aaron into a Serpent* (The Louvre, Paris). After the strain of steady occupation with contemplative and divine subjects, he gladly returned to "quelque chose de délectable"—though tempered by the "noble simplicity and calm grandeur" of his *grande manière* (see Commentary 31).

Immediately after sending the last of his *magnum opus* to Chantelou, in 1648, Poussin painted *Rebecca and Eliezer at the Well* (colorplate 31) for his patron Pointel; it is a work full of joy and pleasure, an apparition of graceful young girls.

The mood in which Poussin produced this pleasant, idyllic scene that is centered around a cortège of young women, expressed with the greatest formality, may also be seen in a few other paintings. The *Finding of Moses* (The Louvre, Paris), painted for Pointel in 1647, has the quality of an epic in contrast to Poussin's earlier, charming version for Le Nôtre (The Louvre, Paris). The scene takes place in a colorful setting in the extended landscape of the Nile, with pyramids and palm trees in the distance and a special anecdotal

Figure 67. CHRIST AND THE ADULTEROUS WOMAN. 1653. Oil on canvas, 48×76³/₄″. *The Louvre, Paris*

Figure 68. DEATH OF SAPPHIRA. 1654–55.
Oil on canvas, 48×78³/₄″. *The Louvre, Paris*

Figure 69. Raphael: BLINDING OF ELYMAS. 1515–16.
Cartoon, watercolor and charcoal on
paper laid down on canvas. *H. M. the Queen, on loan to
Victoria and Albert Museum, London*

addition, a hippopotamus hunt (more visible in the excellent preparatory drawing; fig. 44).

In another *Finding of Moses*, painted for Reynon in 1651 (fig. 65), the young women in the foreground participate in the scene more than they do in the earlier version, and the Egyptian character of the city is more evident, some of the motifs having been taken from the Palestrina Mosaic (fig. 81). This mosaic also supplied the motif of the procession of the priests of

Serapis in the beautiful *Rest on the Flight into Egypt* for Madame de Montmort (fig. 63). The content of the Hermitage painting comes from the legend of the Virgin, but the scene is most amiable and genrelike, with an exotic-romantic flavor supplied by the obelisks, the holy ibises, and the imposing Egyptians who serve the Holy Family. The statuesque forms of the two Egyptian women correspond to the monumental figures in Rebecca's retinue. This "Egyptian" *Rest on the Flight* is one of the most impressive products of Poussin's Maniera Magnifica, although it stands on the threshold of his old age style.

To the category of legendary romance belongs also *Achilles and the Daughters of Lycomedes* (fig. 66): the youthful Achilles, disguised in girl's clothing, excitedly unsheathes the sword which the crafty Odysseus, in the guise of a merchant, had hidden under jewels and other feminine objects. As in the paintings just discussed, this *Achilles* displays the strong, beautiful figures of the three young sisters who examine the precious wares with joyful movements; Laodamia,

Figure 70. FIVE TREES. c. 1635. Drawing, pen, black chalk,
and bistre wash, 9¹/₂×7¹/₈″. *The Louvre, Paris*

turning her head, suddenly realizes that her young friend and lover has given himself away.

During the five or six years that followed directly after the completion of *The Seven Sacraments*, Poussin's production was astonishingly rich in the number and variety of his subjects. This relatively short period includes fanciful, often joyful themes, beginning with *Rebecca and Eliezer at the Well* and ending with *Achilles and the Daughters of Lycomedes*. It includes several dignified but relaxed Madonnas, a number of serious Stoical subjects, and many landscapes composed with seemingly new invention and vision (see chap. XII). But these paintings, however delightful and remarkable, appear almost as by-products in comparison with other paintings of this time which, in the originality of their dramatic solutions and in their ultimate perfection, bring Poussin's oeuvre to a new peak—even among the other glories of his Maniera Magnifica.

Poussin's innate talent as a narrator, a teller of stories, which he had cultivated earlier with such pleasure and success, seems to emerge anew in full force. The tenor and significance of these stories have now changed. The story itself no longer commands primary interest, as it had in the case of the infant Pyrrhus, saved under extremely dangerous circumstances, or in the stoning of the schoolmaster of the Falerii. The Aristotelian high point of the drama, the *peripeteia*—that moment of a story toward which all the action has led and from which all emotion springs—now captures the spectator's full attention.

The outstanding example of this effect (also strongly sensed in *Achilles and the Daughters of Lycomedes*) is the *Judgment of Solomon* (colorplate 33), painted for Pointel in 1648; in this work the theatrical build-up of suspense is particularly artful. The young judge's shocking order has provoked a fearful excitement reflected in the emotions of the bystanders, which are differentiated with a mastery that Bellori particularly notes in his remarks on the painting. On the other hand, the manner is equally striking whereby the frenzied, passionate gestures of the terrified crowd are controlled by a concept of reason that is both idealized and crystallized. All action in the picture is suspended while each figure reacts to the startling judgment. Through the compressed action and clarified structure (that exceeds the famous preparatory drawing in the École des Beaux-Arts; fig. 115), the *peripeteia*, the moment of almost unbearable tension immediately following the climax, has a dramatic effect that is parallel in its tautness to such moments in the tragedies by Corneille.

This tension similarly dominates the other paintings of this group, to which belong *Healing the Blind of Jericho* (colorplate 34; 1650), *Christ and the Adulterous Woman* (fig. 67; 1653), and, lastly, *Death of Sapphira* (fig. 68; c. 1654–55). In *Healing the Blind of Jericho*, the breathless moment just before the miracle takes place is to be seen in the attitudes of the spectators, which are admirably varied; yet all eyes are riveted upon the hand of Christ, with its power to change darkness into

Figure 71. LANDSCAPE WITH FIGURES. 1630s. Drawing, pen and bistre wash, 5⅝×15¼". *The Hermitage, Leningrad*

light. In *Christ and the Adulterous Woman*, the dramatic reversal occurs at the moment when Christ challenges any without sin to cast the first stone (John 8 : 3–11). The *Death of Sapphira* is similarly constructed: Sapphira, the wife of Ananias, discovered as she attempted to cheat the church, was miraculously felled by the words of the wrathful Peter, to the awe and astonishment of the spectators (Acts 5 : 1–10).

Figure 72. ST. MATTHEW AND THE ANGEL. Early 1640s. Oil on canvas, 37³/₄×52″. *State Museums, Berlin-Dahlem*

Figure 73. LANDSCAPE WITH DIOGENES. 1648. Oil on canvas, 63×87″. *The Louvre, Paris*

In these groups of paintings, even more than in *The Seven Sacraments*, the influence of Raphael's tapestries is plain to see. Raphael's *Blinding of Elymas* (fig. 69) shows the same immediate consequences and the *peripeteia* of the *Judgment of Solomon;* Poussin's *Death of Sapphira* is an intentional continuation, in content and in form, of Raphael's *Death of Ananias* (fig. 14) in the tapestry series. The affinity with Raphael's grandiose constructions gives spatial freedom and grandeur to Poussin's paintings, to which he adds landscape backgrounds expanded and deepened into panoramic *vedute*. On the other hand, he crystallizes and arranges Raphael's figures on the proscenium in a typically classicistic manner.

Poussin's *Self-Portrait* (Frontispiece; see Commentary 37), proudly and fully signed and dated in the jubilee year of 1650, is an extraordinary work—a recapitulation and condensation of the perfection he attained in the great period of the Maniera Magnifica. In Poussin's time, portrait painting did not have as high a status as history painting, or the painting of religious and classical subjects; Poussin, dedicated to many-figured history paintings, held the painting of portraits in somewhat dubious esteem. Just as he avoided painting landscapes as a métier until late in his career, so he felt that portraiture did not show the significant human action that gives to a painting its didactic force. In a letter of 1650 to his close friend and patron, Chantelou, he boasted that in twenty-eight years he had not painted one portrait. Only when Chantelou urged him to sit for one, fervently desiring a portrait of his famous friend, did Poussin overcome his declared aversion and condescend to paint it himself. He evidently felt that there was no decent portrait painter in his circle in Rome; even a portrait by Mignard, who was relatively the best, would be a waste of money, since it would be painted in a cold manner, "without force and vigor." Subsequently Poussin made not one self-portrait, but two, giving the first to another friend, Pointel (fig. 117), and the second, which he considered superior, to Chantelou.

This painting contains the essence of all that Poussin endeavored to demonstrate in his most magnificent period: the verticals and horizontals are geometrically co-ordinated into a logical and inexorable scheme that enframes the presentation of his own corporeal and spiritual image (see Commentary 37). He showed himself as he wanted to be seen and understood for all time: as the *peintre-philosophe*, the creative and meditative architect of spatial and human relationships — as the spiritual equal of Corneille and Descartes.

XII. LANDSCAPES

Painters of religious or classical history in Italy did not usually consider the painting of landscape as an end in itself, but as a means of providing a secondary element sometimes needed for completing and embellishing figural compositions. With the important exception of such artists as Annibale Carracci and Domenichino, landscape painting as a genre had been practiced only by such Northern specialists as the Brills or Adam Elsheimer. Poussin, like Rubens before him, turned seriously and repeatedly to the painting of independent landscapes only late in his life, after having resolved complex problems of figure composi-

tion, perhaps as a form of relaxation from the rigors of figure painting. Between 1648 and 1651, years including such great works as *Rebecca and Eliezer at the Well* (colorplate 31), *Self-Portrait* (Frontispiece), and the *Madonna on the Steps* (colorplate 32), Poussin also devoted time to the problems and possibilities of landscape composition. Abraham Bosse wrote in 1649 that he had seen with great delight some landscapes made "par divertissement," which Poussin had recently sent to Paris. These *divertimenti*, like the musical ones by Mozart, must be placed, as Bosse remarks, in the highest rank of the genre of landscape.

Poussin's landscapes that may be biographically documented date from the end of the 1640s, when he was already in his mid-fifties. From this we must not conclude that he did not paint landscapes earlier, even much earlier. We know from Sandrart's amusing description of a sketching excursion to Tivoli at the beginning of the 1630s, in the company of Poussin, Claude Lorrain, and Pieter van Laer (*Il Bamboccio*),

Figure 74. GATHERING OF THE ASHES OF PHOCION. 1648. Oil on canvas, 45⅝×69¼″. *Collection Earl of Derby, Prescot, Lancashire*

Figure 75. After Poussin:
LANDSCAPE WITH THREE MONKS. Engraving.
*The Metropolitan Museum of Art,
New York (Dick Fund, 1953)*

that Poussin was then making sketches from nature. The admirable studies which have been preserved of natural objects—for instance, the study of five trees with deep bistre-washed shadows (fig. 70), or of the Roman arch in the Campagna (fig. 71)—demonstrate the strength of Poussin's feeling for natural phenomena, and this probably remained true throughout his career in Rome. Certainly he had made occasional, "unofficial" landscape paintings of relatively small size before he went to Paris, some of which found their place even on the walls of the *palazzi* of his patrons Cassiano dal Pozzo and Vincenzo Giustiniani. However, none of the paintings of this sort that have been attributed to Poussin—*Juno, Argus, and Io* (State Museums, Berlin-Dahlem), the Domenichinesque *St. Jerome* (The Prado, Madrid), nor the topographical landscape of the *Spoleto Virgin* (Dulwich College Picture Gallery)—has great value or originality. The two landscapes formerly in the Leon Collection, painted possibly 1638–39, also add little to Poussin's glory as a *paysagiste*. The landscape backgrounds of Poussin's other early compositions are much more important for our understanding and appreciation of his great gift in this kind of painting. The trees, bushes, houses, and distant hills that accompany the figure groups were not only an enlargement, a decorative embroidery; they also furthered Poussin's expression of a mood congruent to that of the subject matter. The type of background also changes according to the content and character of these compositions, and may vary within the same period, even within the same year. In Poussin's experimental years—the second half of the 1620s (or somewhat later), and the middle and late 1630s, the years of his "masculine" maturity—his landscape backgrounds are based on a tradition that is partly Roman-Bolognese, but rooted in the Venetian-Titianesque.

The scheme and treatment of Titian's landscapes impressed the youthful Poussin deeply, whereas the influence of Bolognese landscapes or of Raphael's art is prominent in only a few special paintings, such as the *Parnassus* (fig. 24). The mythologies and the romantic subjects that are so preponderant in Poussin's oeuvre in his Roman years before 1640, are saturated in their landscape sections, both morphologically and compositionally, with Titian's atmospheric, vigorous pictorial manner. Already in the late 1620s, paintings such as *Narcissus and Echo* (colorplate 9) show a loose, almost impressionistic treatment of large trees that form a background extremely close to Titian's style. We have already noted the contrast between a massive group of trees closing one side of the composition and the usually smaller opening leading into the lighted distance on the other side; this structural device probably came from Titian's *Death of St. Peter Martyr*, or a similar composition. Poussin, after developing this division and contrast (which is never so emphasized in central Italian art), perfected it in certain mythological

Figure 76. LANDSCAPE WITH PYRAMUS AND THISBE. 1651. Oil on canvas, $76^3/_8 \times 108^5/_8''$. *Städel Institute, Frankfurt am Main*

paintings. The most admirable example, perhaps, is *Aurora and Cephalus* (colorplate 15); the right side, which contains the sentimental and romantic story, dissolves toward the left in a shimmering, uncertain distance. It is important to note that after 1640 this lyrical device does not recur.

Poussin did not exploit his extraordinary talent for the loose technique of bucolic Venetian landscape. He might have developed these backgrounds into landscape compositions such as the *Landscape with the Herd* often attributed to Titian (Buckingham Palace, London), but nothing of the kind happened. On the contrary, the grandiose landscapes that Poussin created after his return from Paris, the ones bringing him fame as a landscape painter, have almost nothing in common with his earlier productions in the genre—not with his brilliant, diffuse, and romantic backgrounds à la Titian, nor with his feebler attempts in a more Bolognese-Roman manner. The grandiose style that Poussin developed for landscape in the 1640s and 1650s is indissolubly connected with the radical change in his artistic attitude (see chap. XI). The monumental figure compositions of the Maniera Magnifica—from *The Seven Sacraments* for Chantelou to *Healing the Blind of Jericho* (colorplate 34)—required backgrounds constructed in a corresponding planimetric system. Consequently, the extended landscapes these paintings contain, such as in the *Holy Family with Ten Figures* (fig. 57), had also to be, as the expression goes, "ge-

ometricized" and crystallized. Only after Poussin had perfected this adaptation of the magnificent style of the landscapes accompanying his figural compositions did he decide to issue independent, large landscape paintings of the same character, in a grand style. Poussin began to paint these landscapes about 1648; he singled out and amplified the type of landscape that he had already conceived to be suitable for the momentous actions of men.

Additional external reasons may have prompted Poussin, at least at that time, to make landscapes an important part of his late work. His rival and compatriot, Claude Lorrain, six years his junior, was approaching the apogee of his fame at the end of the 1640s with a new type of landscape painting, rich and very representational, such as his famous *Mill* (1648; Doria Gallery, Rome) or the *Flight into Egypt* (Gallery, Dresden). Also, in the year 1647, Dominique Barrière engraved and published the famous landscapes that Domenichino had painted in 1608 for the Villa Aldobrandini. Poussin, becoming conscious of the public's great interest in landscape painting (and of its profits), may understandably have wanted to show his friends and the world that he, too, could create landscape pictures that, although basically different from Claude's, had the same excellent beauty. And it was obvious that he could bring unexpected life to Domenichino's rather dry schemes, which anticipate to some degree the rationalistic structures of Poussin's landscapes.

The expression "heroic," with respect to landscape, was coined, as far as I know, by Roger de Piles in 1708, in the excellent remarks on landscape painting in his *Cours de Peinture*. He speaks of the *style héroïque* in contrast to the *style champêtre*, meaning by "*champêtre*" a realistic conception of landscape, showing nature "as one sees it every day." He defines the *héroïque* as a composition of objects which draw from art and nature whatever is great and extraordinary: the buildings are "always temples, pyramids—antique tomb monuments or altars sacred to the divinities." This illusion, says De Piles, can be "*agréable*" and enchanting when it is created by a man with the "*beau goût*" and "*bon esprit*" of Poussin. Although De Piles, the essentially anti-Poussin leader of the Rubénistes, expressed himself rather cautiously in regard to the painter, his term *héroïque* characterizes perfectly Poussin's new landscape style. It well explains the pictorial manner that Poussin conceived for the arid soil and hills of the Roman Campagna. This deserted terrain was consecrated for Poussin, the humanist, by the heroes of Antiquity who had once populated it. It is through his eyes and those of Claude Lorrain, the other great interpreter of the Roman countryside, that later generations up to our own time have seen the Campagna.

Both Poussin and Claude drew the elements of their landscape compositions from nature, from the same Roman nature; as close neighbors, the personal contact they certainly had is reflected generally and sometimes even specifically in their work. On the whole, however, Poussin's drawings show more precise observation: every tree is distinctly and carefully formed. Claude's drawings, on the other hand, reproduce the diffuse, multifarious, and more erratic aspects of nature. The difference between the two masters is even more marked in their finished paintings. The landscapes of Claude, expansive and atmospheric, are filled with a light that permeates the forms, softens the outlines of trees and architecture, and is neither determined nor bounded by the space. The figures in his great compositions have a secondary importance and significance, and reflect only the general mood, be it of a bucolic dance or an elegy on the decay of Rome. Poussin, sometimes from the identical vantage point, constructed a very different landscape that has a thematic, often dramatic character. He distinguishes layers

in light and space; to delineate the figural and landscape elements, he uses a clean light that strikes and reflects rather than saturates; he creates dynamic complexes of color; and, by fixing all details with almost geometric precision, he builds up a landscape that is classical in the fullest sense—clear, balanced, and measurably and intelligibly limited.

All of Poussin's landscape paintings—including those of a marked "heroic" character—belong to the general category of "ideal" landscape. They are ideal because they are both based on nature and "superior to nature" (Bellori). They are "compositions" formulated by his creative and selective mind; thus they differ from each other in shape and significance, but all bear the unmistakable mark of Poussin's masculine and tectonic will. At this perhaps highest point of his development, his landscapes are not lyrical; they do not display the vague and diffused sentiment to be seen in the poetic mood-landscapes by Claude and, even more, by Adam Elsheimer. Instead, as is so often the case with Poussin, reason directs the construction of the chosen scene and makes the mode to which the landscape corresponds as clear and understandable as it is in the figure compositions.

This admirable type of landscape—made anthropomorphic through the presence of human beings—already appears in the early 1640s, when Poussin was almost exclusively absorbed by religious painting. It seems apt that Poussin's first essays in landscape in the Grand Manner should contain religious figures: *St. John on Patmos* (colorplate 38) and *St. Matthew with the Angel* (fig. 72). The idea of inserting the figure of an Evangelist, and later of hermits giving communion to St. Mary Magdalene (an interesting drawing of this subject is in the Royal Library, Windsor Castle), into a landscape has prototypes in the sixteenth century (there are examples by Altdorfer, Polidoro, and, later, Paul Brill). Iconographically, Poussin's two "Evangelist" landscapes may thus be considered transitional.

In 1648, the year of *Rebecca and Eliezer at the Well* (colorplate 31), Poussin started a whole series of landscapes which, popularized through the engravings of Étienne Baudet and Louis de Chatillon, soon became famous. They belong among Poussin's most interesting and beautiful creations. According to Félibien, who is particularly well informed about the work in this period of the artist's life, Poussin produced

Figure 77. LANDSCAPE WITH TWO NYMPHS
AND A SNAKE. 1651. Oil on canvas, 46¹/₂×70¹/₂″.
Musée Condé, Chantilly

Figure 78. After Poussin:
LANDSCAPE WITH A STORM.
Engraving. *The Metropolitan Museum
of Art, New York
(Dick Fund, 1953)*

in rapid succession, during the three or four years after 1648, twelve or thirteen landscape compositions that show an astonishing variety. Félibien's list begins with the famous *Landscape with Diogenes* of 1648 (fig. 73; now thought by D. Mahon, in *Art de France*, I, for stylistic reasons, to be much later); then the two highly praised landscapes with the story of Phocion (colorplate 39; fig. 74); and *Landscape with a Large Road*. Then follow *Landscape with Three Monks* (*La Solitude:* fig. 75), known only in an engraving, and the fantastic

Landscape with Polyphemus (colorplate 42). In 1650 Félibien lists *Landscape with Woman Washing Her Feet* (National Gallery of Canada, Ottawa); in 1651, *Landscape with Pyramus and Thisbe* (fig. 76); the two pendant landscapes, one with a storm (fig. 78) and one with serene weather; and finally, *Landscape with Two Nymphs and a Snake* (fig. 77)—in my opinion, that mentioned by Félibien as being made for Le Brun in 1659. The only landscape (except for the Berlin *St. Matthew;* fig. 72) which was neither engraved nor mentioned in literary sources is *Landscape with Two Seated Figures* (Reinhart Collection, Winterthur). It is difficult to discern a development among the individual pictures or to divide them into groups; they were all painted within a relatively short period and each in its own way is perfect. All of these landscapes share in Poussin's grand style, which transcends the specific and the purely visual. However, it is not only their style that makes these paintings unique; it is the significance of their stories, in some the specifically moral tone, although the variety of moods is great, ranging from passivity to frightening excitement (in such cases as *Landscape with Woman Washing Her Feet*, the meaning may still be hidden). The famous *Landscape with Diogenes* (fig. 73) is of the first type, almost a *veduta*; it shows, very freely, the buildings on the Vatican hill, the *nicchione* of the Belvedere rising above the deep-cut valley of the Tiber, surrounded and framed by masses of green bushes and trees. This eminently passive panorama is in harmony with the scene enacted by the two small figures in the foreground: the cynical philosopher, Diogenes, observing a thirsty boy drinking from the river with his cupped hands, discards his water cup as an object of luxury

that is superfluous in the abundance provided by nature. In the same vein of Stoical retirement from the world, Poussin's *Landscape with Three Monks (La Solitude)*, engraved by Chatillon (fig. 75), presents an image of deep peace, of happiness acquired in amiable solitude. Félibien remarks that the three Carthusians meditating within a narrow valley bounded by rocky mountains—"un désert paisible et charmant"—communicate quietness of soul to the spectator and evoke a desire for similar tranquillity.

But in contrast to those landscapes (such as *Landscape with Woman Washing Her Feet* and *Landscape with a Large Road*) where undisturbed nature prevails, there are others in which Poussin depicts excitement, horror, and death. In some cases Poussin combined as pendants two paintings of opposed moods. It is possible that *La Solitude* had as its counterpiece *Landscape with a Snake*, also called *The Effects of Terror* (color-plate 40). In this work Poussin was demonstrating the contagion of fear as it passes from the hideous death scene to each successive group of figures. A mood of terror pervades the entire scene, while the unmoving landscape radiates its eternal serenity.

Also mentioned as pendants in complementary mood were the "landscape in serene and clear weather" (perhaps *Landscape with Three Men*, The Prado, Madrid) and the landscape, known only in an engraving, of a thunderstorm with a great tree hit by lightning (fig. 78). In this *Landscape with a Storm* the atmospheric turmoil, reminiscent of Rubens' *Broken Cart*, sweeps over the whole composition. One thinks of Félibien's remark that Poussin tried to render the "most extraordinary effects of nature no matter how difficult they might be to represent."

The high point of excitement in these landscapes is reached in the large *Landscape with Pyramus and Thisbe* that Poussin painted for Cassiano dal Pozzo in 1651 (fig. 76). Poussin himself seems to have taken some pride in this result of his effort to depict atmospheric turbulence. In a letter to his friend Stella, the painter from Lyons, he described the composition in detail: "I have tried to paint a storm by combining as well as I could the effects of a violent wind, an atmosphere darkened by rain, and lightning in various places, causing great disorder. All the figures reveal their personalities in their reactions to the bad weather. Some flee through the dust, following the driving

Figure 79. MERCURY AND PARIS. C. 1660.
Drawing, pen and bistre wash, 9¹/₈×8¹/₄″. *The Louvre, Paris*

Figure 80. APOLLO SAUROCTONOS. 1660s.
Drawing, pen and bistre wash, $7^1/_2 \times 10^1/_4$".
The Louvre, Paris

wind; others walk with difficulty against the wind, holding their hands before their eyes. A shepherd runs, abandoning his flock at the sight of a lion attacking the other shepherds ... In this turmoil the dust rises in large swirls. A dog barks, his fur standing on end, but he does not dare approach. In the foreground one sees the dead Pyramus stretched out on the ground; before him Thisbe abandons herself to her grief."

In these scenes of meteorological catastrophe Poussin was undoubtedly influenced by Leonardo da Vinci's *Trattato* (as J. Bialostocki has recently demonstrated in *Actes du Colloque Poussin*, I), for which Poussin had made his important and interesting illustrations.

Félibien wrote that Poussin's landscapes present "extraordinary actions which give satisfaction to the mind and at the same time please the eyes." In this statement is his recognition that Poussin, for the first time in the history of landscape painting, had effectively invested the beauty of nature with didactic significance. Another seventeenth-century French critic, the learned and sensitive Fénelon, found the landscapes with Phocion to have the greatest interest; but his praise, in *Dialogue des Morts*, is less for their compositions, which today we tend to appreciate exclusively, than for their moral sentiments. Such paintings as the

Figure 81. PALESTRINA MOSAIC (detail).
2nd century A.D. Mosaic.
Museo Prenestino Barberiniano, Palestrina

Figure 82. CONVERSION OF ST. PAUL. C. 1658. Drawing, pen and bistre wash, $7^1/_4 \times 11''$. *Musée Condé, Chantilly*

landscapes with Phocion (colorplate 39; fig. 74) and Diogenes (fig. 73) teach Stoical simplicity, represent moral anecdotes, and provide examples of virtue. The group of pictures that includes *Landscape with a Storm* (fig. 78) and *Landscape with a Snake* (colorplate 40) exemplifies Poussin's constant sense of the instability of human life and of the catastrophes that can seize man unawares. His view of life demanded that the individual be constantly on his guard; as in *Et In Arcadia Ego* (colorplates 12, 27), these landscapes are mementos of the fatality of life, of the dangers that await the unprepared man.

XIII. POUSSIN'S OLD AGE

The remarkable phenomenon is often discussed that great artists develop in the last years of their lives a sublime style, symptomatically different from that of their youth and maturity. The works in the late or "old age" styles of Titian, Rubens, Rembrandt, and others display in form and idea a deepened, broadened imagination that compensates for the natural uncertainty of vision caused by the decay of the artist's physical powers. Aged artists seem to strive in their late works for totality of impression, and are less concerned with delineating details. Their works are frequently filled with a new, moving lyricism that is a revival of their youthful style, but in a different, often elegiac, tone that contrasts with the clear, more vigorous narration or action expressed in their mature work.

These deficiencies and virtues of old age may be observed in the work of Nicolas Poussin. In his last years he was often ailing and in pain, and in a letter of the 1640s he already complains of the trembling of his hand. One notices in most of his late drawings (now so greatly admired, thanks to the particularly introspective orientation of our time) the shakiness of the broken lines that carry his ideas, now slowly and hesitantly formed. Consciously or unconsciously the old master was able to turn the insecurity of his hand and his lines into an expressive factor of rare beauty. His color also changes: he no longer differentiates hues and shades with the mature precision of a virtuoso, as he had done in the *St. Francis Xavier* that he painted for the Jesuit chapel of the Noviciate in Paris, or in *Rebecca and Eliezer at the Well* (colorplate 31), made later in the 1640s. The color of his late paintings recalls rather the encaustic technique of ancient Roman painting in which the surface of the canvas is unified by a matte-polished, waxy glow.

In a similar way, Poussin no longer modeled his figures on the rationalized physical ideal of classical statues. His late figures of Apollo, Mercury, and the nymphs no longer emulate the smooth elegance of Hellenistic-classicistic sculpture, to be seen, for instance, in his early *Midas and Bacchus* (colorplate 10) in Munich. His interest now extended even to the grotesque, distorted figures he had seen in the amusing scenes of Egyptian life from the Alexandrian Palestrina Mosaic, of which watercolor drawings made after it (now in the Royal Library, Windsor Castle) were also available

to him in Cassiano dal Pozzo's library. From these he may have derived the grimacing features characteristic of many of his late mythological drawings; drawings from the 1660s, *Mercury and Paris* (fig. 79) or *Apollo Sauroctonos* (fig. 80), look almost like caricatures. Poussin also took directly from the same mosaic the procession of the priests of Isis (fig. 81) for the background of the *Rest on the Flight into Egypt* (fig. 63), and he replaced the usual attendant angels by two Nubian women and a boy, who gracefully give food to the Holy Family. However, these sophisticated and exotic embroideries do not have any effect on the general structure of Poussin's late versions of earlier subjects. For example, in the "Egyptian" *Rest on the Flight* (there are several versions, one including an elephant) Poussin has only added Nilotic "local color" to his usual scheme. Moreover, several of the original inventions of this late period are newly composed in an equally conservative manner. The slightly academic arrangement of figures in the late *Christ and the Woman of Samaria*, insofar as we can judge from the engraving, is almost the same as that in the well-known painting by Annibale Carracci (Kunsthistorisches Museum,

Figure 83. ACHILLES ON SKYROS. 1656. Oil on canvas, 38⅝×51⅝″. *The Virginia Museum of Fine Arts, Richmond (The Glasgow Fund)*

Vienna). The sketch for the *Conversion of St. Paul* (fig. 82) repeats the scheme of Michelangelo's *Conversion of St. Paul* in the Cappella Paolina; it is transformed by the enormous menacing cloud, a favorite device of Poussin in his old age.

Although the method of narration was never essentially altered, the tenor and feeling of the subjects painted in these later years changed remarkably. The utterly different moods that Poussin could convey by his treatment of the same subjects in his old age style are demonstrated by the two versions of *Achilles and the Daughters of Lycomedes*, one made in 1656 (fig. 83) and the other some years earlier (fig. 66; 1653–54). In the earlier painting, Poussin concentrated almost exclusively on the expressive interplay of actions and gestures, and on a clear spatial construction. In the later painting, however, the quiet figures, in their lonely repose, hardly seem to react to one another; but they are linked in a lyrical and resonant rhythm, and are contained, even embedded, in a rich, large landscape. The anecdotal character of the first version has almost disappeared. What does remain is the narcissistic aspect of the young hero in a wonderful shining helmet, bound in the spell of his own warlike image in the mirror and observed by the two shrewd Greeks in the background.

The subjects of these religious and historical paintings in the last phase of his life, between 1656 and 1664, all require a relatively clear and traditional approach, although stylistically and compositionally they betray the characteristic symptoms of an old age style. In only a few of the latest mythological and landscape paintings, and in certain extraordinary drawings where Poussin was more or less unhampered by matters of content, his personal, passionate feeling is revealed and the figures begin to seem symbolic of his transcendental meditations. The paintings that manifest the new quality are *Blind Orion Searching for the Rising Sun*, of 1658 (fig. 84), the *Birth of Bacchus*, of 1657 (colorplate 45), and his last work, the fantasy *Apollo and Daphne* (colorplate 48). To these must be added the incomparable, mysterious cycle, *The Four Seasons* (colorplates 46, 47; figs. 128, 129), painted in the last years before his death. Whatever their specific meaning, these paintings are the product of Poussin's peculiar and individual conception at this late stage of his life.

In spite of the fact that the *Blind Orion* has been highly praised since the time of William Hazlitt and, more recently, has been intelligently analyzed (E. Gombrich, in *Burlington Magazine*, LXXXIV), in my opinion it does not quite rank with the few great masterpieces of this last period. Nevertheless, it is part of the psychological and stylistic change that leads irrevocably to Poussin's final and anticlassical manner. Characteristically, he did not turn for this landscape to one of the curious legends of the hunter Orion, easy to find and to understand in Ovid's *Fasti*, but (as Gombrich discovered) to the sixteenth-century mythographer Natales Comes; this writer, in the manner of the ancient Euhemerus, interprets the legends of the gods and heroes in the terms of natural phenomena— storm, sunshine, rain, and so on. From Comes' *Mythologiae* Poussin took the story of the giant whose blindness is his punishment for a terrible misdeed; Orion, guided by one of Vulcan's young servants standing on his shoulders, gropes toward the east to regain his lost eyesight from the rays of the rising sun. Poussin probably wanted not only to depict the spectacle of the helpless giant, but also to express the natural forces incorporated in him: for Orion, according to the legend, was the son of three fathers, Jupiter, Neptune, and Apollo, who represent a mixture of earth, water, and air. Poussin's painting seems to be filled with appropriate atmospheric humidity. The thickening rain cloud enveloping the shoulders of the giant is most expressive, and upon it stands Diana, through whose intercession Orion was later placed in the sky. Under the constellation Orion, one can expect rain, storm, and thunder. Previously Poussin would have resented the introduction here of Diana, for she belongs to a later phase of the Orion story and has nothing to do with his blindness; her presence surely would have seemed contrary to the unity of the action. But the figure of Diana, goddess of the moon, had a meaningful place as a meteorological symbol in this different conception. The contrast between this landscape and the factual or Stoical-didactic landscapes of the 1650s is surprising, and may be explained only by Poussin's more vague, somewhat pantheistic imagination in this late period.

The grandiose composition of the *Rape of Europa*, preserved in a large drawing, almost a cartoon (fig. 85), is of much greater significance and stature; it is the

Figure 84. BLIND ORION SEARCHING FOR THE RISING SUN. 1658. Oil on canvas, $46^7/_8 \times 72^7/_8''$.
The Metropolitan Museum of Art, New York (Fletcher Fund, 1924)

equal of the magnificent paintings, the *Birth of Bacchus* (colorplate 45) and *Apollo and Daphne* (colorplate 48). This drawing, although made before the two paintings (the project was first mentioned in August, 1649, but we do not know when the drawing was executed), is akin to them in its sublime beauty and puzzling strangeness. In execution it also manifests strongly the signs of Poussin's late manner, and the mask-like divinities at the right, who look at the spectacle unmoved and unmovable, recall the abstract figures in Late Antique mosaics.

The *Rape of Europa* and the two mythological paintings share one important and very odd feature: the introduction of narratives apparently unrelated to the main subject. These passages intrude elements of desperation and menacing death into stories of joy, fertility, and peace. At one end of the long arc of figures in the *Rape of Europa*, maidens place wreaths on the complacent bull, while at the other end a terrified young woman trips in fleeing from a large snake—

gaiety and life are opposed to horror and death. The woman bitten by the snake can hardly be anyone but Eurydice; and here Poussin uses again the motif of ill-omened smoke issuing from a distant castle, which appeared in *Orpheus and Eurydice* (colorplate 41). The combination in one scene of Europa and Eurydice, who are virtually unconnected in Ovid, can only be explained by the innate Stoical pessimism of Poussin as an old man for whom there was no joy or happiness without the possibility of imminent disaster.

The balance of life in its fullest sense against mortal tragedy also prevails in Poussin's marvelous paintings, the *Birth of Bacchus* and *Apollo and Daphne* (colorplates 45, 48). In ancient times, Bacchus was a god of joy, or young life and fertility, but he was also connected with the mysteries of death; similarly in Poussin's painting the melancholy figures of the dying Narcissus and the lamenting Echo temper the joyous arrival of the infant Bacchus into the arms of Mercury, while the flute-playing Pan and the naiads rhythmically grouped in

85

limpid water complement the sweet flowering of nature. Bellori notes that these figures of Echo and Narcissus are not relevant to the main scene, but he says that Poussin included them because the one story almost follows the other in Ovid's *Metamorphoses*.

This is a rather mechanical explanation, and too simple. But in one respect he is correct: the story of Bacchus' upbringing has no connection with the story of Narcissus. Bellori also knew, but did not consider it important enough to mention, that both stories take place in the same location. The lake and the miraculous cave covered with ivy vines and young grapes, where Mercury brings the infant Bacchus, is the same in which Narcissus, coming from the hunt, falls irrevocably in love with his reflection in the clear water. Both scenes are described in Philostratus' *Imagines*, and Poussin certainly knew the magnificent French editions in which it appeared.

In *Apollo and Daphne* (colorplate 48) there is an atmosphere of immobile tranquillity which gives this beautiful painting the appearance of a paradisiac Golden Age. This beauty, however, is not meant to last forever—it is neither complete nor undisturbed. Amidst the general inactivity, one small figure shows a trace of action: Cupid aims his arrow toward the group of nymphs on the right, among whom is Daphne. The "lascivious boy," as Ovid calls him,

avenged himself on Apollo, who had once derided Cupid for his small weapon, by wounding the god with the sharp arrow that "incites to love." But for Daphne, Ovid tells us that Cupid used the blunt arrow that "fugat amorem," driving love out of her, to make her frigid.

The consequences of Cupid's misdeed—Apollo's pursuit of Daphne, her refusal and flight, and finally her metamorphosis into a laurel tree—has frequently been represented in the painting and sculpture of many periods. Poussin himself had earlier made paintings and drawings of the famous climax of Ovid's story. Yet, so far as I know, no one but Poussin, in his last years, depicted the prehistory of the famous chase and transformation, or tried to describe the psychological moment when fate, though not yet awakened, is virtually present, putting everything and everybody in breathless suspense. Poussin's entire composition is saturated with an elegiac mood: in the midst of ideal beauty is the premonition of tragedy. Profound tension permeates the apparently peaceful figures of Apollo and Daphne—the ominous calm just preceding disaster is stressed by adding to the scene a dead youth lying half-hidden in the bushes. The dead boy is Narcissus or, in closer accord with the legend of Apollo, Hyacinthus, the beloved of Apollo, whom Apollo had accidentally killed in a discus match (see

Figure 85. RAPE OF EUROPA. Begun 1649. Drawing, pen and bistre wash, 10¹/₄×22¹/₂". *National Museum, Stockholm*

E. Panofsky, *Bull. de la Soc. Poussin*, III). The eternal calm of this sublimely beautiful painting is jeopardized by the presence of tragedy and death.

These compositions no longer depict the light, more immediate stories from Ovid's *Metamorphoses*—Venus and Mars, or Pan and Syrinx (or even Apollo and Daphne)—that Poussin had enjoyed illustrating in earlier years. It is characteristic of him that he took refuge in less accessible, more complicated writers, like Philostratus, and interpolated Ovidian tales into their stories to make new, mysterious combinations. Quite possibly Poussin had in mind a specific concept for *Apollo and Daphne*, and different literary sources have been suggested. But the appearance of the picture leads one to assume intuitively, without deeper investigation, that Poussin also wished to paint many gods and demigoddesses in a mythological landscape, and thereby to create a mythological dream having little or no precise content, little or no order. This vagueness is perhaps the most beautiful manifestation of his old age style. By their very mysteriousness these crystallized figures re-create in new form the charm which the great storyteller had displayed thirty years earlier in the *Realm of Flora* (colorplate 17).

Among these last paintings by Poussin, *The Four Seasons* (colorplates 46, 47; figs. 128, 129) are wholly isolated by their ideological content. The paintings are not unconnected with the *Birth of Bacchus* (colorplate 45) and *Apollo and Daphne* (colorplate 48), for into all the late mythological pictures Poussin injects a quality of philosophical-religious mystery which does not appear in his earlier works. But in *The Four Seasons* Poussin makes a more positive statement of the dogma of the Catholic Church than may be found in any of his previous paintings.

We still know almost nothing of Poussin's personal commitment to the doctrines of the Church. In his correspondence, some of which is quite personal, there is no significant mention of religious matters. On the other hand, many of Poussin's paintings show his deep interest in, and his understanding of, the iconography of the Old and New Testaments. It may be that Poussin's approach to religious subject matter came from fundamentally the same interest that led him to concentrate on ancient Stoic themes: Germanicus, the subject of Poussin's most personal early work, and Christ both provided him with insight into human life and human tragedy. However, Poussin was surely indoctrinated from childhood with the symbolic phraseology of the Church. When at the end of his life he chose to depict the seasons of the year in the form of a spectacle mirroring the changes in human life, he could easily bring a religious significance to each item without destroying the programmatic connection among the works. It is not improbable that the clerical advisers who were intimate with Poussin just before his death suggested this ecclesiastical "conceit." But Poussin had never before painted such detailed, allegorical conceits; only in his last years, when he broke the limitations of strict clarity and logic, he allowed himself to invest his pictures with hidden and difficult meanings (see Commentaries 46, 47).

People have sometimes wondered why *Winter* (colorplate 47), the last of Poussin's *Four Seasons*, does not show the normal snowy landscape. It may be that he knew that winter in the Levant was characterized by torrential rain, and wished to give, as far as possible, the correct local color to Old Testament stories. This rationalization, though it was once stated in the French Academy, is only half true, for Poussin chose to represent winter as a time of tempest and death, in palpable and necessary contrast to the blooming life of spring and the exuberant fullness of summer and fall. In accord with the religious content investing the other seasons, Poussin equated with winter the almost complete destruction of mankind, namely, the Deluge recorded in the Bible.

To illustrate a terrible accident that nature could unexpectedly inflict upon humanity was by no means foreign to Poussin's mind in his later years. In 1651, in his landscape showing a thunderstorm and a tree hit by lightning (fig. 78), he had tried to depict the effect of wild elements unleashed upon surprised individuals. But *Winter* goes far beyond individual misfortunes, and Poussin here depicts the cosmic terror of catastrophe itself.

CONCLUSION

Poussin—the narrator of mythological tales, erotica, and bacchanals, the lyricist and the psychologist, the painter of action and of the stories of Moses from the book of Exodus—changed after his return from Paris in 1642. By nature a man of reason and meditation,

Poussin's classicistic precision reached its height in his Maniera Magnifica, crystallizing action with the utmost penetration. The influence of Stoical discipline on the conduct of life—Seneca's *Moral Letters* seen through the moral philosophy of such writers as Charron—is never so strong as in the works of the 1640s and the early 1650s, and extends even to the landscape paintings.

Connected in some respects with this Stoical philosophy, a psychological disposition develops in Poussin's last period that seems in some way to corrode the more inhuman and geometricizing quality of his artistic conception of the 1640s and 1650s. J. Bousquet (in "Les Relations de Poussin avec le milieu romain," *Actes du Colloque Poussin*, I) gives a description of Poussin as a misanthrope and a "sauvage," but one can find other features in his behavior as an old man that are almost pathological. His psychic disposition, which made him permanently aware of the fragility of life and the caprices of Fortune, can be characterized by the modern term "anxiety"; the snake lurking in the grass *(latet anguis in herba)* is a symbol of evil that we meet surprisingly often in Poussin's last paintings. The sense of insecurity, of the unpredictable vicissitudes of fate in this world, became an obsession which to a great extent dominated the spirit of the aging *peintre-philosophe*. Even in 1648, the time of his greatest production, Poussin suffered from occasional attacks of despair. When he received news of the terrors of the Fronde, for example, he exclaimed: ". . . but I am afraid of the malice of this century; virtue, conscience, and religion are banished among men. Only vice, deceit, and self-interest now reign. All is lost—I despair for the good. Everything is filled with misery."

It has been recently suggested that Poussin had contact with "skeptical" literary and philosophical groups in Paris, and perhaps also in Rome. Their theories and opinions (which never departed from the context of the Church) may perhaps have had an influence on the more and more introverted mind of the aging Poussin. Be that as it may, Poussin's special state of mind was natural in a man of his character who was awaiting death—for him, pagan fate had almost greater importance than Christian Providence—and it penetrates his art, imbuing it with a divine vagueness. In this spirit, Poussin places the humanist corporeality of his figures and objects in a world that is unreal and undefined, beyond rationalism and civic virtue—a world that manifests, through a kind of mystic transparency, his last fears and his last loves.

DESCRIPTION OF POUSSIN

by Giovanni Pietro Bellori,
in *Le vite de' pittori, scultori ed architetti moderni*, Rome, 1672

"... Poussin's conduct of life was most orderly ... it was his custom to rise early in the morning and exercise for an hour or two, walking sometimes through the city, but almost always on the Monte della Trinità, the Pincio, not far from his house. One ascends by a short slope delicious with trees and fountains, and from there one has the most beautiful view of Rome and her pleasant hills, which together with the buildings form a scenic theater. There he held curious and learned discussions with his friends. Returning home, he painted without intermission until noon, and then after his midday meal he painted again for several hours ... In the evening he went out again, and strolled at the foot of the same hill, in the piazza frequented by foreigners who gathered there. He was always surrounded by intimates who followed him, and by those who, attracted by his fame, wished to see him and have a friendly talk with him. It was his custom to deny no one his company. He was willing to listen to others, but his own discourse was then most grave, and received with attention. He spoke often about art, and with such clarity and understanding that not only painters, but also interested laymen, came to hear from his own lips the most beautiful interpretation of painting, discussed as the occasion offered and not with the intention of teaching. He had read and observed so much that he never spoke of anything of which he had not a satisfactory knowledge. His words and ideas were so original and well organized that they did not seem improvised, but appeared to be based on study and meditation. The reasons for this were his talent and wide reading, not only of stories, fables, and subjects of his special erudition, but also of other liberal arts and of philosophy. His memory of Latin, though imperfect, was useful to him, and he knew Italian as well as if he had been born in Italy. He was perspicacious in understanding, discriminating in selection, and retentive in memory, and these are the most desirable gifts of genius.... He was tall and well proportioned in all parts of his body ... his complexion was rather olive, his black hair became gray with age, and his eyes were blue; his sharp nose and wide forehead gave his face a noble and yet modest appearance ...."

BIOGRAPHICAL OUTLINE

(After Charles Sterling, Biography, *Catalogue*, Exposition Nicolas Poussin, Musée du Louvre, Paris, 1960, pp. 197–283.)

1594   Nicolas Poussin born near Les Andelys (Normandy). His father, Jean Poussin, was a native of Soissons; he had served in the royal army during the civil wars, and recently settled near Les Andelys.

1600–09   Given some higher education including Latin, but he early showed a passion and talent for drawing.

1611–12   Quentin Varin came to Les Andelys to paint altarpieces. Is said to have encouraged Poussin to become a painter.

1612   Poussin secretly departed for Paris, may have stayed in Rouen as apprentice to the elder Jouvenet.

1612–21   Worked in Paris briefly under the Flemish portraitist Ferdinant Elle, and in the atelier of the history painter Georges Lallemand. Studied prints after Raphael and Giulio Romano, ancient sculpture, and Roman and Venetian paintings in the Royal Collection, to which he was introduced by Alexandre Courtois. Went to Poitou to make paintings for a young patron's château, but plan opposed by young man's mother. Illness caused a year's return to his parents. Cured, he returned to Paris, made some Bacchanals in Château de Cheverny. Admired paintings by Primaticcio at Fontainebleau. Studied anatomy and perspective. First attempt to go to Rome ended in Florence, and he returned to Paris, where he lived at Collège de Navarre.

1621–22   Gave up attempt at a second trip to Italy at Lyons, perhaps because of debts.

1622   Received commission from the Paris Jesuits for six frescoes in tempera, in celebration of the canonization of Ignatius of Loyola and Francis Xavier. These decorative paintings were successful (now disappeared).

1622–23   This commission brought him to the attention of Giovanni Battista Marino, who had been at the French court since 1615. Marino admired his inventiveness and the vivacity of his execution. Poussin often worked at Marino's house, made drawings (so-called Marino Drawings) of subjects suggested by him. Commissioned by archbishop of Notre-Dame de Paris for a *Death of the Virgin;* painting has disappeared, but is known through Saint-Aubin's sketch in an 18th-century guidebook. Employed at the Luxembourg under Nicolas Duchesne, with young Philippe de Champaigne. Left for Italy after completing this work. Probably spent several months in Venice and arrived in Rome in March, 1624.

1624   Marino recommended Poussin to Marcello Sacchetti, through whom he was presented to Cardinal Francesco Barberini, nephew of Pope Urban VIII.

1625   Went through difficult period after departure of Cardinal Barberini for France and death of Marino. Studied anatomy from surgeon Nicolas Larcher; read Vesalius. In December, Cardinal Barberini returned briefly to Rome, probably commissioned *Conquest of Jerusalem* (now disappeared).

1626   Lived with Flemish sculptor Duquesnoy. Measured and drew ancient statues, modeled in clay. Studied Raphael, Giulio Romano, and Titian. Continued studies of geometry, optics, and perspective, and obtained access to library of the Barberini.

1627   Received first important commission from Cardinal Barberini, *Death of Germanicus.* Began to be interested in Domenichino's linear and constructed style, attended his school.

90

1627–28 According to Giulio Mancini, Poussin made many small paintings for private houses.

1628 Received an important commission for St. Peter's, the *Martyrdom of St. Erasmus*, which originally had been commissioned to Pietro da Cortona.

1629 During an illness, was attended by Jacques Dughet, a Parisian pastrycook living in Rome, and his Italian wife.

1629–30 Completed the *Martyrdom of St. Erasmus* and painted the *Madonna Appearing to St. James the Greater*, called the *Madonna du Pilier*, commissioned for Valenciennes.

1630 Poussin was unsuccessful in a competition for the commission for a fresco in S. Luigi dei Francesi. September 1, married Anne-Marie Dughet, daughter of Jacques Dughet, in S. Lorenzo in Lucina.

1631 Lived on Via del Babuino with wife and her brother Gaspard Dughet, the famous landscape painter. Poussin probably already a member of Academy of St. Luke. After Domenichino left for Naples, Poussin drew from the live model in the atelier of Andrea Sacchi. Through the trial of the art dealer Valguarnera in the summer of 1631, certain important paintings can be dated in the preceding year: the *Plague of the Philistines* (*Plague of Ashdod*), the *Triumph of Flora*, and the Midas paintings.

1633 The *Adoration of the Magi*, exceptionally signed and dated, was possibly a reception piece for the Academy of St. Luke.

1634 Studied Zarlino's *Istituzioni Harmoniche*, basis of his theory of the "modes."

1635 Final year Gaspard Dughet is known to have lived with him. Poussin very interested in landscape, made many studies from nature. Particularly intimate with Cassiano dal Pozzo, drew from statues and reliefs in his collection and worked in his collection of medals and books. Probably through dal Pozzo, borrowed manuscript of Leonardo's *Trattato* from Cardinal Barberini's library, and made drawings of figures from it. Now well established, sent paintings throughout Italy and to Spain. Of the four *trionfi* for Cardinal Richelieu mentioned by Bellori, two Bacchanales were finished and sent to Paris by mid-May, 1636.

1636 Jean Dughet, Gaspard's younger brother, came to live with Poussin. Became Poussin's secretary, and made many engravings of his works.

1637 Commission for *Schoolmaster of the Falerii* for Phélipeaux de la Vrillère.

1637–38 *Pan and Syrinx* for Nicolas Guillaume de la Fleur, and began the series of *Seven Sacraments* for Cassiano dal Pozzo.

1638 Approached by Chantelou and Jean Le Maire (on behalf of Richelieu and Sublet de Noyers, *Surintendant des bâtiments*) to return to France. Poussin to direct decoration of the royal palaces, assisted by Duquesnoy.

1639 Terms accepted, and received letter from Louis XIII himself. Preparations for trip, and work on commissions for important Italian patrons.

1640 Richelieu and Sublet de Noyers sent Paul Fréart de Chantelou to Rome to make sure of Poussin and Duquesnoy, or, failing them, to find other artists. Poussin finally persuaded by Chantelou. Embarked at Civitavecchia in November, arrived at Fontainebleau and Paris in December. Cordially received by Sublet, introduced to Richelieu. Presented to Louis XIII.

1641 Commissioned to decorate Grande Galerie of the Louvre, to make cartoons for tapestries, to make frontispieces for books from Royal Press of the Louvre, and to do various works for Richelieu and for the chapel of the château of St.-Germain-en-Laye, and for the Jesuit church founded by Sublet. Because of the Grande Galerie commission, artists previously in favor begin intrigues against Poussin.

1642 Progressed with the drawings for the Grande Galerie, executed frontispiece for *Works* of Horace, and finished the *Baptism*, the last of the *Seven Sacraments* for Cassiano dal Pozzo. Promising to return, he started for Rome in September, arriving there in November.

1643 Reinstalled in Rome. Death of Louis XIII and the consequent fall of Sublet. Poussin virtually released from contract in France, but busy with commissions for Chantelou.

1644 Death of Urban VIII caused Cardinal Barberini and Cassiano dal Pozzo to lose influence. Poussin inclined to return to France, unable to get previous favorable terms. Poussin very retiring because of the political situation, and worked mainly for French patrons.

1645 The banker Pointel became one of Poussin's most important French patrons in Rome.

1646 Poussin began the new series of *Seven Sacraments* for Chantelou, which were completed early in 1648, and painted other religious subjects, such as the large *Crucifixion* (in Hartford).

1647–49 Visit of Félibien to Rome.

1648 Poussin began his great systematic series of landscape paintings and the series of monumental Holy Families.

1649 Painted his *Self-Portrait* for Pointel. Complained of being busier than ever in his life, reproached by Chantelou for delays in serving him.

1650 Poussin did the famous *Self-Portrait* for Chantelou, as well as *Healing the Blind of Jericho*, the *Assumption of the Virgin*, and the *Vision of St. Paul*.

1651 A French edition of Leonardo's *Trattato* contained engravings after drawings of nude figures by Poussin.

1652 Because of poor health, Poussin did little work until late in the year.

1655 Cardinal Fabio Chigi elected Pope Alexander VII; interested in art and favorable to France. Poussin again named First Painter to King of France, payment received for the year 1643.

1657 Cassiano dal Pozzo died in October. Poussin painted the signed and dated *Annunciation* for Alexander VII.

1658–64 Works of Poussin's old age. In October of 1664, Poussin's wife died. In the same year, 1664, the *Abbé* Nicaise, Canon of Ste. Chapelle, Dijon, was a frequent visitor.

1665 Poussin partly paralyzed and unable to work. In September he suffered from fever, hemorrhage, and abscesses; he never left his bed again. In November, he drew up his final will, in which he asked to be buried without pomp in the parish church of San Lorenzo in Lucina. Poussin died November 19.

COLORPLATES

HOLY FAMILY
(PEARSON MADONNA)

Oil on canvas, 39³/₈×29¹/₂"

c. 1629

Landesmuseum, Karlsruhe

Among the Holy Families that Poussin painted in his early Roman years, the two best-known and most charming examples are the so-called *Pearson Madonna* and the *Reinhart Madonna* (fig. 86). In contrast to Poussin's monumental paintings in the 1640s of the Holy Family, constructed on a broad basis (*Madonna*

Figure 86. HOLY FAMILY (REINHART MADONNA).
1632–33. Oil on canvas, 34⁵/₈×26³/₈".
Collection Oskar Reinhart, Winterthur

on the Steps, colorplate 32), these Madonnas are vertical in shape, lighthearted in spirit, and very fresh and luminous in tonality. The combination of vertical and diagonal movements in both paintings, and the division of the composition into two more or less equal parts with the lower portion reserved for the main group, are typical of the Early Baroque. In both works, St. Joseph is behind the other figures, reading or contemplating in an idyllic spot shadowed by trees. The little St. John in the *Pearson Madonna* devoutly kisses the foot of the Christ Child; in the *Reinhart Madonna* (really a Rest on the Flight into Egypt), the Holy Family is visited by a host of *putti* who offer flowers and fruit to the Child. In both paintings, the Holy Family is near the ruins of an ancient temple of which there remain only one fluted column and part of a marble pedestal. This column is the only classical allusion in an otherwise distinctly unclassical composition; both paintings more resemble a style that was fashionable in north Italy just before Poussin visited Venice in 1624 (see works by Padovanino and Fetti). In some respects they anticipate late seventeenth- or eighteenth-century painting in France. In organization, the *Pearson Madonna* is quite close to the so-called *Inspiration of Anacreon* (fig. 32), which can be dated c. 1629—the background of both paintings consists of massive trees on one side, and on the other side a smaller space opening into a far distance. Poussin derived this compositional device from Titian, and used it often during this period. The *Reinhart Madonna* appears more mature, and should be dated two or three years later.

This painting, recently acquired from the Corsini Collection, Florence, was originally made for Cardinal Barberini. It is mentioned in the Barberini inventory, and was probably painted in 1627.

Except for the first version of the *Capture of Jerusalem* (1625–26; now lost), the *Death of Germanicus* is Poussin's first outstanding history painting made at the commission of a great family, the Barberini. But it is more important that in this painting are first revealed those values which became increasingly significant as Poussin's artistic conceptions matured. He has devised forms of a suitable monumentality for a tragic and elevated theme. His adulation of Roman Antiquity is already clear: spiritually, it is present in the heroic subject itself; formally, in the dependence on ancient prototypes (in this case, one of the Meleager sarcophagi; fig. 6). Poussin greatly admired this Antique form of deathbed scene—a subject "worthy of an Apelles." He repeated it later in two famous pictures, the *Testament of Eudamidas* and *Extreme Unction* (from *The Seven Sacraments*).

The story of the death of Germanicus comes from a passage in the *Annals* of Tacitus (II, 71–72). There may be read the story of the great and noble man who passionately loved and defended his country, but succumbed to the intrigues of his enemies—a subject dear to Stoic ideology. In the *Germanicus*, Poussin anticipated the moralistic-Stoical attitude in his work of the 1640s, such as the *Testament of Eudamidas* (colorplate 35) and the Phocion landscapes (colorplate 39; fig. 74). Germanicus, the beloved Roman general, is shown as he lies dying—possibly, as he himself suspects, poisoned on order of the jealous emperor, Tiberius.

Agrippina, whose role corresponds to that of Atalanta in the Meleager scene, is seated in a mourning posture much like that of the youth at the left in the Meleager relief. But the greater part of the composition is filled with Germanicus' loyal and loving officers and soldiers, who pledge to avenge him. Poussin wanted to record in this scene, as in the later Phocion compositions, the great value and significance of the dying man's redemption through his friends' demonstration of faith and love.

Here, as always, Poussin selected only the important elements from the Meleager sarcophagus, his ancient source. The dark-blue curtain with its heavy folds serves as an impressive foil to the main group and at the same time emphasizes the parallel layers of the composition within the limited space. But the relief-like style does not govern the entire painting; it is slightly softened by the oblique angle of the bed, and on the left, by an arched hall opening into the lighted background, a device often found in Early Baroque compositions. The space is somewhat unclear and crowded, a sign of the early date of the composition.

In the drawing of the same subject (fig. 7), the action is much more expressive and more integrated. The moral value of the moment of oath-taking is in this case emphasized, as in an epigram. At the same time, Poussin here approximates the style of ancient relief more closely, and he figuratively quotes Tacitus' reference to the soldier who grasps the hand of the dying hero. The drawing clarifies and concentrates the painting in a classicistic sense. Thus it could not be a preparatory sketch for the painting, but belongs to Poussin's style of the first half of the 1630s.

COLORPLATE 2

DEATH OF GERMANICUS

Oil on canvas, 58¹/₄×77³/₈″

c. 1627

The Minneapolis Institute of Arts, Minneapolis, Minnesota

(SEE COMMENTARY ON OPPOSITE PAGE)

Figure 87. Annibale Carracci:
TRIUMPH OF BACCHUS. C. 1597–1604.
Fresco. *Farnese Gallery, Rome*

Two paintings are preserved that have to do with Flora: this *Triumph of Flora* and the so-called *Realm of Flora* (colorplate 17); Poussin may have made other such paintings. Félibien mentions a painting of the "love of Flora and Zephyrus," for which there remains a drawing (perhaps only a copy). In the trial of Fabrizio Valguarnera in 1631, there are references to similar themes in connection with Poussin: "a garden of flowers" and a "Primavera." Poussin apparently made various paintings of Flora or Spring; he painted the *Triumph of Flora*, according to Bellori, during his first years in Rome, for Cardinal Omodei.

The Renaissance had long found enjoyment in according a triumph to an abstract virtue (fame or love) or to a god or goddess, the honor reserved in ancient times for a victorious general. As a Triumph of Bacchus also symbolizes revelry and wine, so Poussin's *Triumph of Flora* is an apotheosis and a grandiloquent praise of springtime.

Flora, the amiable goddess of spring and flowers, is celebrated in a procession led by dancing Venus. For the occasion, Venus has lent to Flora her *amoretti*, who pull her golden chariot and gather flowers to make her crown (Bellori). Behind Venus is her lover, Adonis; he carries the red anemones which Venus later caused to spring from his blood, and offers his flowers to Hyacinthus who, mortally wounded in his game with Apollo, bends down, so that a *putto* may wreathe his head. In the center Flora graciously accepts the tribute of Ajax, the warrior metamorphosed into the larkspur. Just behind him is the naked youth Narcissus, who also offers his flower. In the right foreground, bending down to pluck heliotrope, is Clytie, enamored of Helios (Apollo).

Annibale Carracci's *Triumph of Bacchus* in the Farnese Gallery (fig. 87) certainly influenced Poussin. But Poussin's composition is much more fluid and unified, unlike Annibale's additive composition. Poussin duplicated the movements of arms and legs to stress the sense of a regular progression. In spite of the elaborate, calculated composition, there is no feeling of artificiality, and the whole procession has a free, gay rhythm.

The figures move in a relief-like space parallel to the surface of the picture and they, as well as the blue hills echoing their arrangement, are in clear, distinguishable layers. The two reclining figures may be Crocus and Smilax (Ovid, *Metamorphoses*, IV, 283); they resemble the familiar *repoussoirs* of Venetian painting (especially Tintoretto's); Annibale also used them, though at opposite ends of the composition. It has been noted that Poussin integrated these two figures so fully with the formal composition that it is difficult to say whether they are only spectators, put into the picture for purely formal reasons, or members of Flora's cortege.

The painting anticipates in some respects the series of large Bacchanals which Poussin painted in the mid-1630s for Cardinal Richelieu. It shares with those grandiose compositions an over-all spirit of enthusiastic revelry that comes from the masterly organization of a large number of figures. However, this organization is more fluid than in the later paintings, and it is even less refined than in the *Realm of Flora* (colorplate 17). The composition of the *Triumph of Flora* has an Early Baroque quality like that of the *Death of Germanicus;* and it must be dated not long after *Germanicus*, c. 1627.

COLORPLATE 3

TRIUMPH OF FLORA

Oil on canvas, 65×94⁷/₈″

c. 1627–28

The Louvre, Paris

(SEE COMMENTARY ON OPPOSITE PAGE)

In the 1620s, the chapels of the nave of St. Peter's, recently constructed by Carlo Maderno, were to be completed with altarpieces. For this purpose, the *fabbrica* of St. Peter's awarded commissions to a large number of painters residing in Rome, including such foreign artists as Valentin and Vouet. Poussin, on being recommended by Cardinal Barberini, received the commission for a Martyrdom of St. Erasmus, but not until Pietro da Cortona, who originally held it, was shifted to the more important Chapel of the Sacrament where, in turn, he replaced Guido Reni. Cortona was paid 1,000 scudi; Poussin had to be content with less than half that amount, 400 scudi, which included a "bonus" of 100 scudi for good services, paid to him in the second half of 1629. Cortona's part in the commission is interesting, because the works of Poussin and Cortona have affinities in this period,

Figure 88. Pietro da Cortona: MARTYRDOM OF ST. ERASMUS. c. 1627. Drawing, pen and ink, 14¹/₄×9¹/₈″. *Gabinetto dei Disegni, Uffizi, Florence*

even their general color scheme. When one compares Poussin's *St. Erasmus* with contemporary Italian, especially Roman, paintings, its general disposition is closest to Pietro da Cortona's frescoes in the Church of Sta. Bibiana (1624–26). In *St. Bibiana Refusing to Sacrifice to Idols* (fig. 20), the central figure, who exhorts St. Bibiana, even has a gesture corresponding to that of the high priest in Poussin's painting. Moreover, a sketch of the *Martyrdom of St. Erasmus* (fig. 88) has been attributed to Pietro da Cortona, which has a composition similar to Poussin's—including the gesture of the high priest. Accordingly, Poussin must have used for his *Erasmus* altarpiece the main features of a composition which Pietro da Cortona had begun —at least in preliminary sketches—and left for his successor. This circumstance would explain the classicistic-Baroque style of Poussin's *St. Erasmus*, for the same is to be seen in early work by Pietro da Cortona, a painter schooled partly on Veronese's art. But the severe, candid manner of Poussin's painting is rather different from Pietro da Cortona's more fluid and decorative forms (G. Briganti, in *Paragone*, XI).

Poussin does not focus on the repulsive disembowelment *per se* of the saint, and he avoids the horrors which are to be found, for instance, in Pomarancio's scenes of martyrdom in S. Stefano Rotondo. What is impressive about Poussin's painting is its technique, its "salon elegance" almost comparable to that of the *Inspiration of the Poet* (colorplate 16). The shining surface of the armored man on horseback might be associated with Guido Reni's style, and indeed it seems to be derived from a figure in Reni's fresco in S. Gregorio Magno. Poussin appears here to have completely mastered his craft.

However, the painting is not, and has never been, unanimously appreciated; Poussin himself seems to have complained that the picture did not receive proper recognition. Sandrart apparently did not like this painting, but, being a follower of Caravaggio, he was naturally prejudiced. On the other hand, Bernini remarked some forty years later that in this picture "there was a profundity and solidity of knowledge," and that if he (Bernini) were a painter, "this picture would make (him) deeply envious." It seems that Bernini actually had interested himself in getting the commission for Poussin, and had recommended him to the Pope in the face of Guido Reni's criticism.

COLORPLATE 4

MARTYRDOM OF
ST. ERASMUS

Oil on canvas, 114⁷/₈×73¹/₄″
1628–29, signed
Picture Gallery, Vatican, Rome
(SEE COMMENTARY ON OPPOSITE PAGE)

Figure 89. DEATH OF ADONIS. c. 1630. Oil on canvas, 22$^1/_2$×50$^3/_8$″. *Museum, Caen*

Probably painted at the end of the 1620s, this *Lamentation* and the *Deposition* (The Hermitage, Leningrad) are Poussin's only securely attributed representations, during this early period, of the Passion of Christ. The *Lamentation* was engraved by Vuibert in 1643 (A. Blunt, in *Revue des Arts*, VIII).

Like *Narcissus and Echo*, this painting is imbued with Venetian light and atmosphere. The composition, with figures concentrated on the right side and a view on the left into a distant romantic landscape, has a character that allies it with the group of equally Venetian, mostly mythological, subjects painted at the end of the 1620s. It is closest to the *Death of Adonis* (fig. 89) in composition and feeling (we cannot be sure which composition serves as model for the other, the Chris-

tian or the pagan). The position of the body of Christ and that of Adonis, the head fallen back from the raised chest, is probably taken from a Meleager sarcophagus in the Capitoline Museum, but not the famous one Poussin used for *Germanicus*. In spite of similarities in the *Death of Adonis* and the *Lamentation*, it is not necessary to infer that Poussin expressed thereby a symbolic relationship between the two.

The painting is vigorously and impressively composed, but it has not the religious, tragic force of the *Entombment* which Poussin painted more than twenty years later (fig. 56); the somber tones of the late work are in accordance with Poussin's doctrine of the modes, and the full forms are those of the High Renaissance.

COLORPLATE 5

LAMENTATION

Oil on canvas, 39³/₈ × 56³/₄"

c. 1628

Pinakothek, Munich

(SEE COMMENTARY ON OPPOSITE PAGE)

NYMPH CARRIED
BY A SATYR

Oil on canvas, 37³/₈ × 28³/₄″

Late 1620s or early 1630s

Gallery, Cassel

This relatively small painting belongs to a group of bucolic, erotic mythological subjects that represent nymphs and satyrs in a landscape. These pagan genre scenes—a nymph riding on a goat, or groups sitting and drinking—originate in ancient representations on cameos and gems; Annibale Carracci's playful scenes in the Camerino of the Farnese Palace were inspired by the same source, and likewise his decorations on the lids of precious clavichords.

There is some question if Poussin came to paint these charming scenes as a by-product of his great Bacchanals of the mid-1630s, or if they belong to those Antique scenes in a Venetian manner which Mancini described. With their light character and small size, they became popular works and they come to us in several copies; it is not always easy to decide which one is the original. It is even possible that Poussin made more than one copy himself.

This scene of a ménage on the move, searching for a picnic place—the naked girl piggyback on a kneeling satyr, preceded by one sweet little *putto* and followed by another and by a bearded satyr who bends under his load of a basketful of provisions—is painted with sensuous splendor. It has also a certain bourgeois humor, and the striking effect of the blond flesh tones against the dark foliage, which Poussin inherited from Titian, prepares the way for comparable eighteenth-century scenes—for Watteau and Boucher.

This painting was sold by Poussin to Fabrizio Valguarnera for 110 scudi at the beginning of 1631.

Poussin described the painting, during the trial of Valguarnera, as representing "the miracle of the Ark in the temple of Dagon." It is usually known as the *Plague of Ashdod*. The First Book of Samuel (5 : 1–9) relates how the Philistines confiscated the Israelites' sacred ark of the covenant and placed it in the temple of the Philistine god, Dagon. Next morning they found the statue of Dagon fallen on its face before the ark. They set the image of the god aright, but the following morning it was again overturned, this time broken. The priests and the people were so frightened that they hesitated even to enter the temple; simultaneously, the city was afflicted with a plague which struck all its citizens, "both small and great."

All these elements of the story are to be seen in Poussin's painting. At the left in the middle ground is the ark of the covenant, and further left is the fallen idol of Dagon. On the street below is the multitude, fearful of setting foot in the temple. The rest of the painting shows scenes of the plague—one recognizes from their clothing patricians and commoners alike, among the plague-stricken and among those ministering to them.

Poussin was surely impressed by Marcantonio Raimondi's engraving, the *Plague of Phrygia* (fig. 90), which he had studied in Paris. What interested him was the right-hand part of the composition, which impressively represented a plague-stricken family before a group of buildings. Plague scenes fill the whole foreground of Poussin's paintings, but they are subtler and psychologically more differentiated than in Marcantonio's conception.

The *Plague of Ashdod* is Poussin's first of many narrative scenes from the Old Testament in which expressions and passions (the *affetti*) are brought into prominence. The finely dressed, sophisticated young man on the left, for example, is terrified by a rat, which is designated in the Biblical account as the bearer of the pestilence. In the center is the pathetic group of a dead woman and the child who searches in vain for her breast; the man bending over them and holding his nose makes clear the horror of her condition. Poussin's dead woman and child anticipate the similar group in Delacroix' *Massacre of Chios*.

The composition of the whole, with its small figures of victims on the staircase at the right, still has much of the spatial conception of the High Renaissance (for example, Peruzzi's *Presentation in the Temple* in Sta. Maria della Pace, Rome). Poussin used the spatial arrangement of this forum again, in his first version of the *Rape of the Sabine Women*. In the later version, after 1635, he closed off the background completely and designed the architectural elements parallel to the picture surface. For the first time, in the *Plague of Ashdod*, he filled a pictorial theater with deeply emotional figures, adopting a device that becomes characteristic of many works of the 1630s, such as the *Rape of the Sabine Women*, and several paintings of scenes from the Book of Exodus showing the wanderings of the Israelites (J. Costello, in *Journal of the Warburg and Courtauld Institutes*, XIII).

Figure 90. Marcantonio, after Raphael: PLAGUE OF PHRYGIA. Engraving. *Bibliothèque Nationale, Paris*

COLORPLATE 7

PLAGUE OF ASHDOD

Oil on canvas, 58¹/₄×78″

c. 1630

The Louvre, Paris

(SEE COMMENTARY ON OPPOSITE PAGE)

Poussin's painting, although it is very large, consists mainly of one group, almost over life-size, and one other figure which slightly overlaps the second plane. This reduced number of figures stands in surprising contrast to previous representations of the tumultuous scene, which usually show numerous soldiers slaying the children on the order of Herod. Poussin painted another version, now in the Petit Palais, which is not unlike a battle scene or a Rape of the Sabine Women. In comparison to this crowded composition, the Chantilly picture here reproduced looks as if it must be the second version—for second versions, as we know from other instances in Poussin's art, are always strongly stylized, having an almost abstract character. The model for the *Massacre of the Innocents* is Raphael's famous composition (fig. 91), which Poussin knew well; he has elevated it to a new dramatic and psychological sphere, while retaining its regular alignment. However, Guido Reni's famous painting of the same subject (fig. 16) probably provided Poussin with the immediate stimulus for his Chantilly picture. In the preparatory drawing (fig. 92) he followed Reni's model for both the architectural setting and the actions of at least two figures. The drawing has extraordinary vigor and movement, and has been made with very sharp pen strokes. It is tragic, but the tragedy lies in the action and is thus to some degree transitory. In the finished painting, however, the cruelty and the terror are static and eternal. Poussin has here turned to Hellenistic sculptural groups full of crystallized pathos,

such as the famous *Gaul Killing Himself and His Wife* (fig. 108). The face of the desperate mother is frozen in terror, like a theatrical mask; her white arm is outstretched imploringly and accusingly. The fleeing mother, with her dead child hanging from her hand, throws back her head and makes a distinctive gesture with her right arm that is modeled after a figure in a Roman relief. Poussin could have seen such a relief embedded in the wall of the Palazzo Giustiniani; the figure is also similar to a characteristic figure on Medea sarcophagi, of which the best example is in the Louvre (see R. Wittkower, *Studies in Western Art*, III).

ABOVE: Figure 91. Marcantonio, after Raphael: MASSACRE OF THE INNOCENTS. Engraving. *Bibliothèque Nationale, Paris*

RIGHT: Figure 92. MASSACRE OF THE INNOCENTS. c. 1628–29. Drawing, pen and bistre wash, $5^3/_8 \times 6^3/_8''$. *Musée Wicar, Lille*

The pathetic story of Narcissus, told at length by Ovid in eloquent verse (*Metamorphoses*, III, 339), was a favorite topic in paintings of the sixteenth and seventeenth centuries. The beautiful youth, relaxing from the hunt, sees his reflection mirrored in a still pond. Unable to distinguish between his own face and its enchanting reflection, he falls in love with his own beauty and dies of his desire. Ovid connected with this story the legend of the nymph Echo "with the sonorous voice," who loved Narcissus and mourned her rejection so deeply that she wasted away until only her voice and her bones remained; even her bones then turned to stone. Poussin was apparently the first to include Echo, when showing the death of Narcissus. It has recently been suggested that Poussin may have known François Habert's poem, "Histoire du beau Narcisse," of 1550, but nothing directly connects the two works.

In Poussin's painting, Narcissus lies at the edge of a lake, dead or dying from the exhaustion caused by his desire; already springing up around his head are the narcissuses into which he was changed. The greater part of the background is hidden by the thick trunk and widespread branches of an old oak tree, illuminated rather impressionistically from behind by flickering sunlight breaking through gray storm clouds. This splendid, agitated segment of nature is like the brilliant pen and bistre sketches of sunlit trees and bushes that Poussin made from nature in the Roman Campagna. Beside the tree a very young, thin Echo reclines on a big rock, fading away; on the other side a winged Cupid, holding a burning torch as if at a funeral, looks sadly in the other direction.

Poussin's admiration for Venetian painters, especially Titian, may be seen in both the style and lyrical content of this painting. The posture of the dying Narcissus is similar to that of the *Dead Christ* by Paris Bordone (fig. 11); but it is also much like the figure of a falling giant in Perino del Vaga's fresco in the Palazzo del Principe (Doria-Pamphili), Genoa. However, the element of the landscape and the light are plainly Titianesque, and indicate a date of about 1630.

COLORPLATE 9

NARCISSUS AND ECHO

Oil on canvas, 29¹/₈×39³/₈"

c. 1629–30

The Louvre, Paris

(SEE COMMENTARY ON OPPOSITE PAGE)

MIDAS AND BACCHUS

Oil on canvas, 38⁵/₈×51¹/₈″

c. 1630

Pinakothek, Munich

The story of King Midas as the judge of the musical competition between Apollo and Pan was frequently illustrated, but this more jocular tale of Midas and Bacchus (Ovid, *Metamorphoses*, XI, 92) seems to have been chosen only by Poussin. The story runs that Midas, after being initiated into the Bacchic rites, feted the old Silenus when, by mistake, the latter was brought to him as a prisoner. Grateful for this favor done to his foster father, Bacchus granted Midas his free choice of a gift. The foolish king asked that everything he touched be turned to gold. The conse-

quences, described so delightfully by Ovid, were calamitous. The poor king had to return to Bacchus and implore to be liberated from his golden burden. Bacchus sent him uphill to the headwaters of the river Pactolus; there, by washing himself, Midas could transfer his gold to the liquid of the stream.

We know of three paintings that Poussin made from this story: this rather large picture of Midas kneeling before Bacchus, and two small paintings of the scene at the river Pactolus (see colorplate 11; fig. 94).

The larger painting portrays Midas, in his royal diadem, on his knees as he implores Bacchus. The god, in the guise of some Hellenistic figure of Bacchus, seems to adopt a rather philosophical attitude, explaining to Midas that riches and gold have chimerical value. To illustrate this conception, the attendants of Bacchus—nymphs and Silenus—are sleeping happily after having emptied their cups of wine. Silenus is napping at a table, half in shadow, and a beautiful Titianesque nymph is stretched out in sleep; beside her, a drunken *putto* lies on his stomach. The peacefulness of this bucolic idyl is enhanced by children frolicking with a goat, and by a shepherd playing his flute in the shadow of trees in the background; it contrasts with the worldly greediness of King Midas. But the clemency of Bacchus is also shown in this picture, for in the background, just in front of the shepherd, the king is kneeling to wash off the fateful gold, as Bacchus had bidden him.

In 1630 Stefano Roccatagliata, testifying at the trial of Valguarnera, the diamond thief and art dealer, acknowledged owning a copy of a large painting with

Figure 93. Titian: DIANA AND CALLISTO. c. 1559. Oil on canvas, 74⁷/₈×81¹/₂″. *Collection Earl of Ellesmere, on loan to National Galleries of Scotland, Edinburgh*

figures representing the story of Bacchus and King Midas. This may be assumed to be the work here reproduced (J. Costello, *Journal of the Warburg and Courtauld Institutes*, XIII). Local color is emphatic, but the tonality of the whole is rather cool. A date just prior to 1631 would fit the style of the work very well, placing it with other works such as *Nurture of Bacchus* (colorplate 18).

The composition of this painting of *Midas* is very similar to Titian's *Diana and Callisto* (fig. 93). In both, a nude body shimmering against dark foliage pre-dominates over the other figures, which are in parallel groups balanced to right and left. In Poussin's painting, Bacchus' gesture toward Midas is like that of Diana toward the unhappy Callisto. The backgrounds of both paintings open into romantic views threatened by a turbulent sky. Titian here seems more "Baroque" than Poussin does: his diagonals suggest the emotional agitation of his figures, whereas Poussin used the calmer balance of vertical and horizontal. I would suppose that this *Midas* is somewhat later than the two smaller Midas paintings (colorplate 11; fig. 94).

COLORPLATE II

MIDAS BATHING
IN THE RIVER PACTOLUS

Oil on canvas, 38³/₈×28¹¹/₁₆″

c. 1629–30

The Metropolitan Museum of Art, New York

During the trial of Valguarnera, a smaller painting of "King Midas with another small nude figure" was mentioned by Roccatagliata, who was also an art dealer, in connection with the large painting of *Midas and Bacchus* (colorplate 10). He probably referred to the small painting in Corsica (fig. 94), which has only two figures. The reclining crowned figure in a mantle must be King Midas after he had washed off his fateful golden touch. He looks pensively at the half-naked youth who kneels at his feet, searching for gold in the water he has scooped from the part of the river where Midas washed.

Better known is the delicious small painting here reproduced in color. Midas, without his crown, washes himself in the river Pactolus, which is personified by the reclining river god. Two fat *putti* at the right splash water into an urn. This vigorously painted picture was not mentioned at the Valguarnera trial, but it was listed in the 1677 inventory of the Massimi Collection as the companion piece to *Et In Arcadia Ego* (colorplate 12). Both paintings are saturated with rich color in the Venetian manner, and their quality is equally high. The figures of river gods in both works strengthen their relationship as pendants and make the landscape more mythological than real, in Poussin's typical fashion.

Figure 94. 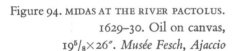 MIDAS AT THE RIVER PACTOLUS.
1629–30. Oil on canvas,
19⁵/₈×26″. *Musée Fesch, Ajaccio*

ET IN ARCADIA EGO

Oil on canvas, 39³/₄×32¹/₄"
1629–30
Chatsworth Settlement, Chatsworth, England

There are two paintings of this subject: this first version is small in size and shows the shepherds' discovery of a tomb monument in Arcadia. The second (colorplate 27) is considerably later, and shows the shepherds meditating on the tomb.

The idea of "the tomb in Arcadia" goes back to Virgil; in the Renaissance, the Neapolitan poet Sannazaro described in his pastoral, *Arcadia*, published in 1502, the tomb of a shepherd in Arcadia, to which other shepherds came to make sacrifices. This tomb was near the river Alphaeus, and in the Chatsworth version the river god has a prominent position (E. Panofsky, "Et In Arcadia Ego," *Meaning in the Visual Arts*, 1955; originally published 1936).

The words "Et In Arcadia Ego"—"I, also, in Arcadia"—are not in themselves ancient; in fact, the phrase was apparently not coined before the seventeenth century. Its precise interpretation was even then a matter of question; Félibien and Bellori have different explanations of Poussin's paintings. The controversy still continues today; one may read the quotation as if it emanated from the dead shepherd in the tomb, "I, who am now dead, also lived once in Arcadia"; or from Death itself, "I, Death, exist even in Arcadia." Poussin's visualization seems to substantiate the feeling and mood of either interpretation.

The first painting of the subject, Guercino's *Et In Arcadia Ego* (fig. 34), provided Poussin with a thematic model for his later composition in Chatsworth. The shepherds in both works seem to have found the tomb quite by accident; they are shown in the midst of their surprise at discovering, in the shadow of large trees, a sarcophagus with a skull resting on its lid, and a half-hidden inscription. In Poussin's delightful painting, the two half-naked shepherds and the charming young shepherdess in her flowing white gown (reminiscent of an ancient statue of Flora) do not seem deeply disturbed by the *memento mori;* they regard the tomb with more curiosity than awe. Only the river god, like the similar figure in *Midas Bathing* (colorplate 11), adds a somewhat pensive note. The scene in the Chatsworth painting is informal and transitory; very Titianesque and "blond" in its light and color, it is brilliant and dramatic. The style of the work is relatively early, about the beginning of the 1630s; it may be compared with such other bucolic paintings of this period as the *Inspiration of Anacreon* (fig. 32), and *Midas Bathing in the River Pactolus* (colorplate 11); the latter was originally designed as a pendant to this *Et In Arcadia Ego*, and both paintings once belonged to Cardinal Camillo Massimi.

The painting *Mars and Venus* also belongs to the group of Poussin's erotic mythological compositions from the late 1620s and the early 1630s. His study of Titian is to be seen in the rich landscape background with darkly shadowed clumps of trees. A canopy is stretched over the amorous couple to protect them from the sun as they sit on a grassy bank, surrounded by exuberant *putti*. In the "mythological" landscape on the other side are a river god and a naiad (fig. 95; see W. Friedlaender, in *Gazette des Beaux-Arts*, XXII).

The story of Venus and Adonis is narrated by Ovid in *Metamorphoses*, but not the story of Venus and Mars. Poussin's composition must be based on Statius' *Thebaid*, although he probably used the excerpt quoted in Cartari's *Images of the Gods;* there it is told that Mars recited a beautiful hymn in praise of Venus, saying that only she could give him "repose from battles, sacred joy, and unique peace of soul." Despite the amorous solace he has found in her arms, he must obey the behest of the Fates and the Supreme Father. From this story, Poussin's imaginative, perceptive mind formed his charming mythological idyl of the love of Mars and Venus.

The 1616 edition of Cartari's book contains a woodcut after an ancient cameo showing Mars leaving Venus (fig. 96); Poussin's representation is very similar to the motif and attitudes of the main group.

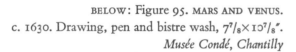

RIGHT: Figure 96. MARS AND VENUS. Illustration in Cartari, *Le Imagini de i dei degli antichi* (Padua, 1616). Woodcut

BELOW: Figure 95. MARS AND VENUS. c. 1630. Drawing, pen and bistre wash, 7⁷/₈×10⁷/₈". *Musée Condé, Chantilly*

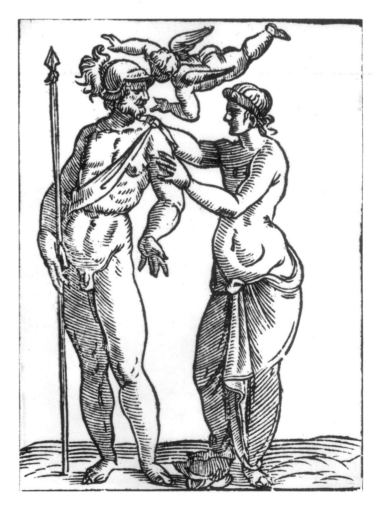

COLORPLATE 13

MARS AND VENUS

Oil on canvas, 61×84″

c. 1630

Museum of Fine Arts, Boston

(SEE COMMENTARY ON OPPOSITE PAGE)

This painting was mentioned in the inventory of Cardinal Mazarin's collection in March, 1661, as "Endymion with the Chariot of the Sun."

Antique fairy tales had a great attraction for the "storyteller" Nicolas Poussin. At the beginning of the 1630s, when Poussin was finally able to work freely and uninhibitedly, he turned with new enthusiasm to stories by Ovid and by others, and enriched them with his Titianesque color. However, he no longer merely outlined the content of the different legends, as he had done in the earlier Marino Drawings; having grown more mature and meditative, he discovered human, even super-human problems in those mythological "stories"—pathos, and the tragic consequences of mortality—and he gave requisite form to his new insight.

The beginning of the romantic story of Luna and Endymion had often been represented before: it occurs frequently on Roman sarcophagi, the moon goddess alighting from her chariot to discover the sleeping Endymion, and falling in love with his beauty. Not so long before, Annibale Carracci had made a charming, sensual representation of the love of Diana for Endymion in one of the grisaille *tondi* of the Farnese Gallery (fig. 97). Poussin's interpretation, however, went

Figure 97. Annibale Carracci: DIANA AND ENDYMION
c. 1597–1604. Fresco. *Farnese Gallery, Rome*

much further. He was less interested in the phenomenon of the magical moonlight that makes the sleeping Endymion's beauty irresistible, almost divine, which later appealed to the romanticism of some of J. L. David's followers, such as Girodet. Poussin was more attracted by the psychological problems of youth and age, sleep and death, that arise from the dangerous intercourse of god and mortal.

Jupiter gave to Endymion, as the beloved of an Olympian, the choice of aging and dying, or of living in eternal youth but forever asleep. Luna in our painting is not the enamored goddess of whom Cartari writes in *Images of the Gods*, but a serene lady implored by Endymion. Her slim body is modeled on that of Luna in an Endymion sarcophagus accessible to Poussin in the Capitoline Museum; also in these reliefs is the *putto* above Luna and the sleeping Somnus.

However, Poussin's painting has an utterly unclassical conception, its artistic atmosphere imbued rather with a romantic, sentimental mood. He is greatly interested in the psychology of expression: the despair and helplessness in the face of the imploring youth; the superiority, tempered with kindness, in the features of the goddess empowered to bestow on Endymion eternal sleep or death. The *putto* on her shoulder, who also occurs in some of Poussin's drawings for this painting, may be urging her departure. Luna's nocturnal reign is finished; already the sun god, Apollo, appears in his chariot drawn by four horses, Aurora flying before it. Against the light of day, Night, a sturdy, winged woman, nude above the waist, pulls close the heavy curtain of the tent of sleep. Somnus is still deep in slumber; at the feet of Night are two children, one dark-skinned and sleeping in the shadow, the other fair-skinned and half-aroused, touched by the rays of the sun. All of these details accord with contemporary iconography.

The composition is somewhat similar to *Midas and Bacchus* (colorplate 10), which was probably painted before 1631. Therefore *Luna and Endymion*, with its extremely painterly style, is from the same period—the early 1630s.

COLORPLATE 14

LUNA AND ENDYMION

Oil on canvas, 48×66¹/₂"

Early 1630s

The Detroit Institute of Arts, Detroit, Michigan

(SEE COMMENTARY ON OPPOSITE PAGE)

Figure 98. Agostino Carracci: CEPHALUS AND AURORA.
c. 1597–1604. Fresco. *Farnese Gallery, Rome*

Just as Luna seduced the shepherd Endymion, so Aurora, the goddess of the dawn who precedes the golden chariot of Helios-Apollo, fell in love with the hunter Cephalus, the young husband of Procris. Their love ends in desperation and death, as described by Ovid in *Metamorphoses*, VIII. Poussin's wonderful painting does not show Cephalus' actual abduction by Aurora in her chariot, as Agostino Carracci's does in his impressive fresco in the Farnese Gallery (fig. 98; part of a larger program, "love in the air," according to Bellori); he concentrates instead on the psychological turning point of the first phase of the long, complicated story: Cephalus repudiating the goddess Aurora. He visualizes Cephalus' faithfulness to his beloved Procris in the manner of a fairy tale, probably of his own invention: a small *putto* holds up to Cephalus a little portrait of Procris; he, enraptured, looks at it longingly while trying to disengage himself from Aurora's embrace. These are the main figures in the picture: the seated goddess, her beautiful body like a Roman statue, almost nude; Cephalus in profile, his posture recalling that of Bacchus leaping from the chariot in Titian's *Bacchus and Ariadne* (National Gallery, London), his head turned sharply and his arm thrust back to deter the amorous Aurora; finally, the little *putto* with Procris' portrait. This group, almost like a sculpture, is placed in a romantic and fantastic landscape; Pegasus, the fabulous winged horse, waits

patiently before Aurora's chariot which is almost hidden among the trees. As Pegasus generally belongs to Apollo, not to Aurora, Poussin probably intended the reclining figure who looks dreamily into the landscape to represent the sun god, Apollo, awaiting the break of day. The river god on the left is not, as has been suggested, Tithonus, the sleeping husband of Aurora, for he has not the gray hair appropriate to his age (which he does in Agostino Carracci's painting). Rather, this is the black-bearded river god Poussin often uses to enhance the mythological character of the landscape. His presence here may suggest water in the sense of Oceanus, from which Aurora rises every morning.

Aurora and Cephalus, one of Poussin's most beautiful and romantic works, belongs to his group of Titianesque paintings which contain a contrast of open and closed backgrounds (see chap. X); these were probably painted at the beginning of the 1630s. A much earlier version of the same theme, elaborately described by Bellori, is preserved in a British private collection (A. Blunt, in *Burlington Magazine*, LXXXIX). Two highly entertaining drawings now in the British Museum (probably copies; see W. Friedlaender and A. Blunt, *Drawings*, III) illustrate the tumultuous scene in which the Horae try to recall the amorous goddess of the morning to her duty, reminding her not to delay the break of day.

COLORPLATE 15

AURORA AND CEPHALUS

Oil on canvas, 38×51¹/₂″

Early 1630s

National Gallery, London

(SEE COMMENTARY ON OPPOSITE PAGE)

In the inventory of Cardinal Mazarin's collection was listed this large painting, now in the Louvre, of "Apollo, a Muse, and a Poet crowned with laurel"; the much smaller painting, now in Hanover (fig. 32), was dubbed "Inspiration of Anacreon" in the eighteenth century. They belong together in the same sense as the two paintings of the *Nurture of Jupiter* (colorplate 28; fig. 111), or *Et In Arcadia Ego* (colorplates 12, 27; see chap. VI). They are versions of the same theme, the Inspiration of a Poet by Apollo; as usual, Poussin's earlier version (in Hanover) appears to be in a more Ionic mode. It is soft and more informal, bucolic and lyric in character. Consequently the charming, rather lightly dressed Muse with her flute, who leans on a tree trunk and benevolently assists Apollo's act of inspiring the poet, is Euterpe, the protectress of lyric poetry. The identification of the inspired poet with Anacreon, the Greek poet of light and earthly verse, was perhaps suggested by a member of the "Anacreontic" school of poetry in Germany. Although certainly not correct, the notion is at least understandable.

This larger *Inspiration of the Poet*, like the other second or final versions of a subject, is more solemn than the so-called *Anacreon*. The figures have become stylized and crystallized, the landscape reduced to two or three tree trunks; the formal and hieratic quality of the action is thus emphasized, as it is in the final version of the *Nurture of Jupiter* (colorplate 28).

In the *Anacreon* (fig. 32) the inspirational act is tangibly portrayed. Apollo raises to the lips of the poet the cup filled with water from the Castalian spring, which has the power to inspire those who drink of it with the true fire of poetry. (The spring, as J. Costello has observed in *The Art Bulletin*, XLIV, is to be seen in the lower left corner of the painting.) Apollo, in contrast to his very casual posture in *Anacreon*, is very dignified in the Louvre painting, modeled more or

less directly on Raphael's Apollo in *Apollo and Marsyas*, on the ceiling of the Stanza della Segnatura. The god dictates in a restrained manner, even imperiously, to the ecstatic listening poet, who holds a tablet in one hand and a pen in the other. The forms and the tenor of the whole composition are elevated in comparison with *Anacreon*. In the foreground are three books entitled *Odysea*, *Illiad*, and *Aeneide*, the works of Homer and Virgil; it has been remarked that epic poetry, which belongs to a higher grade than lyric poetry, is here celebrated, and that the statuesque Muse in her chiton is Calliope, the highest and "most preferred" of the nine Muses (E. Panofsky, *A Mythological Painting* . . ., Stockholm Nationalmuseum Skriftserie, No. 5, 1960). This elevated spirit, together with the cool, elaborate colorism, makes the Louvre *Inspiration* outstanding in Poussin's oeuvre, even among the "second versions." Apparently it was not so highly admired in Poussin's time as it is today. When Bernini noticed the painting, in the Louvre, Chantelou replied, "Oh, that's something he did over forty years ago."

As a young man in Rome, Poussin was interested in Renaissance-humanistic themes, and among these the elevation of the artist was a favorite. The crowning of a poet or writer that took place on the Roman Capitol in Late Antique times was revived in the fourteenth century; it became a much-coveted honor, but in Poussin's inspiration scenes the wreath-bearing *putti* have only secondary importance. The crowning of the poet should be understood as only one episode in the solemn ceremony of Apollonian inspiration.

In spite of their differences, the execution of the two versions need not have been many years apart. The Louvre painting was probably painted in 1630 or 1631, which date would explain its lingering similarity with such large-figure paintings as the *Martyrdom of St. Erasmus* of 1628–29 (colorplate 4); the *Anacreon*, like *Midas Bathing* (colorplate 11), was a year or so earlier.

COLORPLATE 16

INSPIRATION OF THE POET

Oil on canvas, 71¹/₄× 83⁷/₈″

1630–31

The Louvre, Paris

(SEE COMMENTARY ON OPPOSITE PAGE)

In the fifth book of Ovid's *Fasti*, Flora describes her garden "fanned by the breeze and watered by a spring of running water." This garden was a present from her husband Zephyrus, who "filled it with noble flowers (partly metamorphosed personages) and said, 'Goddess, be Queen of Flowers.'"

It was certainly this picturesque passage that inspired Poussin to paint one of his most tender and charming compositions, the *Realm of Flora* or, as Bellori named it, the *Transformation of the Flowers*. The composition could have served, if engraved, as a frontispiece for the edition of Ovid's *Metamorphoses* that Poussin allegedly planned.

The garden is square, enclosed on two sides by an open arched trellis—a motif surely taken from an engraving of the Fontainebleau School (Master L. D. after Primaticcio, according to A. Blunt); the herm of Priapus, the god of the garden, also comes from this engraving, but everything else in Poussin's painting is quite different. The space and proportion is not manneristic; the general aspect is gay and light, bathed in a delicate, almost eighteenth-century atmosphere. From a rock flows a fountain of water to refresh the flowers. Flora, in an olive-green chiton, dances in the center of the garden, surrounded by four *putti* strewing flowers. On the left is the mad Ajax, naked except for his helmet, who throws himself on his sword (Ovid, *Metamorphoses*, XIII, 386 *et seq.*). Next to him, Narcissus regards his image mirrored in the water of an urn held before him by a naiad—not necessarily Echo (*Met.*, III, 344 *et seq.*). Clytie raises her face to the sky to behold her lover, Apollo, in his chariot; disdainful of her pining, Apollo changed her into the heliotrope (*Met.*, IV, 256 *et seq.*). On the right is Hyacinthus, raising his hand to the mortal wound in his head, received while sporting with *Apollo (Met.*, X, 210 *et seq.*). Next to him, the hunter Adonis, with his spear and dogs, points to his thigh, which was gored by a boar (*Met.*, X, 735). In the far right corner are Crocus and the shepherdess Smilax, who were metamorphosed into the crocus and the yew tree because of the impatience of their love (*Met.*, IV, 283).

The *Realm of Flora* differs in style from the *Triumph of Flora* (colorplate 3). The drawing of the figures is more refined, and the painting is artistically more penetrating and sophisticated than the earlier work, in which the figures and scenery have greater freshness and immediacy. Titianesque color has here given way to the more reserved, unified tonality of the whole. Nor is the construction any longer one of relief and layer; the figures are gracefully placed in the square space delimited by the slender trellis and the rock. In the charming atmosphere of the whole there is a certain melancholy for these figures, the victims of their own passions.

These refinements lead one to place the *Realm of Flora* substantially after the *Triumph of Flora*, but the interval between the two paintings is probably no longer than three or four years. The *Realm of Flora* is surely identifiable with the "garden of flowers" (*giardino dei fiori*) mentioned in the Valguarnera trial (J. Costello, *Journal of the Warburg and Courtauld Institutes*, XIII; and J. Thuillier, *Actes du Colloque Poussin*, II). It was commissioned by this gentleman crook in May, 1631, some months after he had acquired Poussin's *Plague of Ashdod*.

COLORPLATE 17

REALM OF FLORA

Oil on canvas, 51⁵/₈× 71¹/₄″

1631

Gallery, Dresden

(SEE COMMENTARY ON OPPOSITE PAGE)

The painting is one of several Bacchic compositions that Poussin painted early in the 1630s, when he was strongly influenced by Titian's Bacchanals. However, it is sometimes dated much earlier. It is close to the so-called *Youth of Bacchus* (Musée Condé, Chantilly), and still more like the *Nurture of Bacchus* (National Gallery, London) which has been proposed as its earlier, unfinished version. Bacchus is surely the chubby boy in the center who, supported by a satyr, eagerly drinks from the bowl offered by another satyr. Behind this group a bacchante leans on a thyrsus, pensively looking on. The goat, led by a little *putto*, belongs to the Bacchic family and also appears in the London *Bacchus*, but Bacchus is certainly being given a drink of wine and not goat's milk. The effects of wine are shown by the drunken, sleeping bacchante with a *putto* at her bosom, who is derived from the famous figure in Titian's *Andrians* (fig. 12). The whole group has still the idyllic, bucolic character of Poussin's amusing, smaller paintings of nymphs and satyrs, such as colorplate 6. This pastoral *Nurture of Bacchus* is very different from his late, serious, and highly mythological representation of the *Birth of Bacchus* (colorplate 45).

TRIUMPH OF PAN

Oil on canvas, 52³/₄ × 57¹/₈"

1635–36

Morrison Collection, Sudeley Castle, Gloucestershire

According to Bellori, among the paintings that Poussin made for French patrons before his trip to Paris "were some for the Cardinal de Richelieu, and particularly four Bacchanals with the Triumph of Bacchus and various fantasies. . . ." We know of only three Bacchanals by Poussin that came to the Château de Richelieu, all of them Triumphs: this *Triumph of Pan*, the *Triumph of Bacchus* (fig. 37), and the *Triumph of Silenus* (often questioned; fig. 101). In a letter of May, 1636, Richelieu was notified that two of the Bacchanals he had commissioned of Poussin had been sent to France.

Richelieu's recognition of Poussin's value as a painter came in the mid-1630s. This great commission pre-

Figure 99. TRIUMPH OF PAN. Mid-1630s. Drawing, pen and bistre wash, 8⁷/₈ × 13¹/₈".
Royal Library, Windsor Castle (by gracious permission of H. M. the Queen)

Figure 100. TRIUMPH OF PAN. Mid-1630s. Drawing, pen and bistre wash,
6⅞×8⅜". *Musée Bonnat, Bayonne*

ceded the resolution of the French government to lure the reluctant Poussin from Rome back to France, and to make him the leader of a concentrated movement in French art. Poussin was fully conscious of the opportunities that Richelieu's commission would open for him, and he did his best in the genre he had already endowed with such splendor.

The uncommonly large number of spirited sketches, especially for the most impressive of the three bacchanalian triumphs, the *Triumph of Pan*, prove that Poussin was animated by great ardor in this task (fig. 99). In contrast to his earlier Bacchic works, the *Nurture of Bacchus* (colorplate 18) or *Bacchanal* (Prado, Madrid), the *Triumph of Pan* is composed more from single mo-

tifs which are separable from one another. The origin of this manner is demonstrated by the amazing diversity of the splendid compositional studies in ink and bistre, in which the same motifs are moved about with great freedom before receiving their definitive place on the canvas (fig. 100).

The herm of Pan is somewhat behind the center, his red face casting a glow over the scene. He is garlanded by a beautiful bacchante who kneels on a goat and reaches into a basket held by a *putto*, her arms stretched out in a diagonal direction. This graceful motif was taken from an ancient terracotta Campana-relief which had also been used in an engraving by the Master of the Die after Giulio Romano's *Feast of Priapus*. The group is flanked by two maenads, one carrying a fawn on her shoulder, the other swinging a tambourine. A corybant blows a long trumpet, and a maenad, riding on a goat, turns to take flowers from a tray carried on the head of a kneeling satyr, while being embraced by another satyr who supports her from behind. In front of the herm of Pan, a nymph is pulling the hair of a satyr who has fallen, and on the right, two youths try to lift up a drunken satyr. The foreground is strewn with bacchanalian paraphernalia: garlands, vases, pipes, masks, and so on. For all of these motifs Poussin has drawn on ancient literature, such as the poetry of Catullus, as well as on ancient sculptures, and they are united in a deliberately ornamental design; the gestures are carefully overlapped and repeated, and a warm colorism pervades the whole. The scene, in the Venetian manner, is set against a screen of thin, black tree trunks through which a mountain landscape may be dimly seen. The curtain of trees in this work, and in *Triumph of Silenus* (fig. 101), is derived from the background motif which Titian used to complete Bellini's *Feast of the Gods*.

Figure 101. After Poussin: TRIUMPH OF SILENUS. Mid-1630s. Oil on canvas, 56^1/$_2$ × 47^3/$_4$″. *National Gallery, London*

The *Triumph of Neptune and Amphitrite*, like the preceding series of Bacchic Triumphs (see colorplate 19), was painted on a commission of Cardinal Richelieu, about 1637. This great triumph of the sea is obviously based on Raphael's *Galatea* in the Farnesina (fig. 102). The visibly seventeenth-century character of Poussin's work separates it, however, from the graceful simplicity and symmetry that pervades Raphael's famous fresco. Poussin's composition, so crowded with figures, looks rather heavy by comparison. He may have wanted to make something unusually spectacular that would be appropriate to the dignity of the Cardinal and his great interest in building up French sea power.

If the attribution to Poussin of two drawings in Stockholm is acceptable (fig. 103), one might conjecture that his original composition was more similar to Raphael's. These lovely drawings (one more expanded than the other) show a sea goddess, supposedly Galatea, flanked by balanced, subsidiary groups of nereids and tritons. Subsequent to making the drawings,

TRIUMPH OF NEPTUNE AND AMPHITRITE

Oil on canvas, 45¹⁄₈×57⁷⁄₈″

c. 1637

Philadelphia Museum of Art, Philadelphia

Figure 103. TRIUMPH OF GALATEA. c. 1635. Drawing, black chalk and bistre wash, 6×8⁷⁄₈″. *National Museum, Stockholm*

Poussin perhaps decided to depict, instead of Galatea, a larger, more pompous *Triumph of Amphitrite*, the official queen of the sea, and therefore altered the symmetry by placing at her right Neptune and his group (similarly engraved by Marcantonio). Neptune stands on his chariot drawn by four wild maritime horses, overtaking Amphitrite's car to win her as his bride.

The goddess of the sea remains at the center of this composition, as in the drawings. Her car, a giant shell, is drawn by dolphins, the ruling fishes especially dear to Neptune's family. According to Hyginus, Amphitrite fled Neptune's amorous proposals, but was found by the Dolphin at the limits of the sea, at Atlantis, and brought back to her future consort (M. Levey, *Journal of the Warburg and Courtauld Institutes*, XXVI). Instead of a crown, an airy veil encircles Amphitrite's head in a majestic arch, a device often used since ancient times in connection with maritime personages. A great dark cloud hovers over the central group and serves

Figure 102. Raphael: GALATEA.
1513. Fresco. *Palazzo della Farnesina, Rome*

as a foil for a host of *putti* flying in the air, some strewing flowers, some shooting arrows, one holding a
torch. The latter is a motif related to nuptials (see colorplate 41) and supports the opinion that this composition actually represents the wedding of Neptune and
Amphitrite. It is probable that the cloud comes from
the smoke of this torch.

Together with Raphael's *Galatea*, which probably
supplied Poussin with his first *idea*, his studious interest in ancient art helped considerably his representation of this great sea triumph. Not only had he orient-
ed himself in the fabulous realm of the sea goddess and

her creatures, through Cartari's *Images of the Gods*, but
he also knew well the relief of *Tritons and Sea Nymphs*
in the *palazzo* of his great patron, Prince Giustiniani.
This relief, or some similar representation, served as
the model for his figures. From this source Poussin put
in the foreground the same little *putto* that Raphael
used. However, Poussin borrowed not the details and
shapes in these monuments of marine mythology so
much as the whole realm of the ancient fairy tale of the
sea. He formed his own brand of "classicism," combining Antiquity and the "divino Raffaello" into his
own seventeenth-century manner.

This Bacchanal is of the same type, joyous but solemn, as the Bacchanals for Richelieu, but it does not belong to that series. It dates from the period of the *Adoration of the Golden Calf* (colorplate 22) or perhaps slightly later, about 1636–37. The dancing nymphs and satyrs at the left side are almost the reverse of the corresponding group in the *Adoration of the Golden Calf*. Poussin had possibly first designed the group of figures dancing before the statue of the golden calf, then extracted them for this Bacchanal and added two humorous scenes at right and left. In the *Adoration of the Golden Calf* the woman's outstretched arm serves only a rhythmical purpose, while in *Bacchanalian Revel* Poussin has placed a bunch of grapes in the hand of a similar bacchante, which she squeezes into the cup held by a fat little boy. To fill out the right side Poussin has invented another jocular incident: a brownish satyr assaulting a laughing bacchante, observed by an amused companion. Behind this group, Pan, as a herm figure, presides good-naturedly over these proceedings, which take place before a dark screen of trees. Poussin has here composed one of his most joyful, colorful bacchanalian revels, and his art in this genre is now at its height.

COLORPLATE 21

BACCHANALIAN REVEL
BEFORE A TERM OF PAN

Oil on canvas, 39×55⁷/₈″

1636–37

National Gallery, London

(SEE COMMENTARY ON OPPOSITE PAGE)

This picture and its pendant, *Passage of the Red Sea* (fig. 43), both painted for Cassiano's cousin Amadeo Pozzo, formerly hung together in Longford Castle. Both are examples of Poussin's forceful representations of the story of Moses in the Book of Exodus, made between 1634–38; in size they are counterparts of his large mythological and Bacchic paintings during the same period (see A. Blunt, *Gallery Books*, No. 21, National Gallery, London).

The story of the *Adoration of the Golden Calf* comes directly from the Bible (Exodus 32). The narrative tells that the people of Israel had become corrupt and had turned from Jehovah; while Moses was on Mount

COLORPLATE 22

ADORATION OF THE GOLDEN CALF

Oil on canvas, 60⅝×84¼"

c. 1636–37

National Gallery, London

Sinai, away from their camp, they worshiped a golden calf that Aaron, Moses' brother, had fashioned from the golden earrings he commanded the people to take from their ears. When Moses returned from Mount Sinai with the Tablets of the Law, he discovered his people adoring the calf and dancing wantonly around it. In his anger, he threw the Tablets to the ground and broke them.

The prototype for Poussin's work is the fresco of the *Adoration of the Golden Calf* in the Loggias of the Vatican (fig. 104), in which the men and women of Israel kneel around the pedestal that supports the small statue of a calf. In the upper left-hand corner Moses is about to break the Tablets of the Law in wrath at the blasphemous scene. Poussin had made a painting of the same scene, signed and dated 1629 (fig. 105), in which he followed the general outlines of the Loggia fresco, but he used figure types that are decidedly Bolognese, similar to those of Lodovico Carracci. For this later version, Poussin chose a more exciting moment of the story—a moment which, as far as I know, had never been represented before. The adoring crowd, including the traditional "charity" group of a mother and child, is moved to the right; the left side is now filled with a group of men and women who dance so dramatically before the idol that the painting is often called *Dance Before the Golden Calf.* The motif of the dancing figures is obviously derived from dancing groups in Renaissance paintings, in particular the Muses in Mantegna's *Parnassus* (The Louvre, Paris), and the dancers in Giulio Romano's *The Goat* (Palazzo del Tè, Mantua), both based in part on well-known ancient models. Poussin again used this group,

Figure 104. School of Raphael: ADORATION OF THE GOLDEN CALF. 1519. Fresco. *Vatican Loggias, Rome*

Figure 105. ISRAELITES WORSHIPING THE GOLDEN CALF. 1629. Oil on canvas, 39⅛×50⅝".
M. H. de Young Memorial Museum, San Francisco (Kress Collection)

which is so prominent in *Adoration of the Golden Calf*, in *Bacchanalian Revel* (colorplate 21), but it is looser and more luxuriant, in accord with the different subject.

The pure relief style that is characteristic of so many of Poussin's compositions is not strong here or in such other compositions of this period as the *Gathering of the Manna* (colorplate 25) and *Passage of the Red Sea* (fig. 43). Poussin wanted to give the impression of a countless multitude of people, divisible into smaller groups which perform specific actions and exhibit specific emotions. The groups are unified through elaborate ornamental devices, most noticeable in the overlapping limbs and bodies of the dancers and of the worshipers around Aaron. Each group has its specific "affective" character, and not least are the splendid figures of Moses and his companion, colorfully contrasted at the left against the dark background. Poussin's theory of the *affetti*, which he discussed in connection with the *Gathering of the Manna* (see chap. VII), is equally valid for the *Adoration of the Golden Calf*.

These particular features are even more evident in the *Passage of the Red Sea*. The title is inaccurate, for the gestures represent the passions of the Israelites *after* their **miraculous** journey.

PAN AND SYRINX

Oil on canvas, 41³/₄×32¹/₄″
1637–38
Gallery, Dresden

The story of Pan and Syrinx (Ovid, *Metamorphoses*, I, 689 *et seq.*) is similar to that of Apollo and Daphne; in both cases the nymph scorns the amorous advances of her pursuer. Impeded by the waves in the river through which Pan was chasing her, Syrinx begged her hamadryad sisters to metamorphose her. Just as Pan seized her body, it changed; instead of a nymph, he held a bunch of reeds in his arms. When he sighed with disappointment into the reeds, his breath produced light, plaintive tones. Their sweet, melodious sound so charmed the god that he cut some of the reeds into unequal lengths and fashioned from them the pipes of Pan, thus finding a way to keep Syrinx with him always.

The contrast in this painting is sharp between Syrinx' white, smooth body and the leather-skinned, fur-covered body of Pan. Poussin's scene is patterned closely on the type used for Apollo and Daphne; the river god, Ladon, into whose arms the frightened nymph flees, could equally well be Peneus, the father of Daphne. The river nymphs, who have a larger role in Ovid's text, are only in the background of Poussin's painting; instead two large *putti* are playing in the foreground, and serve as a form of *repoussoir*. The cool, restrained tonality of the painting is fresh and characteristic; especially beautiful are the enclosing trees which sparkle against the sky.

Félibien placed the painting in the year 1637, and associated it with *Schoolmaster of the Falerii* of the same year (fig. 27). Both paintings exemplify Poussin's theory of the modes (see chap. VII).

RAPE OF THE SABINE WOMEN

Oil on canvas, 60⁷/₈×82⁵/₈". c. 1635
The Metropolitan Museum of Art, New York

Figure 106. Gian Bologna: RAPE OF THE SABINE WOMAN. 1583.
Marble, height 13′6″. *Loggia dei Lanzi, Florence*

There are two versions of *Rape of the Sabine Women:*
the first one (fig. 107) was made for Cardinal Omodei
(for whom Poussin also painted the *Triumph of Flora*);
the one here illustrated in color belongs, according to
Félibien, among the paintings made before 1637.

The well-known, often-represented episode of the
Sabine women abducted by the Roman soldiers is
described by Livy and Plutarch. The population of
the newly founded city of Rome was made up of soldiers and outcasts from other towns; there was an ur-
gent need for young women, if a new community
were to be created. But the outlying towns refused to
give their young women to the Romans in marriage.
Romulus, the Roman leader, was consequently obliged
to resort to a ruse: he invited the neighboring Sabines
to a *consualia,* consisting of games and sacrifices in hon-
or of a newly discovered sanctuary of Neptune.
When the Sabines and their families had assembled,
Romulus raised his mantle, thus giving the signal for
each soldier to seize a Sabine maiden. The Sabine men
and their families were allowed to escape unharmed
and the maidens soon became so reconciled to their
fate that they later acted as peacemakers between the
warring Roman and Sabine armies (this episode is
shown in a famous painting by J. L. David in the Louvre, Paris).

The story was used in the *quattrocento* merely to
lend an instructive scene to the decoration of wedding
chests. In the sixteenth century it gained a more "heroic" character; it served to exemplify the much-admired patriotism and resolution in early Rome that
permitted any act, even a ruthless or barbarous one,
which would assure the future of the nation. The
strongest, most popular representation of this sentiment, Gian Bologna's statue (fig. 106), was publicly
displayed in the Loggia dei Lanzi on the Piazza della

Signoria in Florence and baptized "*Rape of the Sabine Woman*"; it shows heroic action, the struggle of women against masculine brutality, with a sexual connotation. At the same time, it is the perfect solution to a purely artistic problem that was first posed by the motif of Hercules and Antaeus: the design of a tightly enclosed group comprising two or three figures.

Poussin had a vivid interest in sculptural problems during these early years, and he made several spirited pen-and-bistre sketches of the motif of a man lifting a woman, based on Gian Bologna's statue and on fig-ures from the relief on its socle. He used variations of the motif in his paintings. But in addition to Late Mannerist models, Poussin also went back to his be-loved Hellenistic Antiquity for particular groups, and used (in reverse) the famous marble of the *Gaul Kill-ing Himself and His Wife* (fig. 108) for the main group in the right foreground.

However, to formulate sculptural groups and to arrange them on the picture plane was only one aspect of Poussin's fascination with the subject. He was not satisfied with depicting primarily the tumult of the

Figure 107. RAPE OF THE SABINE WOMEN. c. 1631–32. Oil on canvas, 62¹/₂×81″. *The Louvre, Paris*

scene from Roman history, as Luca Cambiaso and Lodovico Carracci had done before him. Poussin was the first to treat the subject in an analytic and psychological way, stressing the immediacy of the surprised reaction to Romulus' one measured gesture, and the diverse passions the gesture evoked.

In the earlier version (fig. 107) Poussin had already characterized with his usual care and intelligence the actions and passions of the different groups of figures. In the second version he elevated the tone of the scene from savage assault to ceremonial dignity and new historical accuracy. Romulus in the first version is only an officer who, by raising his mantle with a sharp movement, gives the signal for attack. Romulus in the later painting wears a heavy, ceremonial garment and stands motionless, isolated between the fluted columns of the temple of Neptune; he seems almost to perform a solemn religious act. Corre-

spondingly, the architectural setting is no longer a public square, but the forum of a great city, and the basilica in the background is of the sort that Poussin could reconstruct from ancient sources (J. Costello, in *Bulletin of the Metropolitan Museum*, V).

As a painting, Poussin's first version has the character of a primitive, late fifteenth- or early sixteenth-century work, as does that of the *Plague of Ashdod* (colorplate 7). The second version is cooler and more intellectually precise, with all its forms remarkably clarified in light and color. The painting of the same subject by Poussin's great Roman rival, Pietro da Cortona (fig. 21), may have had some effect on the second version. It is possible that the larger figures and general radiance of Pietro's Baroque masterpiece inspired Poussin's new freedom. Both paintings mark important points in the development of the High Baroque style: Cortona's painting is a brightly illuminated, decorative ballet in the coloristic Baroque manner; Poussin's is a stage presentation of the classicistic Baroque. I cannot accept the recent attempt of Denis Mahon (*Gazette des Beaux-Arts*, 1962) to reverse the chronological relationship of the two versions. The tenor of the painting in the Louvre (c. 1631–32) seems to me a development of the relatively archaic scheme of the *Plague of Ashdod* (c. 1630–31), especially in the design of the architecture; the Metropolitan Museum painting has all the aspects of a second version: it is more solemn, more stylized, more classically definitive.

Figure 108. GAUL KILLING HIMSELF AND HIS WIFE. 230–220 B.C. Roman copy of Hellenistic original. Marble, height 83".
Terme Museum, Rome

GATHERING OF THE MANNA

Oil on canvas, 58⁵/₈×78″
1638
The Louvre, Paris

This large painting, one of the earliest that Poussin made for Chantelou, was probably finished at the end of 1638. It is perhaps not one of Poussin's most agreeable works, but it is a spectacular paradigm of his style in the late 1630s, when he was investigating the psychological reactions of masses of people. Consequently, it attracted great attention among his analytical-minded contemporaries, and indeed it later served Charles Le Brun as an exemplar for the entire system of French academic classicism. Le Brun analyzed the painting before the French Academy in 1667, discussing it in terms of four categories: disposition, drawing and proportion, expression, and color and light. Disposition included "local color"—the barrenness of the desert in the morning light—and the organization of the scene whereby one can survey the whole, yet the individual groups and figures remain clearly distinguishable. As an example of drawing and proportion, Le Brun stressed the fact that the main figures had suitable ancient prototypes—*Niobe*, a *Diana*, *Apollo Belvedere*, *Laocoön*, and so forth. Expression meant for Le Brun that the thoughts and emotions as well as the actions of the individuals were revealed: reflection, greedy

haste, and kindness. Finally, color and light combine to emphasize and subordinate the appropriate figures and groups, and to create depth and atmosphere. Le Brun concludes by comparing the paintings to a theatrical performance in which there is unity of action: the essence of the entire drama resides in the moment Poussin has depicted, when the preparatory actions —the despair of the starving Jews—are still in evidence, and the necessary "conclusion"—their salvation by the manna—is already at hand.

Poussin would undoubtedly have been satisfied by this academic discussion. Indeed, a similar analysis is already implicit in his letter of 1637 about the painting to his friend Stella. Poussin wrote that the commission pleased him greatly because it gave him the opportunity to express "hunger, joy, admiration, respect; a crowd of women and children, people of different ages and temperaments—things, I believe, that will not displease those people who can read intelligently." Neither in Poussin's own remarks nor in the commentaries of the French Academy is there any mention that the miracle of the manna should be considered a symbol of the Eucharist.

MADONNA ROCCATAGLIATA

Oil on canvas, 27×17¹/₂"

1641

The Detroit Institute of Arts, Detroit, Michigan

Poussin states in a letter of May, 1642, that this painting was made for Stefano Roccatagliata.

This small, beautifully colored work is the most classicistic example of a Holy Family in Poussin's oeuvre. It no longer has the Venetian charm of the few Madonnas he painted around 1630; nor is it Raphaelesque, with the rigidity sometimes seen in Poussin's Holy Families from the late 1640s and '50s. He made the painting during his short sojourn in Paris, when he was dominated by a strong impulse toward classicism.

The pose of the Madonna is both original and classicistic, her foot resting on the base of an ancient tripod. Poussin used the motif, which he derived from a Nike, for various figures at this time; one instance is the standing figure of the Madonna in the small painting of the *Holy Family with St. Elisabeth and St. John* (Musée Condé, Chantilly), to which belongs a beautiful drawing with nude figures (fig. 109); other examples are the drawing of *Victory and Fame* (Städel Institute, Frankfurt am Main), and his frontispieces for the editions of Horace (fig. 10) and Virgil. The Madonna wears heavy draperies and sits in an Antique chair, her head bent over the Child; her pose is that of a Roman statue, but it is reminiscent also of Donatello's *Shaw Madonna* (Museum of Fine Arts, Boston). A thick curtain hangs behind her, and St. Joseph leans on the sill of the open window with a landscape beyond.

Figure 109. HOLY FAMILY WITH NUDE FIGURES. 1641–42. Drawing, pen and bistre wash over black chalk, 8³/₈×6³/₈". *Royal Library, Windsor Castle (by gracious permission of H. M. the Queen)*

COLORPLATE 27

ET IN ARCADIA EGO

Oil on canvas, 33³/₄×47⁵/₈"
1639–40 or 1642–43
The Louvre, Paris

In contrast to the pastoral character of the earlier *Et In Arcadia Ego* (colorplate 12), this painting expresses a philosophy of death which Bellori perspicaciously called "la felicità soggetta alla morte" (happiness subjected to death), meaning that death is always present, even in happy Arcadia. The entire painting has the form of an elegiac meditation, its theme suggested by the tomb.

These are not common shepherds with a sensuous girl, but thoughtful young men who read and interpret the inscription and a female figure who resembles a classical priestess. The skull that in the earlier version crowned the tomb is omitted here, and the tomb is now a classical, rectangular block with a gabled lid. The group of figures is restricted to the space of a relief, and it is perfectly balanced. The inscription is the focal point of the composition, presenting its moral with epigrammatic clarity. Poussin's mature style is now clear in the finely delineated figures, especially the young woman, and in the clear, translucent colors. The landscape is not yet stylized in the cubic manner of the later paintings, and mainly provides a foil for the four figures placed significantly in the foreground; the intention has been to make the epigram very distinct. Therefore the date of the painting, which was formerly thought to be much earlier, is probably within the period shortly before or shortly after Poussin's visit in Paris. In the same manner as the second version of the *Nurture of Jupiter* (colorplate 28), the classicistic conception of this painting reflects a purely philosophical, elegiac sentiment. The painting was bought by Louis XIV in 1683.

150

To protect the newborn Jupiter from Saturn, his voracious father, Jupiter's mother gave the baby into the custody of two nymphs, Amalthea and Melissa, who nourished him on honey and goat's milk (occasionally

Figure 110. Giulio Romano: INFANT JUPITER GUARDED BY THE CORYBANTES ON CRETE. C. 1534. Oil on panel, 41⁷/₈×69¹/₈″. *National Gallery, London*

Figure 111. NURTURE OF JUPITER. Mid-1630s. Oil on canvas, 37³/₄×47¹/₈″. *Dulwich College Picture Gallery (by permission of the Governors of Dulwich College)*

the goat is called Amalthea). When Poussin was considering this subject, he had no need to consult literary sources, such as Virgil or Cartari. He could turn to Giulio Romano's compositions of the subject (fig. 110; engraved by Bonasone; another version is in Hampton Court). Poussin's first *Nurture of Jupiter* (fig. 111), probably dating from the mid-1630s, is very close to Giulio's painting in Hampton Court: in both works a nymph takes honey from a tree, and in Poussin's picture, a bearded shepherd and the other nymph hold the goat between them to feed the infant directly from its udder. To make the landscape more "mythological," Poussin adds the river nymph who looks with detached amusement at the scene. Poussin's version is looser, blonder, and more charming and bucolic than Giulio's rather tight composition, and its contrast to his second version is striking.

The definitive version of the composition illustrated in this colorplate (two other versions have recently come to light) is a masterpiece of Poussin's stylization and restriction. Together with the second version of *Et In Arcadia Ego* (colorplate 27), it is one of his most epigrammatic paintings. It consists of three adult figures and one child, all placed impressively in the immediate foreground. One of the nymphs, Amalthea, kneels on the left and feeds the child, who in this case does not drink from the udder, but from a pitcher. The central nymph, Melissa, reaches behind her for the sweet honeycomb. On the right, closing this extremely measured and balanced composition, is a shepherd milking the goat.

The painting is almost like a sculptured relief, the composition filling the space from right to left; the large, vertical beehives limit the painting on the left, and the oblique tree with its widespread branches, so reminiscent of trees in Hellenistic reliefs and Roman landscape paintings, emphasizes the right side. Only above the goat's back can a distant landscape be seen.

The *Nurture of Jupiter*, its every feature so justly calculated, was probably painted in the period of Poussin's most developed, stylized classicism, either before his trip to Paris, or shortly thereafter.

COLORPLATE 28

NURTURE OF JUPITER

Oil on canvas, 38¹/₄ × 52³/₈"

1639–40 or 1642–43

State Museums, Berlin-Dahlem

(SEE COMMENTARY ON OPPOSITE PAGE)

EXTREME UNCTION

Oil on canvas, 46¹/₈ × 70¹/₈″

1646–48

Collection Earl of Ellesmere, on loan to the National Galleries
of Scotland, Edinburgh

On April 15, 1644, Poussin wrote to Chantelou that he had begun to paint the *Extreme Unction*, first in the new series of Seven Sacraments which the artist decided to undertake for Chantelou when Cassiano dal Pozzo, the owner of the first series (1636–42), refused to allow it to be copied.

Extreme Unction is not based on a specific passage in the New Testament, yet this scene has clearly been placed in the time of Christ. In the present case, as in another deathbed scene from Antiquity, the *Testament of Eudamidas* (colorplate 35), a shield hangs above the dying man; the monogram of Christ that it bears indicates that the warrior was not only noble, but a Christian, a *miles christianus*. The entire disposition of the painting, as well as every detail, corresponds with ancient usage, as envisioned and reconstructed by Poussin. The broad curtain, which in the Meleager sarcophagus divides the space into layers and acts as a foil for the figures, is more spread out than had been the case in Poussin's earlier deathbed scenes. The bed is placed on a platform *all'antica* (in the ancient manner), as Bellori emphasized in his very elaborate description. So also are the poses of the mourning, prostrate women at the foot of the bed and of the priest, whose figure resembles that of the bent old man with one foot raised on a block, on the Meleager relief (fig. 6).

Because the scene has sacramental meaning, Poussin has given it a ceremonial fullness that is absent in the civilian tenor of his other deathbed scenes, the *Death of Germanicus* and the *Testament of Eudamidas* (colorplates 2, 35). Fundamentally, this *Extreme Unction* and its counterpart in the first series (Belvoir Castle) share the same iconography. But the priest now anoints the hand, not the head, of the dying man, and this change permits the whole torso to become dramatically visible. Otherwise, the principal difference between the first and second versions is the greater number of figures in the second, richly interwoven by their repeated gestures; in the first version, each figure is relatively isolated.

Since the scene has both artificial light (the candles required by the liturgy) and daylight (partly obscured by the heavy curtain), the light in this darkened room poses a special problem. The lighting is not determined by strict naturalism, and it stresses such important elements as the shimmering shield emerging like a radiant circle between the dark curtain and the shadowed wall. Poussin delineates the emotion-filled movements and gestures of the participants by strong chiaroscuro, which allows the lesser figures to blend into the shadows. For such reasons, the painting became one of Poussin's most admired works. Bellori wrote: "In this pathetic and mournful composition, Poussin displayed such strong expressions and passions that the eyes and the soul of the spectator are drawn to the passions as well as to the thoughts of his great art."

154

EUCHARIST

Oil on canvas, 46¹/₈×70¹/₈″

1647

*Collection Earl of Ellesmere, on loan to the National Galleries
of Scotland, Edinburgh*

On September 1, 1647, Poussin wrote to Chantelou that he was at work on the *Eucharist*, the sixth of the second series of the Seven Sacraments. A second letter, November 3, mentioned to Chantelou that the painting had already been dispatched to Lyons.

The *Eucharist*, one of the last pictures of the series,

is here presented as a Last Supper. Before the sixteenth century, the Last Supper generally illustrated the moment of Christ's announcement that Judas would betray him. When the Reformation made the Church defend the validity of its sacraments, the connection between the Last Supper and the Passion as a whole was de-emphasized; it became more customary to show Christ consecrating the bread, or giving Communion to the Apostles. Poussin's *Eucharist*, painted in 1641 for the chapel of the Château of St.-Germain-en-Laye (fig. 112; now in the Louvre, Paris), contains no reference to the Last Supper or to Judas, but to the liturgical moment of consecration, the Apostles gathered around their priest. In both series of Seven Sacraments, however, Poussin has chosen to give the Eucharist its narrative and historical context. The Apostles lie at table *all'antica* (see chap. X), some still reacting to Christ's earlier warning: "One of you shall betray me." In the background, as the Gospel of St. John relates, Judas scurries away. But in accordance with the rationale of the whole cycle, Poussin focused attention on the sacramental climax of the Last Supper, the Consecration of the Host: with an unmistakable gesture, Christ points to himself, saying, "This is my body."

Figure 112. THE EUCHARIST. 1641. Oil on canvas, 10'8″×8'2³/₈″. *The Louvre, Paris*

REBECCA AND ELIEZER
AT THE WELL

Oil on canvas, 46¹/₂×77⁵/₈″

1648

The Louvre, Paris

Perhaps the most idyllically beautiful example of Poussin's Maniera Magnifica of the 1640s is the large painting, *Rebecca and Eliezer at the Well*. Pointel, a patron of Poussin's who was in Rome in the 1640s, was allegedly very enthusiastic about a painting by Guido Reni that represented the Virgin as a young girl, sitting amidst a circle of girls, all busy at some handwork—the so-called "Sewing School." With this assemblage of attractive women in mind, Pointel asked Poussin to make a similarly charming work for him. Poussin, who had once compared the columns of the Maison Carrée in Nîmes to the statuesque bodies of the beautiful women he saw there, was much attracted by this proposition; he used the meeting of Eliezer and Rebecca at the well as the pretext for painting a display of the columnar bodies of young maidens—Rebecca's companions—in many poses; they are busily fetching water or leaning on the cistern, and they all look curiously at the stranger.

The story is told in Genesis (24 : 1–28) that Abraham sent his trusted servant Eliezer to seek a wife for Isaac in Abraham's homeland. Eliezer prayed to God for help, and asked that the girl who would be the right wife for Isaac should show herself by giving him drink and watering his camels. Poussin chose to paint the moment when Eliezer reveals to the maiden that

she has fulfilled his sign, and will become the wife of the son of the Israelites' patriarch.

The psychological differentiation that Poussin expressed in other paintings of this time, such as *Healing the Blind of Jericho* (colorplate 34), may also be seen here, in the eloquent gesture of the envoy, the modest response of the maiden, and the attention shown them by the other girls.

At one of the often rather pedantic discussions in the French Academy, Poussin was blamed for omitting the camels that were customarily represented with the subject of Rebecca. Perhaps Poussin did not wish to disturb the psychological values of the scene, the subdued emotions so finely distinguished, by adding strange, exotic animals. Camels do appear in the very early version (c. 1627; Coll. Denis Mahon), and in the late, less psychological version owned by Anthony Blunt.

The painting is one of the first to display a broad stylized landscape; the town is Nabor, its sumptuous buildings separated by a hilly vista in the center. Poussin must have taken great pleasure in this painting for its color scheme is especially differentiated, showing a careful observation of complementary tones. The statuesque girl leaning in front of the pillar of the fountain suggests in her sensuous warmth a figure by Rubens, an instance which is rare in Poussin's art.

COLORPLATE 32

MADONNA ON THE STEPS

Oil on canvas, 27×38¹/₂″

1648

The National Gallery of Art, Washington, D.C.
(Kress Collection)

The painting was made in 1648, according to Félibien. There is another version with equal claim to authenticity in the Bertin-Mourot Collection, Paris.

Two interesting drawings allow us to follow the creative process behind the composition of the painting. The sketch in Dijon (fig. 113) shows the outline of the group as it appears in the painting, including the seated figure of Joseph on the right, but the crouching Elisabeth is still lacking. The fragment of a wall with an opening is an indication of what later develops into a more complex architectural structure, and there is already, perhaps, a hint of the large vase. In the more advanced drawing (fig. 59) the group is now complete, and an architectural background has been added

that limits the space. The motif of the opened wall, at the left in both drawings, has been transferred in the painting to the center, where it forms a kind of halo around the head of the Christ Child; in place of the wall at the left there are now the columns of a Roman temple. The staircase, its massive, bastion-like side foreshortened, now forms a backdrop of geometrical shapes behind the figures. Finally, a simple ledge supporting certain precious objects has replaced the unclear division of the foreground steps, seen in perspective in figure 59. The composition has been adapted to yield a more unified surface in the finished painting, and it is now surprisingly similar to the ancient painting, *The Aldobrandini Wedding* (fig. 9).

Figure 113. MADONNA ON THE STEPS.
c. 1646. Drawing, pen and bistre wash,
5¹/₈×7¹/₂″. *Museum, Dijon*

The *Aldobrandini Wedding* basically influenced Poussin's space construction. He had allegedly made a copy or copies of it, and he obviously remembered it when making his scheme for the construction of the *Madonna on the Steps*—this can be proved from both the general configuration and the details. It is clear from the sketches that Poussin worked toward a solution which would approximate the spirit of Antiquity expressed in the fresco. Even the division between closed and open spaces, and between solids and voids, is generally similar in both paintings. Poussin took over and perfected the incomplete triangle of the central group in the ancient fresco, making the function of Joseph's

figure similar to that of the "genius," the right side of a triangle. He even interrupted the horizontal line of architecture with a rudimentary vertical that extends above the entablature, in imitation of the Roman painting. Poussin seems also to refer to the ancient composition in treating specific figures and objects: the Madonna, placed in relation to an architectural element seen in perspective; the character of her headdress; Elisabeth, leaning forward; the unusual position of Joseph with his foot extended (the Louvre drawing contains an even closer parallel; fig. 59); the cylindrical vases that replace the fountains in the fresco.

Figure 114. Michelangelo: LUNETTE OF NAASSON. 1508–12. Fresco.

The main affinities between Poussin's painting and the ancient work are that the two-dimensionality of the surface is maintained as much as possible in both, and that both present the figures against a severe, planimetric background. In Poussin's *Madonna on the Steps*, the wall which is primitive and quite simplified in the fresco has been translated into the formal vocabulary of the seventeenth century. Of course this new vocabulary had other sources as well. The group of the Madonna and Child has correctly been associated with Raphael's *Madonna of the Fish* (The Prado, Madrid), but the composition is looser than Raphael's, and resembles more closely Andrea del Sarto's *Madonna del Sacco* (fresco in SS. Annunziata, Florence). Joseph's strange position is based not only on that of the Aldobrandini "genius," but also, formally, on Michelangelo's amusing figure in the Naasson lunette on the Sistine ceiling (fig. 114). Only in Poussin's preparatory sketches, however, is Joseph's casualness so evident, one leg bent and the other extended. His

Sistine Chapel, Vatican, Rome

pose in the final version has more dignity, the bent leg hidden behind the profile view of the other. The entire group, painted in fairly strong, simple tones, is isolated against the neutral colors of the architecture. The group in Poussin's painting, as in the Aldobrandini fresco, is seen from below, which elevates its effect psychologically. Poussin's method, although it stems from the ancient work, actually corresponds to the new geometric theories formulated by Abraham Bosse (partly originated by Albrecht Dürer), and we can understand Poussin's praise for the work of this interesting theorist.

The problem of how to preserve an impression of depth without disturbing the unity of the surface is here admirably solved on the basis of the ancient example. The *Madonna on the Steps* is the most perfect, most imaginative testament of Poussin's method of transposing into his own language the ancient conception of space and volume. (See G. Kauffmann, *Poussin-Studien*, Berlin, 1960.)

Poussin painted the *Judgment of Solomon* in 1649 for his friend Pointel. In this painting the tension is more highly concentrated than in the other paintings of action made at the end of the 1640s and after, such as the *Death of Sapphira* (fig. 68) and *Healing the Blind of Jericho* (colorplate 34).

The biblical story (I Kings 3 : 16–28) relates that two harlots came to Solomon for a judgment, one asserting that during the night the other had substituted her dead child for her own living child. Since each mother claimed the living child as her own, the wise young king chose a subtle psychological test to distinguish the true from the false mother: he ordered that the living child be halved by a sword and divided between the two women. Poussin chose to depict the moment when the rightful mother, rather than see her child slain, cries out, "Give her the living child and in no wise slay it." The false mother maintains, "Let it be neither mine nor thine, but divide it."

A preparatory drawing in the École des Beaux-Arts

(fig. 115) gives us astonishing insight into Poussin's procedure at this period. The splendid scene is crowded and noisy. The faces of the figures look almost like ancient masks, and Solomon, miraculously, is out of proportion to the others. The whole drawing has a strange affectation. The finished painting retains the entire disposition of the drawing, and partly its detail, but it is drastically simplified. The chorus is greatly reduced in number, and the architecture, made more severe, is brought into one plane. The judge Solomon, normal in size, is placed at the apex of the triangle established by the declaiming women. The two full-bodied contestants seem to speak in alexandrines and to act like great tragediennes of the Comédie Française.

The painting is perfect in all respects, almost too perfect. Of all Poussin's paintings, it is perhaps the most typically French. Poussin himself considered it (as Bellori relates) his best picture. Nowhere else in his oeuvre do the calculated, consciously figured forms have such a tense vitality.

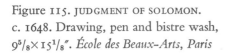

Figure 115. JUDGMENT OF SOLOMON. c. 1648. Drawing, pen and bistre wash, 9⅝×15⅛″. *École des Beaux-Arts, Paris*

COLORPLATE 33

JUDGMENT OF SOLOMON

Oil on canvas, 39³/₈×59″

1649

The Louvre, Paris

(SEE COMMENTARY ON OPPOSITE PAGE)

Figure 116. HEALING THE BLIND OF JERICHO. C. 1650.
Drawing, pen and ink, $4^3/_8 \times 7^5/_8$″. *Musée Bonnat, Bayonne*

This work was painted about 1650, for Reynon. It clearly belongs to the Maniera Magnifica, and received high praise from Poussin's contemporaries in the French Academy, and from Bellori and Félibien. It represents a rather uncomplicated miracle from the Gospel of Matthew (9:27–31), wherein Christ heals two blind men by touching their eyes. Christ lays his hand on the first blind man's forehead, pressing the eye with His thumb. Poussin differentiates with great penetration the various reactions to Christ's gesture: the first blind man seems confident as he kneels, humble and devout, before Christ; the second stretches his arms forward, full of expectation as he gropes his way toward the miracle. (Poussin's interest in the psychol-ogy of these figures may be seen in a number of studies, several in the Royal Library, Windsor Castle; see also fig. 116.) The faces of three of the bystanders show a mixture of interest and incredulity; the fourth, an old Hebrew, bends down to study the event more closely. Christ's three companions on the right observe the mira-cle with complete faith. A woman holding a child is pass-ing the scene on the left, and looks on curiously.

The tectonic structure of the landscape corresponds exactly to the careful interrelation of the figures, and seems to accompany them in an almost musical way. The proud town of Jericho, from which Christ had just departed, is built up layer by layer toward its towering fortress.

COLORPLATE 34

HEALING THE BLIND OF JERICHO

Oil on canvas, 46⁷/₈×69¹/₄″

1650

The Louvre, Paris

(SEE COMMENTARY ON OPPOSITE PAGE)

TESTAMENT OF EUDAMIDAS

Oil on canvas, 43¹/₂×54³/₈″

c. 1650

State Museum of Art, Copenhagen

Lucian, writing in the second century A. D. in his *Toxaris*, a dialogue on friendship, cites the example of Eudamidas, a citizen of Corinth, who was extremely poor, but who had good friends of greater wealth. On his deathbed Eudamidas dictated his will: "I leave my mother to Aretaeus, to support and cherish her in her old age, and to Charixenus my daughter, to bestow in marriage with the largest dowry that he can give out of his own means." When the will was read, many found it ridiculous. But the two men were neither surprised nor dismayed; they undertook their heritage as the fruit of their friendship, and provided for Eudamidas' mother and daughter as their means allowed. Lucian cites the unshakable confidence of Eudamidas in his friends as one of the highest examples of the sanctity of friendship.

Poussin's scene shows Eudamidas lying on his deathbed. The physician, an impressive figure, stands behind him and feels the pulse in his chest; a scribe in a white garment sits beside the bed, writing down the testament as dictated to him by the dying man. At the foot of the bed is the mother, her daughter's head resting in her lap. The room displays the utmost poverty; the wall is bare save for the insignia of the *civis* (citizen)— the round shield, crossed swords, and spear. The whole group, as in Poussin's other deathbed scenes, is arranged in a severe relief style. The strong light coming through a window at the upper left makes the chiaroscuro almost Caravaggesque.

The painting belongs to a series representing the Stoic moralities that especially attracted Poussin after he had been in Paris. The ideal of friendship was a Stoical virtue much valued in Poussin's circle of patrons. He succeeded in expressing this neo-Stoical sentiment with the utmost simplicity and dignity; at the time of the French Revolution, when the moral had such importance, Jean Pesne's engraving of this composition became much in vogue. It inspired J. L. David and his school, as well as Ingres; Napoleon Bonaparte, characteristically, was so enthusiastic about it that he took a copy of the engraving with him on his Egyptian campaign. "If one has seen this austere composition, and the *Death of Germanicus*," he said to Vivant Denon, his art commissioner, "one will never forget them. . . . One must bring back our school of painting to the ways of Poussin."

MADONNA WITH A BASIN

Oil on canvas, 38⁵/₈×50³/₄″

c. 1650

*Fogg Art Museum, Harvard University, Cambridge,
Massachusetts*

According to Félibien, a picture having this subject was painted for the Duke of Créquy in 1651; Félibien probably referred to the work now in Chatsworth, but the version here illustrated must be close to this date. It has the magnificence of Poussin's grand style. In contrast to the relatively fluid design of his earlier lyrical Madonnas, this monumental composition is a calculated showpiece. Nine figures are loosely interconnected, strung out on a narrow relief stage which is sharply limited by a tomblike monument rising behind the main group. At either side of this curious, impressive stone structure opens a dioramic view of great forms in a Roman landscape, beyond a body of water; on the right are the cubical roofs and buildings of a mountain town.

The Madonna, clad *alla Romana*, is in the center. Leaning against the monument behind her is Joseph, with the solemn face of an august Jupiter Capitolinus. These figures dominate the others in the composition; they rise above the playful group of four happy, earthly children who bring fruit and flowers, and above the tight-knit group of the Christ Child, the young St. John, and the crouching St. Elisabeth.

Between these two groups is the shining brass basin at the foot of the Madonna; she has just finished bathing her little Son, an act which here may be, as in other cases, a symbol of purification. The Mother looks smilingly down at Him as He is grasped by St. John. The monumentality of the composition does not preclude its atmosphere of intimacy and relaxed happiness.

The color in this beautiful painting shows an enamel-like surface which, in my opinion, Poussin adopted in imitation of ancient painting.

SELF-PORTRAIT

(for Colorplate, see Frontispiece)
Oil on canvas, $38^5/_8 \times 29^1/_8$"
1650, signed and dated
The Louvre, Paris

About 1650 Poussin made two self-portraits; the earlier version, for Pointel, was finished in 1649, and may be the painting now in the State Museums, East Berlin, which may best be appreciated in the fine engraving by Jean Pesne (fig. 117). The half-length figure of the artist is before a marble plaque showing a monumental inscription and flanked by *putti* who hold a garland of laurel leaves. This severe, classical background is decoratively impressive, but the figure has the informality usual in Poussin's first or earlier versions. Like most seventeenth-century portraits of artists and writers, the sitter's pose is rather casual; he holds a long pen in his left hand, and seems about to write or sketch in a book entitled *De Lumine et Colore*.

The process by which Poussin crystallized his self-portrayal into the final version for Chantelou "in the Jubilee Year, 1650" (as the inscription reads), is astonishing and admirable. This portrait (see Frontispiece), typical of Poussin's second versions, bears the mark of

being definitive. When Bernini saw the picture in Paris, he praised the excellent likeness. Besides mere resemblance, however, this monumental portrait demonstrates the high point of development in Poussin's art. Poussin must have been suddenly inspired to complete this masterpiece, for in March, 1650, he wrote grudgingly to Chantelou that it was not finished because he was lazy and took no pleasure in the making; yet two months later he informed Chantelou that the portrait was finished, and that everyone loved it and wanted a copy. Poussin was proud of it, and so pleased with the place of honor Chantelou gave the portrait in his house, that he cited as a parallel the "portrait of Virgil in the house of Augustus" —an honor which dignified both the artist and the patron.

As we know from Poussin's other landscapes and figure paintings in the Maniera Magnifica, to which this portrait also belongs, Poussin was a master at

Figure 117. Jean Pesne,
after Poussin: SELF-PORTRAIT. 1649.
Engraving

Figure 118. Titian: PORTRAIT OF JACOPO DE STRADA.
1568. Oil on canvas, 49¹/₄×37³/₈″.
Kunsthistorisches Museum, Vienna

suggesting three-dimensional effects by placing parallel layers one behind the other, thus reducing devices of foreshortening and perspective to a minimum. Here he employed this technique in a most original way. The layers which make an effective foil for the half-length figure consist of framed canvases of different sizes, stacked together irregularly. These frames form a co-ordinated system of horizontals and verticals that encloses and to a degree determines the construction of the head and body. The severe, abstract-geometrical background contrasts with the volume of the portrait bust, shown in its full, corporeal vitality. Some deviations from the strict vertical and horizontal axes soften slightly the severe rigidity of the whole composition: the hand and book meet at an oblique angle and the head is slightly tilted, turned in a proud gesture. One thinks of the words of Auguste in Corneille's *Cinna:* "I am master of myself as of the universe, I am it and I will be it. . . ."

The canvases behind the figure are blank except for the narrow strip visible in the one on the left wherein may be seen the bust of a woman, her shoulders embraced by two hands. On her head is a diadem with an eye in the center, symbolizing painterly vision. Bellori's explanation of this figure is probably correct: he identifies her with Painting, and the two embracing hands with Poussin's friendship for Chantelou, for whom he made this painting as a present.

It is not impossible that Poussin, for the structure of his self-portrait in the Louvre, made use of Titian's famous *Portrait of Jacopo de Strada* (fig. 118), which has a special place among Titian's late portraits. Titian's work is connected with Poussin's by the relation of the planimetric background, its wall decorated with interwoven cubical forms, to the realistic, lively, three-dimensional figure in the foreground. (The oblique portion of Titian's composition, containing the presentation statue of a figure of Venus, has a Baroque character that is in contrast with the classicistic dignity of Poussin's design.)

LANDSCAPE WITH
ST. JOHN ON PATMOS

Oil on canvas, 41¹/₈×53¹/₄"
1640s
The Art Institute, Chicago

This large landscape is one of the first of Poussin's landscape paintings in the 1640s and early 1650s; it is probably the earliest of the six landscapes that Chatillon engraved.

St. John reclines in the foreground on the island of Patmos, writing his Gospel on a large tablet. He has retired to the lonely grandeur of deserted Greek ruins, and is surrounded by stones—flat rocks, stones hewn in geometric form, and such architectural fragments as cubic pedestals and the cylindrical drums of columns. In the background are better-preserved architectural remnants, half-hidden behind a pine tree whose broad branches are silhouetted against the sky. Only in the far distance can one distinguish the mainland and a lively town.

This painting and *St. Matthew and the Angel* (fig. 72) anticipate by a few years the mature landscapes, with their severe construction in layers and their broad sweep, which begin about 1648. In comparison with earlier landscape paintings by the Brills and by the Carracci and their school, the *St. John* and the *St. Matthew* have, in their depth and breadth, a grandeur distinctly new. These vistas, however, are not yet as expansive as they later become; its crowded elements seem loosely organized. The lighting is rather abrupt in St. John, especially the sharp contrasts between the highlights on the marble ruins and the deep shadows in the wooded areas.

St. John on Patmos can be dated c. 1644–45; *St. Matthew and the Angel* may be one or two years earlier.

174

This version of the painting is probably a seventeenth-century copy of the original; there are other examples in the collection of the Earl of Plymouth (now thought to be the original) and of Philip Johnson. There is a pendant to it, the *Gathering of the Ashes of Phocion* (fig. 74). According to Félibien, Poussin painted "two landscapes with the story of Phocion for M. Cerisier of Lyons" in 1648. Bernini saw and admired these paintings in the Parisian house of this rich merchant.

The figures in these landscape paintings illustrate the episode at the end of Plutarch's *Life of Phocion*. The Athenian general and statesman was, according to Plutarch, a model of civic virtue in his private and public life—a typical Stoic *exemplum virtutis*, similar to the Roman Cato. During a period of deep unrest and political ferment in the state of Athens, Phocion remained above reproach and even refused the handsome benefices offered him by the king of Macedonia. He served as their governor forty times, and often saved the town of Athens from destruction. But he was finally accused of treason by his enemies in the town's lower classes, and was sentenced to die, like Socrates, by the poisonous hemlock. As an additional disgrace, Phocion's burial within Athens was forbidden; his noble wife had to gather his ashes clandestinely from the pyre near Megara, and bring them back to her home.

Many neo-Stoic writers in France who were Poussin's contemporaries were attracted to the story of Phocion and his fate because of his impeccable behavior and because of the ingratitude of the populace toward a man of such character and merit. Many of Poussin's paintings show that he was fascinated by the cruel reverses of fortune; in the case of Phocion, these caused an honored and respected man to die a traitor's death. The unjust treatment and belated recognition of the "honnête homme" is the subject of two other Stoical pictures by Poussin, the *Death of Germanicus* (colorplate 2) and, in some respects, the *Testament of Eudamidas* (colorplate 35).

In telling the story of Phocion, Poussin did not choose the emotional, highly charged execution scene. He preferred to illustrate the simpler, quieter, and undramatic episodes after Phocion's death: the body transported to the distant funeral pyre near Megara, and Phocion's wife piously gathering the ashes. To dignify and magnify these rather inconspicuous scenes, Poussin presented the figures in extremely grandiose and elaborate landscapes. The two men on the road carrying the corpse of Phocion to Megara are already some distance from Athens, for behind them lies the wide suburban area containing big flat stones in the sunlight. The panoramic background displays the full breadth of the town with its many buildings arranged "neither too confusedly nor too symmetrically"; it is based in part on Poussin's research, and has been elaborated by his rich imagination. The bastioned Acropolis is on a hill far beyond, but there are two diligently designed temples clearly visible within the city; the line of figures before one of them is the procession of cavaliers in honor of Zeus, which Plutarch tells us occurred on the day of Phocion's execution. The painting that shows Phocion's wife gathering his ashes has a similar topographical view, this time of Megara. In both works everything is clearly cut, in almost geometrical form; the space is delimited, and every object may be seen and understood. One can almost "read" these landscapes as Poussin planned his figure paintings to be read.

This kind of descriptive picture interested the famous French writer Fénelon, archbishop of Cambrai, whose *Dialogue des Morts* contains an eloquent, observant account of everything that exists or happens in Poussin's paintings. At the end of the dialogue between Poussin and the Athenian painter, Parrhasius, Fénelon lets the latter exclaim: "... after so many centuries, Poussin, you have given to Phocion a greater honor than his own city, Athens, could have, even had she given him on the day of his death the most sumptuous funeral."

COLORPLATE 39

FUNERAL OF PHOCION

Oil on canvas, 44⁷/₈×68⁷/₈"
(original painted 1648; this probably a 17th-century copy)
The Louvre, Paris
(SEE COMMENTARY ON OPPOSITE PAGE)

LANDSCAPE WITH A SNAKE

Oil on canvas, 47×88¹/₄″

c. 1648–51

National Gallery, London

This landscape, a recent acquisition of the National Gallery, was painted in 1651, according to Félibien. It is one of the last of the so-called "heroic landscapes" that Poussin made during the late 1640s and the early 1650s. "Heroic" is quite an apt term for these paintings with their grandiose hills and large trees, the small river, and the marvelous light of the sky (see chap. XII). *Landscape with a Snake* has all these characteristics; its subject also belongs among those expressing Poussin's intense interest in the accidents that can befall unsuspecting and innocent men (another example is *Landscape with Pyramus and Thisbe*, fig. 76).

The subject of the painting may be based (as G. Tervarent has suggested in *Gazette des Beaux-Arts*, II) on Ovid's story of Cadmus (*Metamorphoses*, III); a dragon of Mars strangles one of the young men whom Cadmus, after their arrival in Boeotia, sent to search for fresh spring water. The snake in Poussin's painting would be the fearful dragon of the Cadmus story. For this experiment in the representation of psychological reaction and emotion, Poussin used only the fundamental element of Ovid's story: the serpent strangling one or more of Cadmus' fellows. He does not show Cadmus, but the man who discovers the killing, and other figures unrelated to the Cadmus story. Fénelon, with his interest in psychology, was captivated by the painting and discussed it in his *Dialogue des Morts*.

It is remarkable that Poussin in his later years was so fascinated by the horror associated with snakes. There is a large snake in *Landscape with Two Nymphs* (fig. 77); Eurydice is bitten by a snake (colorplate 41); a snake is in the large drawing of the *Rape of Europa* (fig. 85); finally, a frightening serpent dominates the lower part of *The Deluge* (colorplate 47). But in *Landscape with a Snake* Poussin wanted to illustrate not only the young man's horrible death, but, more particularly, the chain reaction of terror that the cruel sight produced in others. In the foreground on the left, the serpent, almost as large as a python, coils around its victim; on the right is the man who inadvertently comes upon the hideous spectacle and runs away in terror; in the middle ground a woman is startled by the fleeing man, though she has not seen the actual death. Soon after the painting was completed it received the subtitle, "The Effects of Terror"—and rightly so. A drawing in the Louvre is quite clearly preparatory for this *Landscape with a Snake*, but it has no direct connection with any story. John Shearman has demonstrated rather convincingly that the idea for the landscape anticipated that for the story (*Actes du Colloque Poussin*, VI, 1961).

Poussin made for Pointel a pendant to this exciting picture, intentionally contrasted in character; possibly this was "*La Solitude*," *Landscape with Three Monks* (formerly in the collection of Prince Paul of Yugoslavia; fig. 75).

The *Landscape with Orpheus and Eurydice* is in Poussin's late, though not last, style, and was probably painted in the early 1650s. (It is certainly wrong to identify this painting with the "grand paysage" mentioned by Félibien as having been made for Le Brun in 1659; rather, in my opinion, Félibien refers to the beautiful *Landscape with Two Nymphs and a Snake;* fig. 77.)

Of all the episodes in the legend of Orpheus, this scene, Eurydice bitten by the snake, is here represented for the first time, so far as I know. Iconographically it follows the beginning of Book X in Ovid's *Metamorphoses*. Hymeneus, the god of weddings, wrapped in a yellow, "crocus-colored" cloak, was summoned by Orpheus to the shore of the Ciconians to celebrate Orpheus' wedding with Eurydice. However, Hymeneus came reluctantly, and did not bring good luck. The festivals were joyless and there were bad omens: Hymeneus' wedding torch sputtered, and the smoke brought tears to the eyes of the participants. From this comes the great cloud of smoke which hangs over the castle of the Ciconians (much resembling the Castel Sant'Angelo in Rome) where the wedding had been celebrated. The painting follows Ovid's narration of this unhappy story:

> The outcome of the wedding was worse than the beginning; for while the bride was strolling through the grass with a group of naiads in attendance, she fell dead, smitten in the ankle by a serpent's tooth.

Poussin shows Orpheus playing his lyre as he sits on a rock on the shore of the lake, at some distance from the town. Seated on the ground at his feet and listening to his song are two young women, the Ovidian naiads. The man behind them is probably Hymeneus, elegantly attired in a voluminous white mantle *(amictus)* over a reddish robe (rather than the crocus-colored garment described by Ovid). Hymeneus stands watching Orpheus, and behind him trips Eurydice, looking back in terror at the small snake that has bitten her and now glides away. In and around the lake which separates the main group from the monumental town and *arx* of the Ciconians are many small figures, mostly naked, who enjoy the pleasures of a summer day, swimming, sailing, fishing, or lounging in groups. In their *joie de vivre* they are in striking contrast with the tragic event in the foreground. Typical of Poussin's later style, the picture is closed on the right by an impressive group of trees, from one of which hangs a bright red cloth and two quivers (not torches, as I previously thought). With these belongs the "still life" on the ground, a cloth, precious vessels and baskets, flowers, and two wreaths, all surely connected in some way with the central group of figures.

This Ovidian fairy tale takes place in a landscape filled with almost magical light, which gives magnificence and classic dignity to the story. The idyllic, animated setting that Poussin has created for his tragic tale seems to stress the contrast between the living and the dying which so obsessed him in his later period. There is a connection, although an enigmatic one, between this painting and the drawing of the *Rape of Europa* (fig. 85; see chap. XII).

LANDSCAPE WITH ORPHEUS AND EURYDICE

Oil on canvas, 48⁷/₈ × 78³/₄"

1650s

The Louvre, Paris

(SEE COMMENTARY ON OPPOSITE PAGE)

COLORPLATE 42

LANDSCAPE WITH POLYPHEMUS

Oil on canvas, $58^1/_4 \times 77^1/_2$″

1649

The Hermitage, Leningrad

In Ovid's *Metamorphoses* (XIII, 738 ff.), Scylla, the sea deity, receives a visit from the sea-goddess Galatea; while Galatea combs her hair, she tells her sad tale of Polyphemus, the lovesick Cyclops, who played on the flute and sang praise of her beauty:

> "You are whiter, Galatea, than the snowy petals of the 'liguster,' more flowery than the fields, slenderer than the alder-tree . . ."
>
> ". . . All the mountains," says Galatea, "felt the sound of his rustic piping; the waves felt it too. I, hiding beneath a rock and resting in the lap of my Acis, heard the words he sang at a great distance and well remembered them."

In Poussin's *Landscape with Polyphemus*, the giant Cyclops is sitting on one of the two distant, jagged cliffs that jut into the Sea of Sicily. He has set aside his tree-like staff (as in Ovid's description) and taken up his pipe of a hundred reeds; their sound rings in the cliff-enclosed valley and is heard by all the inhabitants, who are seen here as diminutive figures. In the foreground, unseen by Polyphemus but listening intently to his song, is a female figure who seems to comb or wring out her wet hair. She forms the center of a triangle completed by two other partly draped figures, and she immediately brings to mind Ovid's

description of Galatea hiding behind a rock as she listens to the voice of her terrible suitor.

Galatea is "milk-white," as her name implies and as she is described in the first line of Polyphemus' song. She even, according to Cartari, has white hair. However, when Raphael painted his famous fresco in the Farnesina he did not differentiate the color of Galatea's flesh from that of other figures (fig. 102), and Poussin followed Raphael's example—his Galatea is even slightly darker than her two companions, and her face is decidedly sunburned. Her hair is very dark, almost bluish, in contrast to the light, reddish hair of the others; thus she is characterized as a sea-goddess, one of Nereus' daughters and a companion of the Tritons, whose hair is described by Cartari as the color "of a morass." A sea creature, Galatea does not wear a wreath of reeds, for this decoration is reserved for deities of rivers, where reeds grow. One can hardly doubt that the central figure of this triangle, so admirably formed in the foreground, is Galatea in her ocean-blue garment, and that the whole scene corresponds to Ovid's story of Galatea. She is visibly listening to the sound of the pipes and the song of the Cyclops, and plainly does not want to be seen, for she is hiding behind the

Figure 119. NYMPHS SPIED UPON BY SATYRS. 1660s. Drawing, pen and ink,
6¹/₈×8¹/₈″. École des Beaux-Arts, Paris

back of the almost-naked figure who sits at the apex of the pyramid. It seems to me that this elegant figure does not represent a casual companion or another nymph, but rather Acis, the youth so beloved by Galatea; it is his terrible death and subsequent metamorphosis into a little river that is told at the end of Ovid's story. His girlish figure might be explained by his youth, which Galatea specifically emphasized: "Pulcher et octonus iterum natalibus actis"—he was beautiful, sixteen years old, and his beard had just begun to grow (a youthful feature esteemed by Ovid and Homer). The near-golden hair of this figure is bound, not loose as is that of the river god in *Moses Found by the Pharaoh's Daughter* (fig. 44); he wears a wreath of reeds and holds a grayish urn, the attribute of a river god (although he arrives at this state only

after his metamorphosis, when his blood turns into the river Acis; see W. Friedlaender and A. Blunt, *Drawings*, III, 158). The third figure is very similar to Acis and also has a wreath around his reddish hair, but he has no urn and may, therefore, belong to a lower category; his gesture seems to warn Galatea of the approach of two satyrs who lecherously spy on the nudes. (Poussin elsewhere uses this jocose motif, taken from ancient sources; fig. 119.) The large urns lying before the group indicate the element of water, and pertain to the habitat of the figures.

The colorful little figures spread throughout the heroic landscape have no symbolic significance, but enliven the natural scene as they do in other mythological and historical landscapes (colorplates 39, 41) by their innocent activities—drinking from a jug, bathing in limpid water, digging and plowing. Here they also receive, at the same time, the powerful sounds of Polyphemus' voice and music without diverting attention from the main theme. But the bearded river god in the left foreground and the two spying satyrs (lured, as so often in similar scenes, by the nymph's nudity) have a different purpose: they indicate that the ambient here is not the real world, but the fictional world of a primitive culture.

Poussin has chosen to render this landscape in serene stillness; nothing moves, and the only interruption is the distant sound of Polyphemus' music. Unlike Annibale Carracci's *Polyphemus* in the Farnese Gallery, Poussin did not choose the violent moment when the giant spies the two lovers and hurls down an immense rock which smashes Acis under its weight, al-

though as a youth Poussin made a drawing of this cruel scene (see W. Friedlaender and A. Blunt, *Drawings*, III, 160). Nor is his intention as lyrical as that of Claude Lorrain, who employed Poussin's motif in one of his most poetic seascapes (fig. 120), so full of shimmering light and divine happiness. The atmosphere of Poussin's closed valley, ringed with jagged, threatening rocks, is heavy with tension and with the premonition of a storm, as it is in his last painting, *Apollo and Daphne* (colorplate 48).

Félibien dates the painting 1649, but it has also been dated, with its presumed pendant, the *Landscape with Hercules and Cacus* (Pushkin Museum, Moscow), within Poussin's old age style; this would perhaps explain the rather unspecific exposition of the story (see chap. XIII) and the androgynous character of this group.

Figure 120. Claude Lorrain: ACIS AND GALATEA. 1657. Oil on canvas, $39^3/_8 \times 53^1/_8$″. Gallery, Dresden.

The five figures in this composition are compressed more tightly into a triangle than are the corresponding figures in broader, looser compositions such as the *Madonna on the Steps* (colorplate 32). Thick tree trunks behind the figures stress the verticality of the group. In spite of its severity and the great dignity and noble bearing of the figures, the whole painting seems peaceful and relaxed. The two children play quietly together with a long ribbon, a motif from Raphael's *Canigiani Madonna* (fig. 121). The rich, extensive landscape on the right, and the modest family house on the left, contribute to the impression of a composed and happy family resting on a summer's day. Antique relief space has not exerted any visible influence here, because the architectural accents of the *Madonna on the Steps* have been replaced by the natural forms of clustered trees in the center.

In the Louvre is another Holy Family in a landscape, *Holy Family with St. John and St. Elisabeth, and St.*

Figure 122. HOLY FAMILY WITH ST. JOHN AND ST. ELISABETH, AND ST. JOSEPH PRAYING. 1656. Oil on canvas, 26³/₄×20¹/₈". *The Louvre, Paris*

Figure 121. Raphael: CANIGIANI MADONNA. 1507. Oil on panel, 52×38⁵/₈". *Alte Pinakothek, Munich*

Joseph Praying; it is much smaller, and its format is vertical (fig. 122). The group is compressed, and the figure of Joseph is upright and stiff; the painting is close to the large, vertical Holy Families in the Hermitage, Leningrad, and in Sarasota (fig. 62). It is probably identical with the landscape of 1656 mentioned by Félibien, "pour un particulier." All these Holy Families are decidedly influenced by Raphael's still rather Leonardesque *Canigiani Madonna*, in which Joseph, leaning on his staff behind the others, provides the apex for a strongly defined triangle.

The *Holy Family with St. Elisabeth and Infant St. John* was probably painted about 1655, a few years after Poussin's other paintings in oblong format of the Holy Family. In the Louvre there is a wonderful drawing for it which can, with the painting, be dated stylistically to the first half of the 1650s.

COLORPLATE 43

HOLY FAMILY WITH ST. ELISABETH
AND INFANT ST. JOHN

Oil on canvas, 37×48"

c. 1655

The Louvre, Paris

(SEE COMMENTARY ON OPPOSITE PAGE)

This *Annunciation*, recently acquired by the National Gallery, is the only late work by Poussin that is fully signed and dated: *"Poussin faciebat anno salutis MDCLVII Alex. Sept. Pont. Max. Regnante Roma"* (made by Poussin in the year 1657, during the reign of Pope Alexander VII in Rome). This inscription does not indicate, as Blunt has suggested, that the painting was commissioned by the Chigi Pope, Alexander VII. Even if the commission had been for the Pope's private chapel in Castel Gandolfo, it would still have been noted by the biographers, considering the painter's age and fame. But the presence of a special inscription in such solemn, ceremonial form must indicate that the painting had an important purpose. Its format, too, which provides a long, dark strip at the bottom for the simple (and characteristic) cartouche bearing the inscription, would have been unusual in the average altarpiece. Finally, the tonality of the painting is, for an Annunciation, extremely subdued—it recalls somewhat the colors of the Dublin *Entombment* (fig. 56).

The iconography of this *Annunciation* is very unusual. The Virgin sits on a cushion placed on a low platform, her legs crossed like an Oriental woman's

Figure 123. ANNUNCIATION. Late 1620s.
Oil on canvas, 29¹/₂×37³/₈″. *Musée Condé, Chantilly*

to indicate the *costume*, the local color. She does not, as is customary, fold her hands on her breast, but holds them out on both sides in a gesture of utmost submission. An open book lies before her; the Holy Spirit, in the form of a dove with outspread wings, hovers in a nimbus above her. The angel Gabriel enters on his great wings from the right, in the French manner; kneeling before her, he points hieratically with his left hand to heaven, and with his right to the Virgin. This archaic gesture is certainly rare in seventeenth-century Annunciations, but in the fifteenth century it occurs in Fra Angelico's *Annunciation* (Academy, Florence). Poussin had also used it before in an *Annunciation* (fig. 123), but this early work is utterly different in feeling and composition from the late, enigmatic painting.

Poussin's great friend and patron, Cassiano dal Pozzo, the famous antiquarian and scholar, had died on October 22, 1657; he was buried in the Dominican church in Rome, Sta. Maria sopra Minerva. On December 24, Poussin belatedly reports Cassiano's death to Chantelou in Paris, with these words:

"Notre bon ami, M. le Chevalier du Puis est décédé et nous travaillions à sa sépulture. . . . M. son frère vous baise les mains." This last remark relates to Cassiano's brother, Carlo Antonio, who was also a great friend of Poussin's. The project for a funeral monument on which Poussin either worked or collaborated at the end of 1657 is, in the opinion of J. Costello (published in *Studies in Honor of Walter Friedlaender*, 1965), the source of this *Annunciation*, painted within the same year. An Annunciation is, of course, an unusual choice for a sepulcher, but the *humilitas* pose relates it to this purpose. The church of Sta. Maria sopra Minerva stood above the ruined ancient sanctuary of the Egyptian Isis, and Poussin's *Annunciation* probably combines the values of three divinities: Mary, Minerva, and Isis. The Virgin's receptive posture may also symbolize Mary as the *sedes sapientiae*, the seat of wisdom.

The monument was never executed for reasons still unknown, but it seems possible that this interesting painting may have been part of the plan.

COLORPLATE 44

ANNUNCIATION

Oil on canvas, 40¹/₂×41¹/₄″
1657, signed and dated
National Gallery, London
(SEE COMMENTARY ON OPPOSITE PAGE)

Félibien mentions a *Birth of Bacchus* made in 1657; there are two versions of the subject. That described by Bellori, earlier in the Orléans Gallery and now in

Figure 124. INFANT BACCHUS ENTRUSTED TO THE NYMPHS. C. 1657.
Drawing, pen and bistre wash, 9×14³/₄″.
*Fogg Art Museum (Gift of Mr. and Mrs. Donald S. Stralem),
Harvard University, Cambridge, Mass.*

Figure 125. Jean Verini, after Poussin: BIRTH OF BACCHUS
WITH VENUS AND CUPID IN THE SKY.
Engraving. *Metropolitan Museum of Art, New York
(Gift of Georgiana W. Sargent, 1924)*

the Fogg Art Museum, shows Jupiter and Hebe in the sky; it was engraved by Jean Dughet. The other version, known only through a drawing and an engraving by Jean Verini (fig. 125), replaces Jupiter and Hebe with Venus and Cupid.

As described in Philostratus' *Imagines*, Semele, the mother of Bacchus, implored Jupiter, her lover, to appear to her in his glory; she was destroyed by the celestial fire emanating from the deity, and Jupiter, snatching their half-formed child from the flames, carried it in his thigh until the baby, Bacchus, was born. Poussin's painting shows Jupiter reclining after his labor, on a bed in the sky; he is attended by Hebe, who restores him with ambrosia (fig. 126).

In the lower left portion of the painting is a wonderful group of naiads rhythmically emerging from the limpid water (fig. 127; compare the swimming women in the Palestrina Mosaic). They are most eager to see the child Bacchus, miraculously delivered by Mercury (in the Verini version, Bacchus even has a halo). Swift-footed Mercury points to Jupiter in heaven, the source of the miracle, while Dirce, daughter of the river god Achelous, accepts with delight the charge to protect Bacchus from Juno's jealous wrath. These groups are composed within an oval set before a grotto or cave, the holy place of Achelous, which contains magic statuettes and sacred vessels; it is densely overgrown with ivy and grape vines, sprouting abundantly with young grapes. Above is a radiant sky (in the other version, Helios appears, drawn in his chariot); Pan, hidden among the trees, joyously welcomes the child by playing the syrinx.

This mythological fairy tale is full of gaiety and joy, new life and fertility. However, the mood changes abruptly in the lower right corner, where a half-naked youth lies on his back dead or dying, his mouth open. Behind him, a woman laments, bent with weeping. These figures doubtless represent Narcissus and Echo,

COLORPLATE 45

BIRTH OF BACCHUS

Oil on canvas, $48^5/_{16} \times 70^1/_2''$

c. 1657

Fogg Art Museum, Harvard University, Cambridge,
Massachusetts

(SEE COMMENTARY ON OPPOSITE PAGE)

as Bellori noted (see chap. XIII). The combination of such contrasting elements is in accord with the imagination of a man nearing the end of his life, for whom even earthly luxury and Bacchic *joie de vivre* must be contrasted with death. Poussin's last work, *Apollo and Daphne* (colorplate 48), and his great drawing, the *Rape of Europa* (fig. 85), follow this pattern. Even in the Golden Age, death is present. Poussin, when he composed the *Birth of Bacchus* (fig. 124), remembered Philostratus (D. Panofsky, *The Art Bulletin*, XXXI).

Figure 126. BIRTH OF BACCHUS (detail, Jupiter). *Fogg Art Museum, Cambridge, Mass.*

Figure 127. BIRTH OF BACCHUS (detail, Naiads). *Fogg Art Museum, Cambridge, Mass.*

THE FOUR SEASONS

The style of *The Four Seasons* is not essentially different from that of the other landscapes which Poussin made around 1650. They have, however, a different programmatic intention. None of Poussin's earlier landscapes is conceived in this way—as part of a series of paintings with a common program—and the earlier works may for the most part be readily understood. But the meaning of *The Four Seasons* is so deeply hidden that the paintings have long been considered to be mere representations of the changing seasons, embellished by pleasing or suitable narratives from the Old Testament. Only recently has it been convincingly suggested that the series illustrates, in addition to the seasons, an allegory of the salvation of mankind through the Church (W. Sauerlaender, in *Münchner Jahrbuch*, dritte Folge, III, 1956).

Spring, first in the series (fig. 128), shows man's status before the Law: Adam and Eve beneath the tree of knowledge in the earthly Paradise. Paradise here prefigures the coming Church; Adam, the coming Christ. In the second, *Summer* (colorplate 46), Ruth and Boaz as bride and bridegroom are shaded by a great tree—the tree of life. They symbolize the relation of Christ to His Church, and the cornfield suggests the consecrated bread, the body of Christ, which is offered in the Eucharist. In *Autumn*, the third picture (fig. 129), a huge cluster of grapes carried from the Promised Land signifies the fulfillment of the Law by Christ; grapes also suggest the consecrated wine, the other half of the Eucharist. The trees that flourish and die in the middle ground symbolize the Church and the Synagogue. The last painting, *Winter* (colorplate 47), or *The Deluge*, is an apocalyptic vision of the Last Judgment; the Ark of Noah in the background symbolizes the Church, which offers salvation to the faithful.

It is possible that Poussin did not formulate this theological program himself, but that it was suggested by one of the learned French clerics who frequented Poussin's house during his last years. There was, however, a tradition in the seventeenth century for the symbolism, both literary and artistic, of the stories of Ruth and Boaz, and of the grapes borne from Canaan; Poussin and his advisers may have developed from this core the more complex cycle of *The Four Seasons*.

Bellori does not mention *The Four Seasons* at all. He seems to have been not much interested in landscape painting, and had surely not been informed of the symbolic significance of this series of works. Félibien enumerates the four paintings and gives a description of *The Deluge*, but he was not acquainted with any deeper religious meaning. Like some of his colleagues in the Academy, he sees decay in these works of Poussin's old age: "Certainly one sees in these four paintings still the form and the genius of Poussin, but one also remarks the weakness of his hand." The spectacular *Deluge* attracted by far the most attention. Loménie de Brienne states (c. 1695) that it is a beautiful piece in its intention, but the execution is not equivalent ("c'est une belle chose pour l'intention, mais l'exécution n'y répond pas"). Some qualities in the other three paintings were appreciated by certain critics at the time, but their pictorial value was not fully understood and admired until the nineteenth century.

193

Figure 128. SPRING. 1659.
Oil on canvas, 46$\frac{1}{8}$×63″. *The Louvre, Paris*

A rich cornfield, ripe for harvest, epitomizes summer. Poussin has developed the bucolic scene with mastery: reapers cut the corn, women set out bread for the noon meal, a hurdy-gurdy player amuses the workers, a team (strangely Antique) of five horses is being driven by a man with a flying whip. Most astonishing from a painterly point of view is the sweeping cornfield, a flat expanse which makes spectators think of Cézanne (who surely studied this painting in the Louvre). In the far distance is a small mountain town—perhaps Petra, the home of Ruth—and the towering peak of Mount Sinai.

In the foreground near a great tree stands Boaz, the landowner from Bethlehem, a noble figure in rich clothing with a turban on his head. The young Moabite widow, Ruth, kneels before him, imploring him to protect her and permit her to glean the ears left behind the harvesters. Boaz, his hand outstretched, orders his foreman, the humble youth with the spear, to stand guard so that Ruth can work unmolested. These three figures immediately reveal the essence of the story: Ruth, a stranger and a foreigner, receives admittance into the community, and eventually marries Boaz, as idyllically narrated in the Book of Ruth. It is significant that the couple belongs among the ancestors of King David, and thus to the lineage of Christ.

The charming, touching "novelletta" of Ruth and Boaz greatly enhances the painting, and the *idea* of summer is expressed with beautiful conviction. The symbolic meaning is so fully integrated with the composition that neither the visual nor the narrative impression is in any way diminished.

COLORPLATE 46

SUMMER (RUTH AND
BOAZ), FROM THE FOUR
SEASONS

Oil on canvas, 46¹/₈×63″

1660–64

The Louvre, Paris

(SEE COMMENTARY ON OPPOSITE PAGE)

For the setting of *The Deluge*, Poussin could turn to Michelangelo's grandiose fresco on the ceiling of the Sistine Chapel. He probably also knew the surprising composition (not without Michelangelo's influence) of *The Deluge* painted about 1616 by Antonio, the youngest of the Carracci, in the Quirinal Palace. In both Poussin's and Antonio's paintings, two great masses of rock enclose the expanse of water in which men and women struggle hopelessly against the rushing tides. The large snake that Poussin often used in his late years to embody evil winds itself over the rocks, adding still more horror to the scene. A foaming cataract connects the two levels of water; the upper waters are calm, the sun breaks through the clouds; the only note of hope is the Ark of Noah, the symbol of the Church.

Poussin's contemporaries praised his manner of imbuing the light and color with so much humidity. A critic said, in Poussin's own time: "Who would not tremble with horror when he looks at this painting; who would not be in the grip of an icy shudder?" (see chap. XIII).

Figure 129. AUTUMN.
1660–64. Oil on canvas,
46¹/₈×63″. *The Louvre, Paris*

COLORPLATE 47

WINTER (THE DELUGE),
FROM THE FOUR SEASONS

Oil on canvas, 46¹/₈×63"

1660–64

The Louvre, Paris

(SEE COMMENTARY ON OPPOSITE PAGE)

Figure 130. APOLLO AND DAPHNE.
Early 1660s. Drawing, pen and bistre wash with alterations in
black chalk, 12¹/₄×16⁷/₈″. *The Louvre, Paris*

Bellori mentions that when Poussin left this painting to Cardinal Camillo Massimi it was not entirely finished, "because of the impotence and trembling of his hand in his last years." In its present state, however, the beauty of the painting as a whole does not suffer from these deficiencies.

At first glance, *Apollo and Daphne* suggests one of those Golden Ages that have been painted since the sixteenth century, especially in the north (one of the last examples is Ingres' *Golden Age*, in Dampierre). They satisfy a certain romantic-classical ideal: the desire to see gods and demigods in the shimmering splendor of their bodies, under a serene sky and amid full bushes and noble trees; as these beings stand, sit, or lie, singly or in groups, on soft meadows near a clear fountain, they enjoy the happiness of pure existence—not speaking, not moving. The famous, serene *Judgment of Paris* from the school of Raphael (engraved by Marcantonio) is another such work; it was possibly Poussin's model for this monumental, romantic-classical composition.

The figures in *Apollo and Daphne* are arranged in an enclosed composition similar to that in the *Birth of Bacchus* (colorplate 45); the form is an extended oval, open toward the back and flanked on both sides by female figures. Apollo, apparently suffering from the deep wound inflicted on him by Cupid (see chap. XIII), is seated in an almost archaic pose on the left. Behind him Mercury, his younger brother, in a variation of the scene described in Philostratus' *Imagines*, steals a golden arrow from Apollo's quiver. A majestic oak tree fills the canvas at the upper left; a female figure in a light blue chiton sits near the tree, grasping a branch for support and gazing toward the thieving Mercury. Another dryad reclines in the branches of the tree: in Giulio Romano's *Cephalus and Procris* (Städel Institute, Frankfurt) a figure has a similar pose, turning her head toward the groups on the right as if something had suddenly caught her eye. Apollo is unaware of the theft, being totally captivated, as Bellori remarked, by his love for Daphne: he stares longingly at Daphne,

who clings to her father, the river god Peneus, imploring him to protect her, exactly as Ovid described (*Metamorphoses*, I). In the foreground are two naiads, one of whom wrings her hair in the ancient manner; they belong with Cupid and Apollo, on the left side of the composition; two other reclining naiads belong to the Daphne group on the right, which includes the two magnificent, standing nude goddesses who tower behind Daphne. Both of these groups are basically triangular, but that form is subordinated to the flowing chain of the figures, who are psychologically interrelated as well. The whole composition of figures, loosely intertwined, is set before a rich southern landscape. Behind are reddish cattle, and beyond are distant lakes and hills. This herd comes from Ovid's legend of Apollo and Mercury; Poussin alluded to it in an early Marino Drawing, and elaborated it in a series of drawings more or less closely connected with this last, grandiose *Apollo and Daphne*.

But the aspect of happiness, as in the *Birth of Bacchus*, is counterbalanced by death. Beneath bushy trees in the middle ground lies a dead or dying youth, again resembling in pose a dying Narcissus. His body, just discovered, is here mourned by a shepherd and shepherdess. This youth is more probably Hyacinthus than Narcissus, because the former was accidentally killed by Apollo, his beloved friend, in a game of discus-throwing (D. Panofsky, in *The Art Bulletin*, XXXI).

It has been clearly and ingeniously proved that Poussin not only followed his main source, Ovid, but also used (as in the *Birth of Bacchus*) episodes from Philostratus which do not appear in Ovid's *Metamorphoses*. But it is doubtful if Poussin originally intended to depict the "unfortunate loves of Apollo" on the basis of Lucian and Philostratus, as E. Panofsky proposed. For, even more than in the *Birth of Bacchus*, this canvas is dedicated to its main theme, Apollo's new love for Daphne. The "jocular" (Bellori's term) episode of Mercury's theft (which Poussin also used in his drawing, *Apollo Sauroctonos;* fig. 80) is not much emphasized, nor is the contrast offered by the tragedy of the dead youth hidden in the bushes. There is a fine drawing for the whole composition (fig. 130) which is rather close to the painting, but it does not contain the dead youth. This episode was possibly inserted as an afterthought.

In the *Birth of Bacchus*, the contrasts between joyful fertility and unhappy death are clear; in *Apollo and Daphne*, they are more subdued. Apollo is here not the radiant sun god, the creator of life, but a frustrated lover. Poussin, to show the first phase of the love story of Apollo and Daphne, followed what he had read in Ovid and other authors, and he wanted to combine these stories symphonically. In his last painting he succeeded in creating a great work of art, and in rendering an atmosphere full of peace and happiness that is nevertheless impregnated with forebodings of catastrophe.

INDEX

Titles refer to works by or attributed to Poussin, unless otherwise noted.

Numerals in roman type signify page numbers; *italic* numerals signify black-and-white figure numbers;

bold-face numerals signify colorplate numbers

Abandonment of Armida (drawing), 50, *40*

Achilles and the Daughters of Lycomedes, 72, 73, 84, *66*

Achilles on Skyros, 84, *83*

Adoration of the Golden Calf, 49, 53, 54, 136–139, **22**

Adoration of the Magi, 42, *30*

Adoration of the Shepherds, 42, *29*

Aldobrandini Wedding (ancient painting), 21, 160–163, *9*

Annunciation (Chantilly), 42, 188, *123*

Annunciation (London), 42, 188, **44**

Antinous, Statue of (engraving after Poussin), 33, *22*

Apollo and Daphne, 22, 26, 84–87, 185, 192, 198–200, **48**

Apollo and Daphne (drawing), 200, *130*

Apollo Sauroctonos (drawing), 83, 200, *80*

Aurora and Cephalus, 26, 47, 77, 124, **15**

Autumn, 87, 193, *129*

Bacchanal (Prado), 132

Bacchanal with the Lute Player, 49

Bacchanal Before a Temple (drawing), 49, *38*

Bacchanalian Revel Before a Term of Pan, 49, 136, 139, **21**

Bacchanals (for Richelieu), 49, 98, 130–134

Bacchus and Ariadne (drawings), 21

Baptism, 57, 65, *49*

Baptism of Christ (Washington, D. C.), 56–57, 62, *47*

Battle of the Horatii and the Curatii (drawing), 68

Bellori, Giovanni Pietro, 13, 15, 27, 30, 33, 40, 61, 65, 73, 89, 98, 126, 130, 150, 154, 164, 166, 190, 192, 193, 198

Bernini, Lorenzo, 14, 32–33, 64, 100, 124, 172, 176

Birth of Bacchus, 26, 84–87, 128, 184, 190–192, 198, 200, *126, 127*, **45**

Birth of Bacchus with Venus and Cupid in the Sky (engraving after Poussin), 190, *125*

Blind Orion Searching for the Rising Sun, 22, 84, *84*

Borghese Warrior (ancient sculpture), 20, 51

Bosse, Abraham, 32, 34, 75, *163*

Caravaggio, 29, 33, 67, 168

Carracci, Agostino, 30, 47, 48, 122, *98*

Carracci, Annibale, 26, 27, 30, 38, 47, 49, 75, 83, 98, 104, 120, 185, *87, 97*

Carrying of the Cross (drawing), 66, *55*

Cartari, Vincenzo (*Images of the Gods*), 22, 49, 118, 120, 135, 182, *96*

Chambray, Roland Fréart de, 22–24, *58*

Chantelou, Paul Fréart de, 22, 23, 33, 35, 37, 39, 51, 55, 57, 58, 60, 63–65, 71, 74, 146, 154, 156, 172–173, 188

Charron, Pierre (*Traité de la Sagesse*), 64, 88

Child Moses Trampling on Pharaoh's Crown, 71

Children's Bacchanal, 25, 49, *36*

Chione Slain by Diana (drawing), 15, *2*

Christ and the Adulterous Woman, 27, 74, *67*

Christ and the Woman of Samaria, 83

Claude Lorrain, 75, 77, 78, 185, *120*

Coloring of Coral (drawing), 48, *35*

Column of Trajan, Scene from the (drawing), 17, 19, *3*

Comes, Natales (*Mythologiae*), 22, 84

Confirmation, 57, 65, *50*

Conquest of Jerusalem (lost), 15, 41, 46, 96

Conquest of Jerusalem (Vienna), 41, 42

Continence of Scipio (drawing), 39, 69, *26*

Conversion of St. Paul (drawing), 84, *82*

Coriolanus, 69

Corneille, Pierre, 37, 38, 64, 73, 75, *173*

Coronation of David, 19, 38, 45–46, *25*

Crucifixion, 27, 65, *54*

Dance to the Music of Time, 39, 46, *33*

Death of Adonis, 102, *89*

Death of Chione (engraving), 15, *1*

Death of Germanicus, 16, 20, 22, 39, 46, 52, 68, 90, 96, 98, 154, 176, **2**

Death of Germanicus (drawing), 19, 20, 96, *7*

Death of Sapphira, 27, 74, 164, *68*

Death of the Virgin (lost), 14

Death of Virginia (drawing), 39, 71, *28*

Deluge, see *Winter (The Deluge)*

Deposition, 43, 102

Descartes, René, 34, 36, 37, 38, 75

Domenichino, 15, 29, 30–32, 53, 75, 77, *17, 19*

Duquesnoy, François, 25, 31, 33, 49

Entombment, 66, 102, 188, *56*

Et In Arcadia Ego (Chatsworth), 34, 47, 82, 114, 116, 124, 150, **12**

Et In Arcadia Ego (Louvre), 34, 39, 47, 82, 116, 124, 150, 152, **27**

Eucharist (Earl of Ellesmere), 21, 57, 65, 156, **30**

Eucharist (Louvre), 60, 156, *112*

Exposure of Moses, 53, 55

Extreme Unction, 24, 57, 96, 154, **29**

Félibien, André, 13, 18, 19, 33, 78–81, 98, 140, 142, 166, 170, 176, 178, 180, 185–186, 190, 193

Fénelon, Abbé, 81, 176, 178
Finding of Moses (for Le Nôtre), 71
Finding of Moses (for Pointel), 71
Finding of Moses (for Reynon; Schreiber Collection), 55, 65, 72, *65*
Five Trees (drawing), 76, *70*
Flight Into Egypt, see *Holy Family in a Boat*
Four Seasons, The, 84, 87, 193, *128, 129,* **46, 47**
Funeral of Phocion, 79, 176, 184, **39**; see also Phocion landscapes

Gathering of the Ashes of Phocion, 79, 176, *74;* see also Phocion landscapes
Gathering of the Manna, 36, 37, 53, 54, 139, 146, **25**
Gaul Killing Himself and His Wife (Hellenistic sculpture), 19, 20, 30, 108, 143, *108*
Gian Bologna, 142–143, *106*
Giulio Romano, 15, 27, 47, 68, 132–133, 138–139, 152, 198, *110*
Giustiniani, Vincenzo, 76, *135*
Guercino, 47, 116, *34*

Hannibal Crossing the Alps (lost), 16, *41*
Healing the Blind of Jericho, 73, 77, 158, 164, 166, **34**
Healing the Blind of Jericho (drawing), 166, *116*
Hercules and Dejanira (drawing), 56, *45*
Holy Family (drawing; Chantilly), 68, *60*
Holy Family (drawing; Stockholm), 68, *61*
Holy Family (Pearson Madonna), 42, 88, 94, **1**
Holy Family (Reinhart Madonna), 42, 94, *86*
Holy Family in a Boat (Flight Into Egypt), 43, *31*
Holy Family with Eleven Figures, 68, *58*
Holy Family with Infant St. John the Baptist, 68, 186, *62*
Holy Family with Nude Figures (drawing), 66, 148, *109*
Holy Family with St. Elisabeth and Infant St. John, 186, **43**
Holy Family with St. John and St. Elisabeth, and St. Joseph Praying, 186, *122*
Holy Family with Ten Figures, 68, 77, *57*

Horace, *Works,* Poussin's frontispiece for, 22, 148, *10*

Infant Bacchus Entrusted to the Nymphs (drawing), 192, *124;* see also *Birth of Bacchus*
Inspiration of Anacreon (Inspiration of the Poet; Hanover), 34, 38, 45, 94, 116, 124, *32*
Inspiration of the Poet (Louvre), 34, 38, 45, 100, 124, **16**
Israelites Worshiping the Golden Calf, 53, 138, *105*

Judgment of Solomon, 73, 164, **33**
Judgment of Solomon (drawing), 73, 164, *115*
Juno, Argus, and Io, 76
Jupiter Swimming to the Naked Callisto (drawing), 48

Lamentation, 43, 96, 102, **5**
Landscape with Diogenes, 79, 80, 82, *73*
Landscape with Figures (drawing), 76, *71*
Landscape with Hercules and Cacus, 185
Landscape with a Large Road, 79, 80
Landscape with Orpheus and Eurydice, 85, 135, 180, 184, **41**
Landscape with Polyphemus, 79, 182–185, **42**
Landscape with Pyramus and Thisbe, 79–81, 178, *76*
Landscape with St. John on Patmos, 78, 174, **38**
Landscape with a Snake, 80, 82, 178, **40**
Landscape with a Storm (engraving after Poussin), 80, 82, *78*
Landscape with Three Men, 80
Landscape with Three Monks, "La Solitude" (engraving after Poussin), 79, 80, 178, *75*
Landscape with Two Nymphs and a Snake, 79, 178, 180, *77*
Landscape with Two Seated Figures, 80
Landscape with Woman Washing Her Feet, 79, 80
Lanfranco, Giovanni, 17, 23–31, 41, 43
Le Brun, Charles, 36, 146, 180
Leonardo da Vinci, 36, 51, 81, *23, 42*

"Libertins," 62
Luna and Endymion, 19, 26, 47, 55, 114, 120, **14**

Madonna with a Basin, 68, 170, **36**
Madonna du Pilier, see *Vision of St. James the Greater*
Madonna Roccatagliata, 16, 66, 148, **26**
Madonna on the Steps, 29, 67–68, 75, 94, 160–163, 186, **32**
Madonna on the Steps (drawing; Dijon), 160, *113*
Madonna on the Steps (drawing; Louvre), 68, 160, 161, *59*
Mancini, Giulio, 15, 16, 21, 24, 31, *104*
Marcantonio Raimondi, 13, 21, 46, 106, 108, 134, *90, 91*
Marcus Aurelius, Equestrian Statue of (drawing), 19, *4*
Marino, Giovanni Battista, 12–15, 22, 30, 40, 41, 45
Marino Drawings, 14–15, 40, 120, 200
Marriage of St. Catherine, 43
Mars and Venus, 22, 25, 118, **13**
Mars and Venus (drawing), *95*
Martyrdom of St. Erasmus, 16, 30, 32, 43, 100, 124, **4**
Massacre of the Innocents (Chantilly), 30, 32, 41, 108, **8**
Massacre of the Innocents (Petit Palais), 108
Massacre of the Innocents (drawing), 108, *92*
Massimi, Cardinal Camillo, 71, 114, 116, 198
Mazarin, Cardinal, 120, 124
Meleager Sarcophagus, 19–21, 96, 154, *6*
Mercury and Paris (drawing), 83, *79*
Mettius Curtius (drawing), 68
Michelangelo, 26–27, 162, 196, *114*
Midas and Bacchus, 19, 25, 83, 106, 112–114
Midas Bathing in the River Pactolus, 47–48, 108, 112–114, 116, 124, **11**
Midas at the River Pactolus, 112–114, *94*
Miracle of St. Francis Xavier, 60
Moses Changing the Rod of Aaron into a Serpent, 71
Moses Found by the Pharaoh's Daughter (drawing), 184, *44*
Moses Striking the Rock (Earl of Ellesmere), 36, 53

Moses Striking the Rock (Leningrad), 61
Moses Striking the Rock (drawing), 46
Moses Sweetening the Waters, 53

Narcissus and Echo, 24, 48, 76, 102, 104, 110, **9**
Nurture of Bacchus (London), 128
Nurture of Bacchus (Louvre), 25, 49, 113, 128, 132, **18**
Nurture of Jupiter (Berlin), 34, 47, 124, 150, 152, **28**
Nurture of Jupiter (Dulwich), 34, 124, 152, *111*
Nymph Carried by a Satyr, 49, 104, 128, **6**
Nymphs Spied upon by Satyrs (drawing), 184, *119*

Ordination (Earl of Ellesmere), 57, 65, *52*

Palestrina Mosaic, 17, 21, 72, 83, 190, *81*
Pan and Syrinx, 36, 52, 55, 140, **23**
Paris Bordone, 24, 110, *11*
Parnassus, 38, 45, 76, *24*
Passage of the Red Sea, 53–55, 138–139, *43*
Pearson Madonna, see Holy Family (Pearson Madonna)
Penance (Earl of Ellesmere), 21, 57, 65, *51*
Penance (drawing), 65, *53*
Phaeton Before Apollo, 56
Phocion landscapes, 21, 22, 33, 39, 79, 81, 82, 96
Pietro da Cortona, 24, 29, 31, 32, 41, 64, 100, 144–145, *20, 21, 88*
Piles, Roger de, 78
Plague of Ashdod, 46, 52, 106, 126, 144, 145, **7**
Pointel, 35, 71, 73, 74, 158, 164, 172
Pozzo, Cassiano dal, 15–17, 19, 21, 22, 41, 46, 56, 57, 59, 60, 62, 69, 76, 83, 188

Queen Zenobia (drawing), 69

Rape of Europa (drawing), 47, 84, 85, 178, 180, 192, *85*

Rape of the Sabine Women (Louvre), 52, 106, 142, 144–145, *107*
Rape of the Sabine Women (New York), 19, 21, 32, 52, 53, 106, 142–145, **24**
Raphael, 13, 15, 26, 27, 32, 41, 45, 53, 63, 65, 66, 68, 74, 76, 108, 124, 134–135, 138, 162, 182, 186, 198, *14, 52, 69, 102, 104, 121*
Realm of Flora, 22, 48, 87, 98, 126, **17**
Rebecca and Eliezer at the Well (Blunt Coll.), 158
Rebecca and Eliezer at the Well (Louvre), 55, 71, 75, 78, 83, 158, **31**
Reinhart Madonna, see Holy Family (Reinhart Madonna)
Reni, Guido, 29, 30, 100, 108, 158, *16*
Rescue of the Infant Pyrrhus, 19, 51, *41*
Rest on the Flight Into Egypt, 21, 65, 68, 72, 83, *63*
Reynon, 71, 166
Richelieu, Cardinal, *see Bacchanals (for Richelieu)*
Rinaldo and Armida (Dulwich), 49, *39*
Rinaldo and Armida (lost), 36
Rinaldo and Armida (Moscow), 50
Roccatagliata, Stefano, 16, 112, 148
Rubens, Peter Paul, 26, 38, 40, 75, 80, 82, 158
Ruth and Boaz, see Summer (Ruth and Boaz)

Sacchetti, Marcello, 15
Sacchi, Andrea, 17, 31
St. Cecilia, 43
St. Francis Xavier, 13, 83
St. Ignatius of Loyola, 13
St. Jerome, 76
St. Matthew and the Angel, 78, 79, 174, *72*
Sandrart, Joachim von, 25, 75, 100
Schoolmaster of the Falerii, 22, 31, 36, 39, 52, 140, *27*
Scipio and the Pirates (drawing), 69, *64*
Self-Portrait (Berlin), 172
Self-Portrait (engraving after Poussin), 32, 74, 172, *117*
Self-Portrait (Louvre), 74, 75, 172–173, **Frontispiece**
Seven Sacraments (first series), 35, 56–57, 62, *47*

Seven Sacraments (second series), 21, 35, 57, 62–66, 71, 77, 154, 156, *49–52*, **29, 30**
Spoleto Virgin, 76
Spring, 193, *128*
Stella, Jacques, 36, 55, 56, 146
Suicide of Cato (drawing), 68
Summer (Ruth and Boaz), 193, 194, **46**

Tasso, Torquato, 14, 49–51
Testament of Eudamidas, 39, 71, 96, 154, 168, 176, **35**
Time Revealing Truth, 46, 60
Tintoretto, 33, 66
Titian, 24–26, 33, 34, 40, 49, 56, 61, 63, 76, 77, 82, 104, 110, 113, 128, 133, 143, *12, 13, 93, 118*
Triumph of Bacchus, 49, 130, *37*
Triumph of David, 31, *18*
Triumph of Flora, 48, 98, 126, 142, **3**
Triumph of Galatea (drawing), 134, *103*
Triumph of Neptune and Amphitrite, 49, 134–135, **20**
Triumph of Pan, 26, 49, 130–133, **19**
Triumph of Pan (drawing; Bayonne), 132, *100*
Triumph of Pan (drawing; Windsor), 132, *99*
Two Draped Female Figures (drawing), 20, *8*

Valentin de Boulogne, 29, 100
Valguarnera, Fabrizio, 16, 98, 106, 112, 114, 126
Venus Arming Aeneas, 56
Venus Surprised by Satyrs (drawing), 48
Victory and Fame (drawing), 148
Victory of Joshua Over the Amalekites; Victory of Joshua Over the Amorites, 40
Vision of St. James the Greater (Madonna du Pilier), 29–30, 43, *15*
Vision of St. Paul (Sarasota), 32
Vouet, Simon, 15, 29, 60, 100

Winter (The Deluge), 87, 178, 193, 196, **47**

Youth of Bacchus, 128

203

BIBLIOGRAPHICAL NOTE

The main sources for the life and works of Nicolas Poussin are: Giovanni Pietro Bellori, *Le vite de' pittori, scultori ed architetti moderni*, Rome, 1672; André Félibien, *Entretiens sur les vies et sur les ouvrages des plus excellents peintres anciens et modernes*, Paris, 1685–88 (ed. Trévoux, Paris, 1725); Giulio Mancini, *Considerazione sulla Pittura*, completed about 1626 (ed. Marucchi and Salerno, Rome, 1956–57); Joachim von Sandrart, *Teutsche Akademie der edlen Bau-, Bild-, und Mahlerey-Künste*, Nuremberg, 1675–79 (ed. Pelzer, Munich, 1925); Paul Fréart de Chantelou, *Journal du voyage du cavalier Bernin en France*, written in 1665 (ed. Lalande, Paris, 1885). A complete edition of Poussin's letters is edited by Charles Jouanny: *Correspondance de Nicolas Poussin*, Paris, 1911.

For a comprehensive listing of books and articles in chronological order, the reader is referred to the Bibliography in the excellent catalogue prepared by Anthony Blunt and Charles Sterling for the *Exposition Nicolas Poussin*, Musée du Louvre, Paris, 1960, pp. 285–328. Of special importance are the two volumes of the *Actes du Colloque Nicolas Poussin*, published in 1960 just before the opening of the exhibition; and the series of articles by Anthony Blunt entitled "Poussin Studies: I–VIII," which appeared in the *Burlington Magazine* between 1947 and 1959.

Publications since the catalogue of the *Exposition Nicolas Poussin* which were of particular use in this work are: Anthony Blunt's subsequent "Poussin Studies: IX–XIV" in the *Burlington Magazine*, 1960 to 1964; Denis Mahon, "Poussiniana," published as the summer number of the *Gazette des Beaux-Arts*, 1962; and Georg Kaufmann, *Poussin-Studien*, Berlin, 1960. Also useful were: volume four of the *Drawings of Nicolas Poussin*, which appeared in 1963; and the catalogue of the smaller exhibition, *Nicolas Poussin et Son Temps*, held in the Musée des Beaux-Arts, Rouen, in 1961, with an introduction by Jacques Thuillier. Additional works are mentioned in the text.